**WALL
STREET
JOURNAL
BOOKS**

# AT HOME IN THE WORLD

## Collected Writings from
## The Wall Street Journal

### DANIEL PEARL

**EDITED BY HELENE COOPER**
*Foreword by Mariane Pearl*

A WALL STREET JOURNAL BOOK
Published by Simon & Schuster
*New York London Toronto Sydney Singapore*

WALL
STREET
JOURNAL
BOOKS

*A WALL STREET JOURNAL BOOK*
Published by Simon & Schuster, Inc.
Rockefeller Center
1230 Avenue of the Americas
New York, NY 10020

For information regarding special discounts for bulk purchases,
please contact Simon & Schuster Special Sales:
1-800-456-6798 or business@simonandschuster.com

Designed by Lisa Chovnick

Manufactured in the United States of America

4   6   8   10   9   7   5   3

Library of Congress Cataloging-in-Publication Data is available
ISBN 0-7432-4317-X

*For Danny's son, who will know his father in words and in spirit.*

May you grow up to be righteous,
May you grow up to be true,
May you always know the truth
And see the lights surrounding you.
May you always be courageous,
Stand upright and be strong,
May you stay forever young,
Forever young, forever young,
May you stay forever young.

—BOB DYLAN

# CONTENTS

## PART ONE

## TALKING TO STRANGERS

**PART TWO**

## I HOPE GABRIEL LIKES MY MUSIC

**PART THREE**

## MR. PRECIS

### PART FOUR

## POISONING THE WELL

**PART FIVE**

## FINDING THE POTHOLES ALONG THE
## INFORMATION SUPERHIGHWAY

**PART SIX**

# NICE LEDE!

## APPENDIX I: FROM THE *NORTH ADAMS TRANSCRIPT*

# FOREWORD

It was in London that I first stepped into one of Danny's offices.

The office floor was divided into little cubicles. Danny wore a stylish suit topped with a splashy tie pulled from his trademark crazy collection. He introduced me to his cramped space, inviting me to lounge in a beach chair that sat beside him, a totally inappropriate piece of office furniture filling most of his cubicle. I sat in that beach chair and took a good hard look at the man of my life as he spun out a tale from another of his reporting adventures in the Middle East, quickly sweeping his fingers over the keyboard without looking at the keys, surrounded by mountains of papers and books. Touchstones from his travels surrounded him. He had spread a big black tapestry that said "Allahu Akbar"—"God is great"—in scrolling red Arabic letters. He had propped a larger-than-life-sized picture of Iranian revolutionary leader Ayatollah Khomeini, brought back from one of his countless trips to Iran. He also had the most amazing collection of little monster figurines perched on a shelf.

I could tell he was a fast thinker, constantly synthesizing new ideas. He was a man who was going to illuminate my life. Sharing his existence would be like turning the pages of a comic book packed with lots of fun, unexpected turns of events and plenty of plane rides. Most important, I felt I had met the man who shared my approach toward the world and stood committed to change the world for the better. Lying in his beach chair, an exotic spot in London's gray, I felt great respect and trust in him.

As a journalist and sojourner of the world, Danny held no prejudices about the people we interviewed and met. He first and foremost considered the human being in front of him, regardless of religion, race or social status. Very suspicious of groups and organizations, he had a natural tendency to trust individuals. Once he started to work on an article, he would literally throw himself at it, working days and nights, tracking facts for weeks and experiencing pure delight when he found the littlest detail that would make the story livelier. He liked to walk on beaten paths and discover tales of the unexpected. He was a hunter of human contradictions, as well as of the small and immense absurdities of existence. In reporting from mosques and villages, deserts and world capitals, he was witness to the difficulties of communication between humans. He was like a tightrope walker, a *funamble,* happily linking worlds with his writings.

As journalists, Danny and I traveled so much that we began to live without acknowledging borders. We were truly citizens of the globe. We were beyond cosmopolitan. Danny was Jewish; I am Buddhist. Danny was born in Princeton, New Jersey; I was born in Paris, France. Danny's father was born in Israel, his mother in Baghdad, Iraq; my mother was born in Havana, Cuba, my father in Amsterdam, the Netherlands. We last lived together in Bombay, India, and last traveled together in Pakistan.

Our commitment to journalism as our means of changing the world deepened every day. The world often seemed to be a mess, but it was our world and somehow our mess. It became clear to us that we enjoyed a privileged position. That enabled us to expose corruption, injustice and ignorance. It empowered us to question vested interests, fundamentalism and untruths. For us—for Danny—journalism epitomized the path for charting a better world future. Danny cherished truth more than anything. He called it his religion. He had undertaken a lifelong struggle against conventional wisdom. In all those respects, Danny was a hero—an ordinary hero.

We were legitimate citizens of the 21st century.

I can only hope that more individuals will think independently, give voice to their thoughts and take responsible action so that this world starts belonging to its people. It is our task to educate, inform and provide keys to people so that they will not be held hostage to the ignorance bred in every corner of the world. It takes courage.

Danny's kidnappers tried to behead freedom. The absurdity of his death belied the life we lived together. We were journalists. We were free. We met people and told their tales to the world. Nobody could harm us. Why would they? We were open-minded and respectful. We were not corrupt. We were not running after power or fame. We were not political or militants. We needn't hide anything. We were ambitious. We believed ordinary people like us could change the world by changing the way people think about each other. We believed you only had to be a journalist armed with intellectual courage, curiosity, a writing talent, a solid sense of humor and a genuine willingness to fight your own limits.

The terrorists who killed Danny stood at the other extreme of what Danny represents. They could only wield their knife and cowardice against Danny's intellectual courage and bold spirit. Danny died holding only a pen. They stole his life but were unable to seize his soul. By killing Danny, terrorists took my life as well but could not lay claim to my spirit. Dead and alive we will never let them win.

I wish you a good journey through Danny's writings. It is my sincere hope that his spirit and values will radiate from all of you who he inspires. I hope that, like me, you will be able to laugh with Danny as he navigates you through the *absurdités de l'existence*. Mainly, I trust that Danny's flame will keep burning in you as it does in me, his wife.

—Mariane Pearl
Paris, France
April 2002

# DANIEL PEARL (1963–2002)

Daniel Pearl was born October 10, 1963, at Princeton Hospital, New Jersey, the second child of Judea and Ruth Pearl. The Pearl family moved to California in 1966. In 1970, Danny had his first violin lesson and, in 1972, his first soccer lesson, beginning two love affairs that would last his entire life.

In 1976, on October 16, Danny had his bar mitzvah in Jerusalem, Israel, and spent the next year living in Rehovot, Israel. He graduated from Birmingham High School in Van Nuys, Calif., in 1981 as a National Merit Scholar, and was ranked 15th in the country for his grade on the PSAT in English.

Danny entered Stanford University that fall and soon afterward cofounded *Stanford Commentary*, a nonpartisan political newspaper. He graduated Phi Beta Kappa one semester early, with a bachelor of arts degree in communications.

Danny's first professional job in journalism was with the *North Adams* (Mass.) *Transcript.* He also worked for the *Berkshire Eagle* and the *San Francisco Business Times.*

He joined *The Wall Street Journal* in 1990, and he covered air cargo from the paper's Atlanta bureau. Three years later he was recruited by the paper's Washington bureau, and two years after that by the London bureau. Beginning in 1996, Danny worked as foreign correspondent for the *Journal*, first from London, then from Paris and finally from Bombay, where he served as the South Asia bureau chief.

Danny met his wife, Mariane, a Dutch-Cuban of French citizenship, at a party in Paris in 1998. The two were married a year later in Paris.

Danny was kidnapped on January 23, 2002, in Karachi, Pakistan, while reporting a story. He died at the hands of his captors. A few months before his abduction, Danny and Mariane discovered she was pregnant; two days before his abduction, the couple discovered the child would be a boy.

In addition to his wife, son and parents, Danny leaves two sisters, Michelle and Tamara. His death is mourned by dozens of relatives, scores of friends, hundreds of colleagues and thousands of people around the world.

# AT HOME IN
# THE WORLD

# PART ONE

# *Talking to Strangers*

*Danny had the ability to see the ordinary as extraordinary. He told me he was interested in the shades of gray in the world, rather than the extremes of black and white.*

—TAMARA PEARL, *Danny's big sister*

Better than anyone, the Pearl family understood how Danny used his natural affection for the unfamiliar in searching for that middle ground. At his son's memorial service on March 10, 2002, Judea Pearl explained:

Thirty-eight years ago, Ruth and I had the great fortune of observing a unique biological phenomenon. The child that we brought home had a peculiar syndrome: he had not one shred of malice in his bones.

This child developed into a young man who filled our lives with joy, humor, love and meaning. We feel fortunate to have been influenced by him so profoundly, and we are lucky to have beautiful memories to guide us in the future.

But where did Danny get this zero-malice affliction? I know it did not come from my side of the family; I am not sure of Ruth's side. But I am pretty sure that it was genetic in nature, because it showed itself when Danny was still in the crib.

When you pulled the pillow from under his head, Danny would not startle; his head would just relax into a new position, as if that is where he wanted to be all along.

If you tried to bully him, he would not cry nor bully back; he would just look you in the eyes till you realized for yourself how silly you looked.

1

When we told him he must sleep with braced shoes, to correct his toeing-in, he did not utter a single complaint. Night after night, for six whole months, he would just bite his lips and ask to be put into those awkward and painful braces.

Naturally, we thought that he was somewhat slow: A two-and-a-half-year-old boy who does not hit back must be, we thought. Therefore, when the nursery school teacher described him as a "born leader" with a six-year-old level of intellect, we made a special trip to the nursery school to make sure that she was talking about our Danny.

His kindergarten teacher later explained Danny's secret. He is like a sponge, she said. Nothing escapes his eyes; he simply sees no reason to show it.

And that was also the secret of his subtle leadership. Kids sought his company not because he was outgoing—he wasn't—but because he was secure, unassuming and unintimidated. He was not intimidated by bullies, or by rules, or by teachers—not even by his parents.

He was not intimidated even when one teacher stuck a swastika in his face and said, "You are wearing the Star of David, Danny? Look what I am wearing!" As Israelis, we were terribly upset. This was our first exposure to anti-Semitism, and we were sure Danny would be scarred for life. We even called experts from the Anti-Defamation League to assess the damage.

But Danny just narrated the incident in his matter-of-fact way, as if saying, "Upset? Why would I get upset if a teacher makes a fool of himself?"

One day Danny came home from school with a booklet full of new safety instructions. Among them we found one popular rule of the 1970s:

"Do not talk to strangers."

After some discussion, we decided that we would not press this rule too seriously with Danny.

Little did we know then that "talking to strangers" would become Danny's hobby, then his profession and, eventually, his mission and ideology.

And he sure learned to talk to strangers:

When he went on his first interview and forgot to put on a belt, he talked the taxi driver into loaning him his belt—just for the interview, of course.

People who we believed to be the epitome of boredom, Danny found to be intriguing.

He talked to strangers in jazz bars, on soccer fields, in barbershops and in train stations.

He talked to peasants and rulers, rabbis and mullahs.

He talked to winners and losers, to special strangers and to ordinary strangers.

He talked to strangers more than he talked to his parents. Little did we know that "talking to strangers" would one day invite this tragedy. Weeks after learning of his abduction, our family and friends were still playing with fantasies of how Danny talks his captors into coming to their senses and ending their silly game.

Until this very day, images of Danny talking them into playing a game of backgammon or humming a little tune are much more vivid than anything I will ever view on CNN.

We now know that the last group of strangers Danny talked to were strangers of a different breed, from a different planet. These were strangers that knew no talking.

They have silenced Danny's voice, but not his spirit—the legacy of Danny's lifelong "talking with strangers" will be forever in our heart.

For eleven years, Danny Pearl introduced readers of *The Wall Street Journal* to beggars and thieves, workers and rulers. Here are a few stories that show his capacity for turning strangers the world over into people we know.

*—H.C.*

# IN INDIAN QUAKE, DEATH HAUNTS THE LIVING

*February 5, 2001*

ANJAR, India—What is India's earthquake zone really like? It smells. It reeks. You can't imagine the odor of several hundred bodies decaying for five days as search teams pick away at slabs of crumbled buildings in this town. Even if you've never smelled it before, the brain knows what it is, and orders you to get away. After a day, the nose gets stuffed up in self-defense. But the brain has registered the scent, and picks it up in innocent places: lip balm, sweet candy, stale breath, an airplane seat.

The smell had become acute around Gujarat state's Kachchh province by Thursday. It was a pretty good gauge of how many bodies were trapped in any particular place. Numbers of dead are thrown about—25,000, 100,000—but nobody really knows. And it isn't just the number that explains why the world's media are here. AIDS will kill more Indians this year but get less coverage here. In India's Orissa state, reports are emerging of starvation from drought. In Afghanistan, refugees are freezing to death in camps. But an earthquake is sudden death, a much more compelling story.

The New Delhi fire department, working to exhume bodies at a collapsed apartment building in the town Gandhidham, assumes an actual corpse is what a journalist would want to see and photograph. "Come closer, come closer, you can see the hand," a firefighter says, beckoning. The spray the firefighters use to mask the smell doesn't really work, and an older member of the crew pulls away and gags. The department has a crane and a hydraulic extrication device, but for some reason, when it's time to search deep in a hole in the rubble, nobody has a flashlight. One firefighter produces a box of matches.

Ragendra Singh, manager of the Shiv Regency hotel in Gandhidham, is standing below a sagging beam that used to be above the second floor. "Come on in, it's perfectly safe," he says. After the earthquake, the second floor collapsed into the first floor. He points out the unbroken windows and says all the guests got out—luckily, there was nobody in room 113, which now has the kitchen from below sticking up through it. "All the televisions were perfectly OK," he marvels. Five days after the earthquake, Mr. Singh and his family resume sleeping inside their suburban home, which has a slight crack in each wall. The door is left open during dinner, and if anybody notices the death smell pushing inside, nobody says anything. The next morning, a faint whiff reaches the roof, where Mr. Singh's father, a retired army colonel pressed back into service for quake relief, shows off his pet pigeons. "Animals can tell when death is coming," he says. "They pray to the gods to take them instead of me."

The earthquake victims weren't all poor people in mud-brick villages. Gujarat includes some of India's richest businesspeople, even if they're not known for flaunting their wealth. The hotel billboards are still standing—"Entertain your corporate clients in style," "Free bowling," "For your hard day's night"—but the hotels are flattened. Owner-occupied villas seemed to survive better than apartments. Temples seemed to survive better than student dormitories. Is it random? Some Indians are pointing the finger at some builders, though the evidence is still circumstantial. "When money-making is involved, they resort to cheap materials," opines Shaukat, translator for this Gujarat assignment.

Even amid the rubble, some people are quietly trying to get on with their lives: A child plays on the remains of a wall. Businessmen set up a sidewalk desk with typewriters and phones salvaged from their shipping office. At the Razdip apartments in Gandhidham, where locals say 40 people died, Ranjena Shah climbs through the top of a pile of rubble, under a slab that used to be her ceiling. Isn't that dangerous? "I don't have any clothing. I'm trying to salvage what I can," she says, pulling out a plastic clock.

The desperate ones are charitable organizations trying to get their work mentioned. "Please flash this to the world. It will be very good for us," says a white-bearded Nirmohananda Avadhuta, with a neatly typed handout about the international religious organization Ananda Marga's work digging up corpses and sheltering survivors at its ashram. "When can we meet? When?" Mr. Avadhuta pleads, at a busy newsstand.

Maybe everyone really just wants to help. But why does Mahantshree Devprasadji Maharajshree, eighth in a line of gurus of the Shree Anandabava Seva Sanstha temple in Jamnagar, already have the photo album ready a day after his visit to the razed village of Jodia? Photos of the guru distributing water barrels and the guru talking with survivors are quickly posted on the Web site along with an appeal for funds. Later, a disciple of the guru phones asking for "advice" on their efforts to "adopt" Jodia. OK, why not send money to a big organization, instead of adding to the chaos among competing aid groups? "Yes, but we don't want to be one of these organizations that tries to do everything everywhere and ends up doing nothing." Seconds later, he talks about expanding from Jodia to other villages. That requires money. Publicity would help.

The ride around the shore of the Gulf of Kachchh, from Gandhidham to Jamnagar, usually takes three hours, but now it's nearly doubled: The bridges have cracks, and white rocks have been laid out to confine vehicles from both directions to a single lane. Clothes lie piled up by the side of the road. Some trucks stop by the side of the road and unload their cargo to whoever gets there first. Kids sell donated bags of water to passing drivers. And that smell: It wafts in from nearly every village now. It sticks around, even days later, in the shoes, the camera bag, the computer bag, the notebooks.

# −2−

## PORTRAIT OF THE ARTIST IN SEARCH OF PATRONS IN THE HIGHEST PLACES

### Andrew Vicari Paints Princes and War Heroes; Flattery Doesn't Get Him Very Far

*July 25, 2000*

RIYADH, Saudi Arabia—There was a time when a court artist could make his career with a single flattering painting of Napoleon on a horse. Modern warfare hasn't been so good to Andrew Vicari.

Mr. Vicari is portraitist to the royal families of Saudi Arabia and Monaco and, by his own reckoning, one of the great living painters. His crowning work was a collection of more than 100 paintings of the generals, diplomats and battles of the 1991 Gulf War. But the Saudis lost interest. The paintings are warehoused at great expense in the south of France, protected by security guards and a $75-million insurance policy. "It has nearly bankrupted me," says Mr. Vicari, who is 62 years old.

And so, Mr. Vicari returns to Saudi Arabia, looking for somebody to buy "the most important work in the history of art since the Napoleonic era." That is how Mr. Vicari described his paintings in an unsuccessful pitch to Saudi Arabia's defense minister, Prince Sultan bin Abdul Aziz.

It was the Napoleonic Wars, in a way, that drew Mr. Vicari into battle. "Have you read 'War and Peace'? Well, you must," Mr. Vicari exclaims in his booming voice, over dinner at the Riyadh Intercontinental Hotel, where he keeps an executive suite year-round as his local studio. The novel inspired Mr. Vicari to spend more than two years painting his own masterpiece, which he called "From War to Peace in the Gulf."

Mr. Vicari realizes he is an anachronism. Born in Wales to Italian parents, he had his first gallery sale at the age of 18. He was outraged to see how much money the dealer kept and vowed to work like the old masters—selling directly to a wealthy patron, preferably royalty. "I went out to America in the 1960s," he says. "I wanted Nelson Rockefeller as my patron, but little did I know he hadn't a bloody clue about art." Translation: The late Mr. Rockefeller liked abstract art. In 1973, a friend took Mr. Vicari to Saudi Arabia, where his traditional oil paintings won favor with royal advisers. He got lucrative commissions for series, including "The Triumph of the Bedouin" and "The Majesty of King Faisal." The Saudis even let Mr. Vicari paint women without veils. And he painted princes, charging $80,000 or more per portrait. "He is bigger than anyone," says Saad Al-Showiman, a Riyadh gallery owner.

On January 15, 1991, the deadline for Iraq to withdraw from Kuwait or face war, Mr. Vicari flew from Paris to Riyadh, feeling an artistic duty: Hadn't Lord Byron died helping Greece win independence from the Turks? he points out.

War life wasn't so bad for Mr. Vicari. He fell into a circuit of dinner parties and receptions that were barely interrupted as Iraqi Scud missiles fell around Riyadh. "It was a great time," recalls Jacques Berniere, French ambassador during the war. "We were all provisional bachelors": diplomats, businessmen, generals and Andrew Vicari (who is, in fact, a bachelor). Soon, Mr. Vicari had everybody sitting for portraits.

"It's partly ego—someone wants to paint you because you're involved in some significant historical event," says retired Lt. Gen. Robert Johnston, an aide during the war to Gen. Norman Schwartzkopf. Mr. Vicari drew them both. And with his friends' help, Mr. Vicari saw battlegrounds firsthand: the just-liberated Saudi town of Al Khafji, the still-burning Kuwait oil-well fires.

Even a war of instantaneous video feeds had room for a few painters. The Imperial War Museum in London commissioned artist John Keane, who caused a stir by painting Mickey Mouse next to a shopping cart full of missiles. The U.S. Army dispatched four painters to portray the everyday life of troops. American artist Susan Crile witnessed the Kuwait oil fires and painted four dozen renditions, most of which she still owns.

"This isn't the easiest thing on earth to sell," says her dealer, Valerie McKenzie of New York's Graham Gallery. "People don't want to acknowledge modern warfare."

Prince Khaled bin Sultan, business-savvy Commander of Joint Forces in the Gulf War, put up $7 million for Mr. Vicari's work, which commenced in a style befitting the artist's patronage. Mr. Vicari set up a one-acre studio in a former bus factory outside Nice, to allow him to work on four battlefield canvases at the same time. He traveled first-class with bodyguards and a biographer.

Prince Khaled, now retired from the Saudi military, sent a brigadier general to inspect Mr. Vicari's work, and set up a committee to ensure that no allied leader was slighted, no important battle neglected. The Gulf War series ballooned in number from 125 paintings to 235. Mr. Vicari's Gulf War series was to tour world capitals—Paris, London, Washington, Cairo, Kuwait City, Riyadh. Peter Cannon-Brookes, a British art curator working on the international tour, says some of the paintings were so large he was having trouble figuring out how to get them into the great exhibition halls in these places.

Then suddenly, in the summer of 1992, the prince pulled out. He settled the outstanding expenses, and took home just seven portraits of himself and his relatives, Mr. Vicari says. Did the Saudis lose enthusiasm because Islamists were grumbling about American troops remaining on Saudi soil? Was Prince Khaled diverting his energy into his memoirs, "Desert Warrior," which tried to correct the perception that the Saudis had contributed little to the fight against Saddam Hussein? Were Mr. Vicari's tanks less impressive than his horses? Nobody answered these questions. "The Saudis are not good about explaining themselves," says Ollie Akel, a former Exxon executive who helped Mr. Vicari with finances. Prince Khaled declines to comment.

Mr. Vicari tried to find another backer, but in Saudi Arabia and Kuwait, he says, "nobody wanted to hear about the war." He landed a commission in China through a diplomat friend, and forgot about the Gulf War. "Then my bank rings me and says, 'You've got to do something, you've got a huge loan out.' " He sold his Monaco penthouse, laid off his staff and stopped staying at the Hotel Crillon in Paris. Once again, he tried to unload "From War to Peace"—insisting, still, that the paintings be sold as a block.

In 1997, British newspapers reported that Iran had offered to buy the paintings for GBP 5 million (more than $7.5 million at current exchange rates) and burn them as un-Islamic. "I think that was Andrew" who came up with that, says Mr. Vicari's former biographer, Daniel Curzi. "They wouldn't have printed it if it was false," retorts Mr. Vicari. "I went into hiding for two months." Not that most of the art world would have noticed. Mr. Vicari's name doesn't appear in major European and American artists' directories, and he says none of his 4,000-odd paintings has ever come up for auction. (*Leonard's Price Index*, however, does list one Vicari landscape as selling at a 1991 U.S. auction for $412; Mr. Vicari says it actually was painted by a student of his who signed Mr. Vicari's name.)

The artist has marked up pages of *Who's Who in the World* to show that he has a bigger entry than Margaret Thatcher and Bill Gates. He has begun to work on an autobiography to be called "Scenes From an Interesting Life" by compiling an index of 500 important people he has met. On June 29, Mr. Vicari reports good news by telephone from Riyadh: Prince Khaled's vizier has just promised the prince will build a museum and buy the rest of "From War to Peace." For how much? "I don't know. It will be a huge sum." So far, Mr. Vicari has heard nothing further. But he is confident, drinking wine in a Paris café and musing about what is next for the "king of painters, painter of kings." He may go to Luxembourg and paint a portrait of the Grand Duke. Then again, he adds, "Vladimir Putin is a great friend. Maybe I'll do something with him."

# 3

# SEARCH FOR MERCY ENDS IN TEARS ON QUIET KOSOVO STREET

*December 2, 1999*

KOSOVO POLJE, Yugoslavia—President Clinton came to Kosovo last week pleading for a little ethnic reconciliation. This reminded me of my first trip here, in June, when I searched in vain for a story about ethnic Albanians and Serbs moving beyond their hatred.

"Reconciliation? I don't think anybody's working on that yet," one relief worker told me. I was undeterred. Albanians should be angry with police officers, soldiers or local militias who shot civilians and burned houses during the war that ended in June. But ordinary people? I didn't even understand how people could tell the ethnic groups apart on the street.

"Albanian or Serb?" I quizzed my ethnic-Albanian translator, pointing to a pedestrian as we drove through Kosovo Polje, an ethnically mixed town near the provincial capital of Pristina.

"Serb."

"How can you tell?"

"The way he walks."

In my search for a pocket of ethnic harmony, I tried the new soccer team (no Serbs), a once-mixed jazz band (no gigs), even a mental hospital. There, ethnic-Albanian nurses told me the Serb staff had fled, told the patients to leave too, and taken the telephones. Hearing that Albanians and Serbs were working together to revive train service, I ventured into the main train station. Serb guards told us to "get lost" after my translator told them his name (names being the other way Albanian and Serbs tell each other apart).

Only one encounter seemed to offer any hope for Serbs and Albanians living together. It took place on a quiet residential street here. And last week, on a return trip to Kosovo, I decided to see if the story had a happy ending.

In the third house on the right lived Rade Volic, a 70-year-old ex-railroad worker. Mr. Volic is a Serb, but the kind who avoids the word "Shqiptar," a slur against ethnic Albanians. His wife, Jelka, who is 64, served me the same dark oriental coffee Albanians serve.

Next door lived Hamit Fazliu, 68 years old, a retired mill worker and ethnic Albanian. He and Mr. Volic, neighbors for 30 years, worked to stay friends, even as neighborhood Serbs were meeting in the late 1980s to discuss harassment by the ethnic-Albanian majority, even as Albanians were losing their jobs and seeing their children thrown out of schools during the 1990s, even as an Albanian guerrilla war for independence and a Serbian ethnic-cleansing campaign began.

On March 27, soon after the North Atlantic Treaty Organization bombing began, Serb vigilantes shot up Mr. Fazliu's house while he cowered on the living room couch. Mr. Volic says he persuaded the vandals not to burn the house. Mr. Fazliu spent the night at Mr. Volic's house, then left Kosovo. In June, Mr. Fazliu's nephew, Bafti Fazliu, showed me the gutted home: glass shards everywhere, the kitchen stripped bare.

In their own tidy home, the Volices showed me a letter their neighbor had written while taking shelter with them. "What will happen, nobody knows, but let this be proof that Rade is a good man, and his wife, and I'm very thankful," it read. Still, the Volices weren't sure they would stay. All around, neighbors were pooling their money to rent trucks to move to Serbia proper.

That was four months ago. KFOR, the NATO-led military force, is more organized now in its efforts to protect Serb villages, but there are few mixed neighborhoods left. My Pristina-based translator said he hadn't spoken the Serbian language in three months.

I visited Mr. Fazliu first. He now had furniture, a television, new cabinets. He said he had made the rounds of neighbors at first, telling how Mr. Volic had helped him. But lately, he was asking Mr. Volic not to speak with him on the street.

"Some of my relatives don't understand," he said, especially the ones who had had immediate family members killed. He said he was trying to help the Volices in quieter ways, buying them bread so they didn't have to go out, helping them find a buyer for their house.

Next door, the Volices greeted me warmly, and asked if I could help them determine if the German-mark notes they were about to receive for their house were real. They had gone with one of the many Albanians who knocked on their door asking to buy the place. KFOR was "very nice," but they were tired of rocks being thrown through the window, and they were moving in four days' time to live near their daughter and son in Belgrade.

It was a tearful moment. The Volices had built the house thinking their children would live there. Over coffee and Serbian grape liquor, Mrs. Volic talked about how happy she used to feel returning home from Serbia proper and seeing the white felt hats ethnic Albanians wore. Now "there are extremists on both sides, and good people suffer," she said. I wished them luck and said goodbye.

My driver was across the street. "I was worried, I thought maybe those Serbs killed you," he said. And then: "The people who bought this place are crazy. They could have it for free. The Serbs are going to have to leave anyhow."

"Thank you, Agim," I said, as we rolled toward Pristina. "Thank you for reminding me that I'm in the Balkans."

# 4

# JOINT FORCE: A TOUGH U.S. COP WITH A DAUNTING BEAT: PEACE IN THE BALKANS

## Officer Grady Places Serbs, Albanians Side by Side—and Gets Mixed Results

### Training in 'Human Dignity'

*December 9, 1999*

PRISTINA, Yugoslavia—The last time Officer Donald Grady II made any headlines, he was losing a racially charged battle to reform the Santa Fe, N.M., police department. Now he has revived his career in an improbable way: building ethnically mixed police departments in the Balkans.

Consider the task. Struggles over the makeup of the police forces helped start the last two Balkan wars. Here in Kosovo, ethnic-Albanian separatists targeted Serb police officers for assassination. Serb police took part in some of the worst atrocities against Albanians during the NATO bombing that ended in June. Since then, attacks on the dwindling Serb population have taken hundreds of lives, including that of a Serb professor dragged from his car by a mob during a recent Albanian celebration.

And Don Grady wants Serbs and Albanians to patrol the streets together.

Now consider the man: a 46-year-old grandfather, six-feet-five-inches tall, black, nonsmoker, nondrinker, notoriously unforgiving with fellow cops. Don't tell Mr. Grady that police scandals such as the Rodney King beating are isolated incidents. "Every system is perfectly designed to get the results that are achieved," he says. In Pristina, Kosovo's chaotic provincial capital, Mr. Grady scolds drivers who pull into the crosswalks and walks on a retaining wall to keep his boots out of the puddles. He has already removed one subordinate for missing deadlines. Mr. Grady, whose favorite movie is "The Wizard of Oz," doesn't like hearing that his plans won't work. And he's scoring some successes in the region. In Bosnia, he got Croats, Serbs and Muslims to patrol together. In Kosovo, as deputy police commissioner of policy and planning for the United Nations mission, he helped put a class of 175 Kosovo Police Service cadets—including seven Serbs—on the street earlier this month. The cadets have gotten along reasonably well, and a second class began last week, with 28 Serbs.

It isn't a real police force yet. Cadets are unarmed, training under the U.N.'s international police officers, who in turn rely for protection on the NATO-led troops in armored carriers. But the soldiers are handing over power to the police. And NATO officers hope the sight of Serbs and Albanians in the same police uniforms will help persuade minorities to stay in Kosovo and stem fears that the West is allowing ethnic cleansing in reverse.

The police deployment has been rough at times. One female ethnic-Albanian cadet got her nose broken by an angry mob when her Tunisian supervisor took her into the Serb section of the divided city of Mitrovica. Bad judgment, says Mr. Grady. Delays and absurdities have marked the overall U.N. operation in Kosovo. The U.N. set pay for local cops at just $26 a week, one-fifth what it pays janitors in the same building. (It's a different budget, the U.N. explains.) Some Serb cadets are picking up monthly cash stipends from the Yugoslav government, while Albanian cadets are believed to be getting money from the Kosovo Liberation Army. That's a clean slate compared with trying to battle entrenched interests in U.S. police departments, Mr. Grady says. "I believe this can work," he says. "It's just a matter of paying attention to the details."

In Kosovo, Mr. Grady produces flowcharts, talks of "float time" and "critical path," and doesn't travel much beyond the 10-minute walks from his apartment to his office in Pristina. But it's impossible to miss what's going on. Renting an apartment from a Serb, he had to get a Kosovo Liberation Army certificate for the door to stop break-in attempts by bandits who see Serb apartments as fair game. An ethnic-Serb cleaning lady stops him in the hall of the U.N. police headquarters one morning and complains that her relatives want to return to Kosovo but can't because they fear attack. He has no ready answer.

"Everybody keeps saying how much better Kosovo is now than before," Mr. Grady says, walking among Pristina's nighttime strollers. "Well, better for whom?"

Like many black officers, Mr. Grady entered policing hoping to help clean it up. Before becoming a deputy sheriff, the Wisconsin native recalls, he'd been slammed against a police-car door by patrolmen looking for another black man. His first stint as police chief was in Bloomer, Wis., where, asked to dole out tickets for snow-shoveling violations, he gave one to himself and several to the mayor. He had learned, in a brief army career, to do things by the book. Hired in 1994 as police chief of Santa Fe, Mr. Grady tried to break up what he called an "old boy network" in the police department, which hadn't had an outsider as chief for decades. He demanded fewer specialists, more community stations and strict enforcement of rules, such as no free coffee. City Hall backed him, citizens wrote letters of support, but police officers held a no-confidence vote, which Mr. Grady lost 103–5.

The battle got national media attention when Mr. Grady insisted officers wear clip-on neckties for safety reasons; Hispanic leaders protested that their round-the-neck bolo ties were a state symbol. Santa Fe's tiny African-American community held a rally casting Mr. Grady as a victim of racism. Race was always in the background, says Isaac Pino, former city manager, who recalls that a city councilor asked whether he really wanted to hire a black man to run a mostly Hispanic department. Still, Mr. Pino, who eventually withdrew his support for Mr. Grady, recalls that "his management style was a little despotic."

Mr. Grady concluded the battle was simply doomed from the start. He resigned, got a Ph.D. in applied management from Walden University, Minneapolis, and put his name up for international jobs, though he had never been abroad. The U.S., which now has 700 police officers overseas, was relatively new to international police work, and the State Department was looking for strong personalities such as Mr. Grady to make a mark. "The Europeans are always complaining we send old, fat cops, so we send him through the door," one U.S. official says. Leaving his wife in their Albuquerque home, Mr. Grady flew off to build a police force in Brcko, a city whose status was left undecided in the 1995 Bosnia peace agreement. There, former colleagues say Mr. Grady's decisiveness won him respect, if not affection. When a Serb mob gathered in front of an international-administration office, Mr. Grady went through the crowd with a translator, asking what was bothering the Serbs and inviting their leaders to come inside to talk. During an August 1997 riot, Mr. Grady saw his car set on fire and his police force trapped. Convinced that someone had obtained a copy of the evacuation plan, Mr. Grady learned to hide information from locally hired staff.

As a U.N. police supervisor, Mr. Grady had broader firing power than a U.S. police chief. He got rid of half of the purple-uniformed Serb police force, relying on Croats and Bosnians to identify radical members. Mr. Grady held police-chief meetings to get Brcko's Muslim, Croat and Serb police to work together, and when Serbs boycotted, he made sure they knew what decisions they had missed.

"How do you make a child go to school with somebody they know hates them? You show him the benefits," Mr. Grady says.

Just as Brcko was showing results, fighting in Kosovo heated up. In the fall of 1998, it became clear the province would soon have an international police force. The State Department sent Mr. Grady to the Vienna-based Organization for Security and Cooperation in Europe to start planning. His scheme was to get a new local police force running quickly by having internationals train local officers one-on-one and gradually giving them more autonomy over three years. Mr. Grady even sent a team to refugee camps in Albania to find candidates for a new Kosovo police force.

The U.N. ended up getting the police job instead of the OSCE, but the U.N. adopted Mr. Grady's basic plan. The U.S. fought with European officials to put an American near the top of the U.N. police mission: again, Don Grady, who got local police as part of his portfolio. Police recruitment was already under way when Mr. Grady arrived. The U.N. got 23,000 applications, but almost all from Albanians. A few Serbs who did apply turned up on lists of war criminals. Doubts arose within the U.N. whether building a local force quickly was a good idea. But Mr. Grady was so optimistic that he pushed for hiring more older police—to give the force a natural retirement rate in years ahead.

In the academy, Serbs got hard stares and threats from Albanian classmates, and went absent for several days. The OSCE, which runs the police academy, coaxed them back, and the training—which included "human dignity"—drew them closer. In an anecdote that quickly made the rounds of international officials, a group of cadets went into town and encountered neighborhood youths who asked, "Where are the Serbs?" Albanian cadets told them, "We're not Serb or Albanian, we're Kosovo police." Still, at a graduation ceremony, the crowd applauded only Albanian names.

Mr. Grady has an integration plan. Set up a meeting among Albanian officers and a Serb moderate, let them exchange concerns. Then move to small groups, perhaps five Albanian officers meeting five Serbs to talk about local problems. Then put an Albanian officer into a Serb area, for a few minutes at first, then eventually full-time, relying on the support of the Serbs from the meetings. At some point, replace this officer with another Albanian. "It's not a complicated process," Mr. Grady says.

An "information collection and analysis team" works the cafés and gauges ethnic tensions. Kevin Smith, one of the officers in the unit, says he managed to find a few moderate Serbs and Albanians sitting together as friends in divided Mitrovica. Their advice: It's much too early to put an Albanian in a Serb area.

Already, though, Mr. Grady's ideas are being tested around Gnjilane (pronounced "Jee-Lahn"), a region south of Pristina where four Serb cadets are training as officers. Serbs are being murdered every few days—with bullets, hand grenades, mortars—and nobody will admit to being a witness, the Gnjilane police station's mostly American commanders say. They respond to calls using a color-coded map, with green shading for Serb villages, yellow for Albanian, red and green for the few remaining mixed villages.

The tattered police station is in the same spot as always. Most of the officers were Albanian until November 19, 1989, when the Yugoslav government fired the Albanians, former police employees say—part of Yugoslav president Slobodan Milosevic's crackdown on autonomous Kosovo. The owners of two shoe stores across the street say they often heard screams coming from the station's upstairs rooms. They say Serb officers demanded cash from them, on the excuse that they weren't allowed to hold deutsche marks, though local Albanians are divided over whether any of the current Serb officers were involved in abuses.

One recent Tuesday, a joint military-police patrol pulled over a weaving truck. Mile Filipovic, a Serb who had been a longtime traffic officer before joining the Kosovo Police Service, asked the driver for his registration—in the Serbian language. The Albanian truck driver shouted, "I know you, and I'm going to kill you tonight," and was arrested by the peacekeeping troops for the threat, police officials say. Mr. Filipovic got a lecture.

The next day, during roll call, Serb cadets protested that nobody told them they had to speak Albanian. The station's Serbs had two days off, and rumors circulated that Mr. Filipovic wouldn't come back Saturday.

Saturday morning, American patrolman Manny Stinehour drives into Mr. Filipovic's all-Serb village to pick him up. At the front porch, the cadet's wife insists her husband didn't have problems with Albanians before. "It's a learning experience," Mr. Stinehour tells her, as her husband appears in the blue uniform, buckling his belt for work.

Mr. Stinehour, of German–Puerto Rican descent, quit his job as a patrolman in Killeen, Texas, to take a one-year Kosovo posting, which pays better than most U.S. patrol jobs. Riding past Gnjilane's street markets, Mr. Stinehour says he's known suspects back home to spit out slurs like "big nose Mexican" while he's arresting them. He figures the big problems in a community usually come from outsiders: in Killeen, gang members; in Gnjilane, terrorists.

Riding with Mr. Stinehour today is Lubisa Mitrovic, a Serb 19-year police veteran who has a different view. Though Mr. Mitrovic is friendly with some Albanian colleagues, he says, "The Albanian cadets know who is doing the shootings. I don't know why they won't tell us." Mr. Mitrovic says he still drives to a Serbian town every month to pick up his old $260-a-month pension from the Yugoslav government, and isn't sure the extra pay from the U.N. justifies the risk. "If Mr. Stinehour weren't here and I walked this street now, it's 100% that I'd be kidnapped, even in a police uniform." (Mr. Grady says he recently helped convince the U.N. to raise local police salaries by 50%.)

Success here will be partly a question of avoiding the worst. Gary Carrell, regional police commander for Gnjilane, was a police monitor in Banja Luka, a Bosnian town where three Serb policemen were car-bombed in a postwar power struggle. He's concerned that the names of four Albanians detained for recent kidnappings might correspond to names of four of his cadets. He's upset that the U.N. hasn't yet provided all of the 327 international officers he was promised. But he's glad to have an idealist such as Mr. Grady on his team.

"We need people like that," Mr. Carrell says. "It's easy to say, 'It will never work out, why bother.' This is a long, painstaking process."

Or, as station commander John Selby puts it, "Our civil war was 130 years ago. This is just three or four months."

# 5

# THIS FILM HAS A BUS, EXPLOSIONS AND VEILS: CALL IT 'IRANIAN SPEED'

## Tehran's Take on Hostages Has an Interesting Twist: Americans Hold Passengers

*November 19, 1996*

TEHRAN, Iran—Sixteen years after the fact, the full story of the Iran hostage crisis is about to reach the silver screen.

The audience meets the protagonists in the opening sequence. But these hostages are on a bus, not in an embassy. And they're Iranian, not American. Their captors? U.S. soldiers, of course. "Sandstorm," an Iranian film scheduled for release here in February, doesn't devote any screen time to the 52 American hostages who were held for 444 days by militant students after the November 1979 storming of the U.S. embassy.

Instead, the film focuses on 44 Iranian bus passengers who were detained for about three hours in April 1980 after their vehicle stumbled upon a remote desert site, where American helicopters and planes were grouping for a planned assault on Tehran that failed miserably.

As in any good suspense film, there is the obligatory cast of sympathetic characters: a health worker riding the bus because her car broke down, pilgrims on their way to a holy site, a bus driver who comically mistakes the invading planes for UFOs.

Things turn nasty when the Americans surround the bus and start slapping the passengers around to find out if any are revolutionary guards. The hostages argue in hushed tones whether to run away or cooperate with their captors. They rush off to tell authorities when they are freed, and the Americans flee. Later in the film, one passenger who returns to the site is martyred when he stands too close to a U.S. helicopter that blows up.

The plot is historically accurate—albeit with the details embellished in the great movie-making tradition. The film's writers say that focusing on the bus injects some needed drama into the actual events. After all, the Americans never did encounter any Iranian soldiers during their aborted mission. They flew home after losing three helicopters to dust storms and equipment problems; eight Americans died in a midair collision during the retreat.

Dwelling on Iranian "hostages" is "revisionist history," says Wade Ishimoto, a top commando during the 1980 mission and now a special-operations expert at the Sandia National Laboratories in New Mexico. "In terms of the law, we took some hostages," he acknowledges, but "our intentions were totally different" than Iran's hostage takers. The only harm he recalls coming to the bus passengers: The driver, who tried to run away, got bopped on the head, and a passenger's laundry somehow ended up on a U.S. C-130 transport plane and was never returned.

Not that Hollywood hasn't taken a stab at revising the story of the Desert One rescue mission. The only movie to deal with it, the 1986 film "Delta Force," opens with a four-minute sequence recounting the American retreat. Then it spins off into a fictional tale about Arab terrorists who hijack a jetliner to Beirut. "Sandstorm" director Javed Shamaghdari of Mahreb Film Corp. in Tehran marvels: "How could the movie maker actually ignore all the events that happened before those four minutes?"

When asked why his film doesn't deal with the U.S. hostages, Mr. Shamaghdari crosses his arms, leans back in his office chair, and says that they weren't relevant. The U.S. was really trying to pull off a coup—not rescue its countrymen, he says. "It's such a silly excuse for an attack like that."

Mahreb Film had no trouble getting its script approved by Iranian film authorities. While Western audiences have embraced Iranian art films like the poignant "The White Balloon," Iran's Islamic government is pushing for more films that spread the message of the Iranian revolution to the world, especially war movies. Mahreb had already proved itself with the film "On the Wings of Angels," which portrays martyred soldiers as angels. The government helped fund "Sandstorm," and provided some old American helicopters for the filming.

Casting was a challenge, though. Not many Iranians speak and look like Americans. To play a U.S. general, Mr. Shamaghdari hired a university English teacher who had never acted before. The role of U.S. Delta Force founder and commander Charles Beckwith is played by Ahmad Najafi, a hazel-eyed 48-year-old Iranian television star. Mr. Najafi, who has a passable American accent, says he has some sympathy for Americans: He was once married to an American woman, and was in a California hospital recovering from a traffic accident at the time of the rescue mission.

"If we want to go for the truth, let's go for the truth," Mr. Najafi says of his approach to his role, as he smokes Winstons and relaxes in a tan poplin suit and loafers in a hotel lobby. He says he insisted he would take the part only if "it's not going to be like the Americans do to us, showing us with no teeth." For research, Mr. Najafi even started to telephone a surviving commander in the U.S., before realizing that the call might be misconstrued. Instead, he read the late Mr. Beckwith's book, and had a sequence added to the film in which the colonel breaks down and cries over the mission's failure.

For his part, Mr. Shamaghdari is suspicious of Americans. He figures they rate about 15 of 20 points in God's eyes, if Iranians are 18 out of 20. In May, he told an Iranian newspaper that a Swiss diplomat had been accosted near the filming site at Tabas, apparently trying to discover the film's production schedule. (Switzerland represents U.S. interests in Iran.) The Swiss embassy's explanation: The diplomat and his wife were merely passing through Tabas on vacation.

Mr. Shamaghdari wouldn't mind if Americans got a chance to see his film. After all, he says, the sandstorm that scotched the mission—an act of God—saved America from a horrible mistake that the U.S. seems bent on repeating now with its threats against Iran. "It's good for Americans they lost in this one case."

The domestic audience, meanwhile, may give "Sandstorm" mixed reviews. Iran has been trying to revive interest in the 1980 mission, laying plans for a memorial on the site and holding commemorations each April that draw thousands to Tabas.

But many young Iranians find the subject a bore. An 18-year-old girl named Ladan, hanging out recently at the Golestan shopping center in

West Tehran, says her high-school teachers spoke about the failed rescue mission every year during student assemblies, but "we didn't care to listen." Adds Naghmeh, a 16-year-old girl munching an ice-cream cone nearby and trying in vain to recall any details: "There are so many other things to think about, it's not important what happened 17 years ago."

# BEAUTY SHOWS TURN BEASTLY AS SPONSORS BARE LACQUERED NAILS

## A Tiff Over 'L'il Miss Georgia' and 'Achy Breaky Heart' Sashays Into County Court

*February 2, 1993*

JONESBORO, Ga.—At the age of nine, Ashley Kinard has discovered just how ugly the business of beauty can be.

A winner of more than 25 beauty titles, Ashley now finds herself at the center of a war between two beauty pageants. She has watched grown women scheme over her, scream over her, and sue each other. Last October, while waiting to go on stage to sing "Achy Breaky Heart" at the Jonesboro Fall Festival, she learned that the Starlite USA pageant company had stripped her of her "Little Miss Georgia" crown. The reason: She allegedly broke a contract by singing the Billy Ray Cyrus hit at the same festival the previous day as "1992 National Overall Most Beautiful" queen for Starlite's archrival, Prestige Pageants.

"She cannot perform as Little Miss Bookcase on Saturday, then Little Miss Georgia on Sunday," says Jan Kennedy, executive director of Georgia Beauty Pageants Inc., which owns Starlite. "It's confusing to the public, it downgrades our title, and we simply will not tolerate it."

Ms. Kennedy's company filed suit in Henry County magistrate court against Ashley's parents to get back the blue sash, rhinestone tiara and the magnetic car emblems that proclaim Ashley "Little Miss Georgia." Her parents have countersued. And Prestige has rallied to her defense, saying Starlite dethroned her over a "blurred technicality." A court hearing is scheduled for next week.

"It's a war," says Stanton Varnadoe, a pageant judge and owner of Exclusively Dressed, a local dress shop where moms routinely drop hundreds of dollars on rayon and lace in the hopes, Mr. Varnadoe suspects, of influencing his vote. Parents aside, he says, "with all the bickering between pageants, it's gotten to where it's a dog-eat-dog situation."

Small wonder. Pageant promoters popped up everywhere in the 1980s, as more and more mothers dressed their tiny tots in white gowns and eyeliner and trained them to sashay. Soon, there were 1,500 beauty contests attracting half a million girls nationwide, says Ted Cohen, president of World Pageants Inc., which publishes a directory of the contests. Then the recession hit. Parents found they had to be choosy. Beauty competitions could cost thousands of dollars, what with Western wear, sportswear, evening clothes and professional pageant coaches, not to mention the typical $200 entry fee, $500 hotel stay, and mandatory good-luck ads in the pageant programs. Many could no longer afford to enter their kids in everything from "Plum Pretty" to "USA's Loveliest Miss." Competition among pageants got cutthroat, says Claudia Tatum, who lives in Atlanta and has been involved with pageants for 20 years. Things are so bad in Florida, she says, that pageant directors would cancel each other's hotel reservations.

The beauty world was a lot prettier in the early '70s, when Sue Jones, Starlite's founder, got started in the business. Her first pageant was a fund-raiser to help her daughter Jan's baton-twirling team travel to South Bend, Ind. When she started producing pageants for profit, she had the run of this town, about 25 miles south of Atlanta, which is the site of the fictional Tara in "Gone With the Wind." What little competition Mrs. Jones encountered in those days was mostly friendly. Directors shared mailing lists and staff, and they took care not to schedule pageants on the same day.

As her daughter, a former legal secretary, started running the business, the field was getting crowded. Some new directors were pageant mothers upset with the quality of judging. Others were entrepreneurs looking for a hot opportunity.

One of those was Kay Beckom, who attended her first Starlite pageant in 1987 as she was deciding to quit the real-estate business. She formed Prestige Pageants, scheduled a pageant in Jonesboro and immediately started butting heads with Starlite. First, rumors circulated she was going to try to put Starlite out of business. Then word got around that she was paying people to avoid Starlite's pageants. Both rumors were unfounded, she says.

For its part, Starlite warned mothers not to use other pageants because they might face "unqualified judges." Prestige started a newsletter, Pageant Patter News, which slammed Starlite's practices, and began scheduling pageants the same days as Starlite's.

They tried to outdo each other in perks and prizes, too. Starlite pageants are aired on a local TV station and its winners are featured in commercials for a dry-cleaner and other businesses. Although it has tougher rules—like no hair pieces—it holds the coveted "Miss Georgia" moniker. "Everyone wants that title," says Anne Kim, whose 17-month-old daughter, Macie, has already been in 10 pageants. But Prestige, some parents say, offers better prizes: a 1993 Hyundai Excel, for example, compared with Starlite's trip to Las Vegas.

Starlite has begun guarding its 15-odd trademarked titles with vigilance, sometimes admonishing girls who wear rival titles like "Miss Georgia Peach." To keep out fly-by-night competitors, the pageant company also helped convince the Georgia legislature to pass a law requiring pageants to post a $10,000 bond. Ms. Kennedy then kept county district attorneys busy by tattling on rivals that didn't list a bond company in their brochures.

Ashley Kinard became a crucial battleground. The youngster, who won her first "Baby Miss" title before she was out of diapers, has accumulated more than 500 beauty-pageant trophies over the years. Judges praised her "beautiful delicate soft features" and her inventive costumes—like the tuxedo she stripped away to reveal a black-and-white polka dot dress in 1991. If Ashley snubbed Starlite, five or six other pageant regulars would follow, contends her father, John. Gail Kinard says Ms. Kennedy asked her not to let her daughter, who won the "Little Miss Georgia" crown in both 1990 and 1992, sing for another pageant last October: "She said, 'Ashley is mine.'" (Ms. Kennedy says she doesn't recall saying that.)

When she did sing "Achy Breaky Heart" for Prestige, Ashley was surprised to see Mrs. Jones and another Starlite official in the audience, snapping photos. The next day, beside the same stage, her aunt gave her a corn dog and broke the news that Starlite had just stripped her of the title and given it to her runner-up.

But the Kinards refused to surrender the sash and tiara, and their spat with Starlite continued. Ms. Kennedy says she will soon disclose information about Gail Kinard that will "freak these people." Meanwhile, Kinard supporters are buzzing about sending a complaint against Starlite to state officials.

In Starlite's office off Tara Boulevard, Mrs. Jones expresses some concern about what effect the beauty battle might have on the beautiful children. "I really hate it—for Ashley," she says, as she helps her daughter search for the videotape of a commercial from which Ashley would soon be excised.

So far, Ashley has managed to keep her composure. She'd like her title back because "it makes me feel like a queen," but she doesn't get as worked up as her parents do. Although her mother can see her growing up to be a soap-opera star, Ashley, who has three schnauzers and a pet rabbit named Starlite, would prefer to be a veterinarian. In fact, she says she plans to leave the pageant circuit for a few years and play more baseball.

—*Laurie M. Grossman*
*contributed to this article.*

# 7

# VANISHING ACTS: HOW 2 FLORIDA FIRMS FOOLED STOCKHOLDERS, AUDITORS AND THE SEC

## Cascade International Was Largely a Mirage, and So Was College Bound Inc.

### Cosmetics and Cram Courses

*July 8, 1992*

If a company is largely a mirage, how long should it take for investors to find that out? With two Florida companies, Cascade International Inc. and College Bound Inc., it took years. Quarter after quarter, the two enterprises continued to win the praise of investors, the loyalty of employees, and the approval of auditors, even though much of their revenue—and all of their profits—apparently were an illusion.

Their stories are bizarre. Cascade International, a women's clothing and cosmetics retailer, had a vanishing chief executive, an imaginary cosmetics division, and millions of shares of bogus stock. College Bound, for its part, kept a secret bank account, and five of every six dollars it supposedly took in for coaching students for college-entrance exams were a fiction, according to investigators.

Still, both companies were able to flourish for mundane reasons—overburdened regulators, inattentive auditors, and an economic slump that encouraged struggling companies to resort to fraud and discouraged employees from blowing the whistle.

"I'm sure there are a lot of similar cases out there," says Howard Schilit, an American University accounting professor who studied College Bound and other apparently fraudulent companies. The hot stock market of the 1980s encouraged small, often struggling companies to turn to the public markets in unprecedented numbers.

Deltec Securities Corp., a New York firm that invested more than $9 million in Cascade International, has cooled to small-growth companies. Cascade International is "an ugly example of things that could happen elsewhere," says John R. Gordon, Deltec's president.

The founders of Cascade International and College Bound started out as typical entrepreneurs, slavishly devoted to their companies, convinced they had winning formulas, and unwilling to accept defeat.

Victor Incendy had the enthusiasm but not the knack for business. He and his wife, Jeannette, launched a company that made lipstick cases in the early 1970s. After two years, its equipment was repossessed. Similar start-ups went nowhere, and Mr. Incendy was always late paying bills, former business associates recall.

Then, in 1985, Mr. Incendy tried a new tack. He gave his creditors stock in a new public company that would sell Jean Cosmetics—lipsticks, blushes and nail polishes—designed by his wife. Eager investors bought in, and Mr. Incendy began buying bankrupt women's clothing stores that could be an outlet for the cosmetics.

By 1989, the retailing downturn was killing Cascade International. Independent retailers, like Fashion Bug, wouldn't accept the company's cosmetics counters, and the Incendys were having problems turning around their newly acquired Allison's and Diana's women's clothing chains. Yet analysts, relying mostly on Mr. Incendy's rosy projections, predicted ever-higher earnings. Mr. Incendy, apparently to buy time, claimed to have more and more cosmetics counters—255 by last year. The truth was closer to six. At the same time, Mr. Incendy created and began secretly selling more than six million shares of unauthorized stock, according to lawyers for the company and its creditors.

Mr. and Mrs. Incendy, now divorced, both disappeared last November and haven't turned up. Cascade International's stock is worthless. The company's Chapter 11 bankruptcy trustee recently closed the remaining 29 stores. They are scheduled to be auctioned off later this month.

College Bound's founders also started out legitimately. Janet Ronkin, a former schoolteacher, wanted her sons to go to medical school, so she tutored them herself for college-entrance exams. (They ended up going to the University of Miami law school.) Then, friends asked her to tutor their children. By 1981, she and her husband, George, were running a thriving little company out of their Plantation,

Fla., garage. The idea was to help students cram for exams, choose extracurricular activities, pick a college, even iron out problems with teachers.

But expanding the concept beyond affluent south Florida was tougher than the Ronkins expected when they began to sell franchises in 1986. By 1988, franchisees were demanding the Ronkins buy them out. Desperate for cash to expand, the Ronkins solved their problem by taking the company public. They raised $30 million from European investors over the years, according to their investment banker.

The Ronkins quickly opened centers throughout the country. Their goal was 15 a quarter—and they sought immediate results. The Ronkins, whose company had moved into gleaming offices in Crocker Center in Boca Raton, often worked until midnight and were back in their twin offices, separated by a sliding door, at eight in the morning. At some point before the fall of 1990, to mask the poor turnout at many of their new centers, they began concocting revenue by transferring money from one bank account to another, according to the Securities and Exchange Commission, which is suing the couple for allegedly defrauding investors. The SEC estimates College Bound overstated its center revenues by $8.9 million, or 489%, last year.

Through their Tampa, Fla., lawyer, John Lauro, the Ronkins deny intentional wrongdoing. Mr. Lauro says they "intend to litigate this case very aggressively." College Bound's centers have all been closed, and the company now is being sold off in bankruptcy court. The highest bid for the test-preparation business is $600,000—less than 0.5% of its value in the Nasdaq market a year ago.

To some, it was obvious the companies weren't what they purported to be. Thomson McKinnon, a brokerage firm that was one of Cascade International's early boosters, became so suspicious of the company in 1987 that it quietly eased its clients out of the stock. Catherine Hall, hired to be Cascade International's in-house attorney in late 1989, testified in May that she quit after four months. She said a call to the company's insurance carrier showed Cascade had far fewer stores and cosmetic counters than it claimed.

Cosmetics-industry officials say they had never heard of Jean Cosmetics, even though the company said in its 1986 annual report, for example, that "Jean Cosmetics is in the formidable company of Lancôme,

Estée Lauder, Elizabeth Arden and other well-established firms." As for College Bound, John Katzman, president of Princeton Review, a leading test-preparation firm, called it the "stealth competitor" because "they don't show up anywhere on the radar map." Others, however, took the company's SEC filings at face value, including James Bax, who sold his 17-year-old professional-testing firm to College Bound in May 1991 for shares that now are worthless. Mr. Bax, who recently had to pay more than $1 million to get the company back, says, "Most people assume, with the government putting its imprimatur on something, that it's certifying that they're OK."

In fact, Cascade International and College Bound's operations flew too low for the government's radar for years. Both companies went public in a way that attracts less scrutiny than an initial public offering: merging into an existing shell corporation. The Incendys, for instance, merged Jean Cosmetics into Cascade Importers, a public company with no operations, and got most of the public company's stock in return. The gambit is popular among entrepreneurs because they can save months of work and hundreds of thousands of dollars by avoiding the formal underwriting of an initial public offering.

Once public, both Cascade International and College Bound did file regularly with the SEC. But the agency's main office gives only about 10% of all annual reports and 7% of all quarterly reports full reviews. And the Miami branch, which has 15 attorneys and one accountant, investigates tips rather than systematically screening for fraud. "Policemen don't stand outside every bank and wait for a bank robbery," says Edward Noakes, the SEC's deputy chief accountant.

Even when the SEC follows up a tip, it can still be slow going. In the case of College Bound, the SEC at first was sidetracked by charges made by stock speculators that some of the company's centers didn't exist. But College Bound officials produced a box of leases and a scrapbook of photos with managers standing in front of their centers. It took the SEC most of last year to discover the alleged bank-account manipulation. SEC officials won't comment on either investigation.

The SEC says that making sure companies' revenues are real is not its job. "The auditors are there to find material fraud," says Mr. Noakes. "We don't do audits."

The auditor for Cascade International was Bernard H. Levy, an amiable Manhattanite who had prepared Mr. Incendy's personal tax returns for years. He worked mostly from his Central Park South apartment, but the company maintained a private office for him at its headquarters in Boca Raton. Cascade International also leased a car for him, according to a company document.

Mr. Levy won't talk about Cascade International now, but in an interview last November, he explained that Mr. Incendy told him to simply write the SEC reports and not to worry about auditing subsidiaries. That was supposedly done by other Incendy accountants, he said. When Mr. Incendy disappeared, Mr. Levy said he didn't have the name of the accountant for the phantom Jean Cosmetics unit.

Last year, Mr. Levy endorsed financial reports that said the company had $11.1 million in profit in the year ending June 30, 1991. The reality, according to the company's bankruptcy examiner, was more like a $7.1 million loss. "Obviously I didn't do everything I should have done," Mr. Levy said in the November interview. "I'm a trusting person."

Professional standards for auditors prohibit such things as driving a company car and trusting the chief executive about subsidiary results. To enforce the standards, a trade group, the American Institute of Certified Public Accountants (AICPA), requires members who audit public companies to let another firm review their work regularly. But neither the SEC nor the National Association of Securities Dealers (NASD), which listed Cascade International and College Bound shares, requires auditors to join the trade group; Mr. Levy didn't.

Gordon K. Goldman, College Bound's auditor until last March, was a member of the AICPA. But Mr. Goldman, a close friend of Mrs. Ronkin's twin brother, never did get a peer review. (The trade group says it is investigating why.) The 47-year-old accountant works out of his house in the borough of Queens in New York City and didn't bother to attend College Bound's only annual meeting last year.

Nobody has claimed that Mr. Goldman colluded with the Ronkins. But he attested to College Bound's claim last year of $5.5 million in net income. The SEC says the company actually had a loss. One thing Mr. Goldman apparently failed to notice was that expense records had been inflated by adding two digits to the left (a $538.48 furniture invoice was listed on a ledger as a $43,538.48 expense, for example, according to investigators.)

Mr. Goldman's only comment: "If you want to bury something, you can bury it. You can bury it in a way that can't be found by someone who doesn't already suspect it."

Currently, "there's no requirement that an accountant look actively for fraud," says Rep. Ron Wyden. The Oregon Democrat has sponsored three unsuccessful bills aimed at changing that. He believes many auditors, large and small, are more concerned with protecting their client relationship than the public.

Many investors believed the companies' ability to get NASD listing meant they were real. Yale Hirsch, publisher of the Ground Floor Newsletter, touted Cascade International in the fall of 1990 without visiting the company or its stores. He says, "When a company is on Nasdaq and is a fairly decent size, you assume they're doing decent work."

But NASD says it doesn't inspect the operations of the 4,000 companies it lists and can't inspect their books. The organization does require each listed company to have at least two "independent" directors on its board, individuals "able to exercise independent judgment." The independence of College Bound and Cascade International's boards was questionable. College Bound was negotiating with one of its two independent directors to buy out his company's 50% interest in 31 Ronkin centers for College Bound stock. Mr. Incendy dominated Cascade International's board and kept it from meeting more than once a year, according to a former director's lawsuit.

In the absence of aggressive auditors and board members, the SEC relies on tips from employees that something is amiss. But both Cascade International and College Bound kept workers well-paid and ill-informed. Maurice Mayberry, who was paid $101,538 last year, had the title of chief financial officer of College Bound. But he didn't do much more than pay the company's bills, according to his deposition in bankruptcy court. He said he didn't track the company's revenues or checking accounts—the Ronkins did—and that, one day, he found he could no longer see the company's bank balances because Mrs. Ronkin had changed the computer password. Center directors didn't know their own profitability, because they deposited checks into shared bank accounts and sent bills directly to headquarters. "I had no idea what my center needed to break even, and no budget to work with," says Mark Bilotta, a former center director in Worcester, Mass. One former College Bound manager recalls asking Mrs. Ronkin for sales reports on the centers, and "she smiled and patted me on the back and said, 'They're doing great out there.' "

At Cascade International, John T. Sirmans was the Incendys' vice president. Mr. Incendy, when questioned about the cosmetics counters, "told me that he would give me the list of his counters when I could give him the list of the Avon ladies from Avon," Mr. Sirmans testified. On other occasions, he said, Mr. Incendy pulled a manila folder from his briefcase and read off figures purportedly from the cosmetics division. "I was fed just enough to satisfy me," said Mr. Sirmans. Money was enough incentive for some people to keep their mouths shut. Unlike the Defense Department and the Internal Revenue Service, the SEC doesn't pay informants. Bernard Lake, who joined Cascade International as a buying manager in 1988, said he knew within three months that the Incendys were "playing a game" of some kind. But, "I got a good paycheck on Friday. I didn't give a damn what they did."

# 8

# TO BE A BLACK COP CAN MEAN WALKING A VERY FINE LINE

## After the Rodney King Verdict, Officers at Work in Atlanta Must Endure Many Taunts

*May 7, 1992*

ATLANTA—Tyrone B. Powell of the Atlanta police was one of hundreds of officers confronting black students protesting the Rodney King verdict in the streets here last week. The students threw bricks, the police lobbed tear gas, and from behind his riot shield Sgt. Powell could see the anger in the protesters' faces—and hear the taunts.

"You should be ashamed," they shouted to him. "You're selling out. . . . You're black before you're blue."

Sgt. Powell doesn't need them to remind him; 24 years ago he was on the other side of the police line. Following the assassination of Martin Luther King, Jr., he says he joined a mob in New York City and threw rocks at the police confronting him. "I remember how angry I was," he recalls. "I understand the people throwing rocks."

The acquittal of the Los Angeles policemen in the beating of black motorist Rodney King, and the violence that followed the verdict, have intensified the already uncomfortable position that many black police officers feel themselves in. No matter how hard they may work to improve community relations, they are part of a justice system that many blacks feel tends to fail them. In some cases, black cops are having to suppress protesters with whom they empathize. In other cases, they are being asked: Are you black or are you blue?

"There's a frustration—they've been out there trying to do a good job and keep the calm, and they're going to be targeted," says Calvin J. Howard, past president of the National Black Police Association. Cpl. Howard, a Dallas policeman for 19 years, says he dreads the rioting he fears will inevitably resume if the Los Angeles police officers aren't ultimately convicted for beating Mr. King. "If my grown children are out there protesting the injustice in the justice system, it's going to be hard for me to turn my nightstick on them."

Atlanta isn't the most likely place for such tensions to arise. The city's mayor and police chief are black, as is 53% of its police force. Atlanta has avoided major racial confrontations over the years.

But last Thursday, blacks reacting to the King verdict tore through downtown, overturning cars, smashing store windows, and beating white people. The next day, students from Atlanta's six black colleges faced off against police officers, many of them black, when the students tried to march downtown again. The police turned them back. Some students complained the officers beat them and provoked them, and black leaders criticized the cops for keeping students from assembling on campus; one called the officers "lackeys."

Sgt. Powell, for his part, ignored the insults and shouted back, "Move! Move! Move!" with his booming voice and stern jaw. "You can't show any emotion on your face," says the 40-year-old officer. But because Sgt. Powell is who he is, he has a good understanding of the protesters. "You think what you're doing right now is going to change the world that second," he says of the protesters. But, "no, it's not."

Sgt. Powell grew up in Harlem, where by high school he had lost his father to tuberculosis, his mother to a heart attack, and most of his friends to violence or drugs. Despite his role in the establishment, Sgt. Powell faces regular reminders that he remains a black man in an often racist world. When he drove around the back of a supermarket once looking for boxes, a white patrolman rushed to stop him, and later said, "You just don't look like a police officer." When he walks into a general store in north Georgia with his wife, who is white, everybody goes silent. He says he would hesitate to take his wife on his Harley Davidson motorcycle for fear of getting run off the road.

"I know racism is alive and well," he says. And that makes putting down the rebellion a wrenching experience.

"I hope I'm always going to be fighting dope dealers and common criminals. That part of the job I can handle," says Sgt. Powell, who carries 72 rounds of ammunition on his belt. "But demonstrations, where people have strong ideals, similar to my own—I hope never to get in a situation like that again."

Don Smith, a senior patrol officer in the same unit, says black officers can't help feeling "ambivalence" about the last week, since many of
them believe the justice system isn't fair to poor people and minorities.
Officer Smith, 33, who was raised in a poor, black section of Atlanta,
says he wishes he could have worked with student leaders immediately
after the King verdict to help channel their rage in a nonviolent way.
When he joined the force 10 years ago, he thought being black would
make a difference. "I was idealistic, young and naive, thinking, 'Well,
this is a person's community, they're going to communicate with me in
an effort to eradicate any problem they may have.' You find out people
are reluctant to communicate with the police." Officer Ray Griffin tries
his best to bridge the gap. He recalls that the police had a bad image in
the neighborhood where he grew up in inner-city Milwaukee. Minor
transgressions triggered verbal abuse from police, and blacks venturing
into the suburbs risked being stopped by patrolmen for questioning.
But when basketball and computer science didn't pan out, Mr. Griffin
found himself applying for a job with the Atlanta police. "I thought, if I
become a police officer, maybe I can make a difference," he says.

In small but important ways, he is. On patrol in southwest Atlanta—
a middle-class neighborhood that is almost entirely black—Officer
Griffin is less an enforcer than a community-relations worker. Watching
a driver squeeze through a red light, he says, "I'll get him next time."
But when a distraught man walks up to describe having car trouble, Officer Griffin drives four blocks to the man's car and starts it himself.

He also stops to chat with local business people, like Stan Blackburn,
who runs a fried-chicken restaurant, and Mike Dean, a security guard at
a Dairy Queen. Rodney King is still the hot topic, and 32-year-old Officer Griffin shakes his head with his friends as they tell him that a new,
more detailed version of the video of the Rodney King beating shows
Los Angeles police beating Mr. King's companion, too. "It's embarrass-
ing, as far as law enforcement goes," Officer Griffin says. But in his patrol car, Officer Griffin is just another man in blue to those outside.
Sunday, a black man flashes his middle finger at Officer Griffin as he
drives by in his patrol car with a white partner. Monday, a black
teenager in a football jersey stands unyielding in the street, blocking Officer Griffin's patrol car from passing through. The two silently stare
each other down for 10 seconds before the youth finally steps aside.

"There's gonna be people out there that don't like the police, period," Officer Griffin says, insisting it doesn't bother him. He disagrees with any suggestion that he's less black because he's a cop. "I'm a black person, but I took an oath to do my job," he says. "It's a job I chose to do." Patrolling the southwest side Monday night, Officer Griffin climbs the stairs of the Allen Temple apartments with a white officer to investigate a domestic dispute. Six young black men, two wearing Malcolm X caps, watch as they approach. When Officer Griffin's colleague extends his hand toward a black toddler and says, "Hey, buddy," one of the onlookers sneers, "There's a little Rodney King."

As the policemen leave the building minutes later, one of the young men challenges Officer Griffin. "Where's your black armband," he asks, "to protest our unjust treatment last week?"

"Where's yours?" the officer responds.

"I've got black all over me," says the young man, pointing to his own arms and legs.

"Well, I do too," says Officer Griffin, getting into his patrol car.

# 9

# MAROONED: THE UPWARDLY MOBILE FIND HOPES DASHED ON SUBURBAN PLATEAUS

## Gwinnett County, Ga., Was a Booming Way Station Until the Growth Stopped

## A New Industry: Pawn Shops

*March 30, 1992*

GWINNETT COUNTY, Ga.—This was once the land of great expectations.

A white-collar haven and one of the fastest-growing suburbs in the country, Gwinnett County, on Atlanta's northern rim, seemed like just the ticket for ambitious couples like Steve and Jean Alhadeff. When the Alhadeffs bought their $70,000 starter home in the brand-new Oakbrook Station subdivision in 1984, it was as much an investment as a place to live. The nearby hum of route I-85 didn't bother them much; it was only a matter of time before Mr. Alhadeff's accounting job would lead to a top finance position and they'd buy a bigger house in a better neighborhood. Ms. Alhadeff didn't bother to read the local paper. After all, they'd be moving on soon.

But now, two corporate cutbacks and a real-estate slump later, the Alhadeffs are stuck. They're in the same house, which is worth roughly the same amount. Mr. Alhadeff, 37, is earning the same income, selling insurance. And Ms. Alhadeff, 41, is trying to accept that they might be marooned in Oakbrook Station for some time. A "For Sale" sign is stashed in their garage.

"To expect that we're going to have this, and in five years that, and in 10 years this—maybe it doesn't make sense," says Ms. Alhadeff.

The Alhadeffs were among millions of people who gambled on booming suburbs like Gwinnett County as the ideal places to advance their lives. The 1980s saw an explosion of such communities, like

Tyson's Corner near Washington, D.C.; Aurora, near Denver; Plano, near Dallas; and Contra Costa, near San Francisco.

These were less suburbs than a new breed of city, with their own places to work and shop and their own electric optimism. Like the others, Gwinnett was a convenient way station for sales executives and young managers moving up through the regional offices of large companies. Land was cheaper here, the schools newer, the streets safer. And the new neighborhoods—with cookie-cutter homes and names like Hasty Acres and Rivermist—had so many newcomers that people didn't feel the need to pretend they planned to stay very long.

For entrepreneurs, places like Gwinnett were gold mines. The country's population doubled during the 1980s, and orange-and-white construction pylons and mud from new subdivisions filled the streets. Ten new banks emerged as if from nowhere, as did restaurant franchises, day-care facilities and office parks. Technology start-ups grew, and the managers often split off to start their own firms.

"If you didn't make money in Gwinnett you were an idiot," says Leonard Cyphers, a businessman whose ventures included video and auto-parts stores. "People were picking up $20 bills off the ground."

Now the recession and some new demographic realities have left Gwinnett a much different sort of place. It's still growing, but the feeling of guaranteed upward mobility is disappearing, perhaps permanently. Many people feel stuck: in their jobs, in their homes, in Gwinnett. For many couples, the traditional family life they came to Gwinnett to pursue is being derailed. And some neighborhoods are spiraling toward urban decay, with pawnshops anchoring their half-empty shopping centers.

Residents of Gwinnett, with their young, transient profile, are in some ways emblematic of baby boomers everywhere. The loss of expectations here helps to explain the persistent slump in consumer confidence and the malaise that has surfaced in recent political polls. It will take more than slow economic growth to cure that.

"There has been a day of reckoning in these growth suburbs," says Mark Baldassare, a professor of urban and regional planning at the University of California at Irvine, who studies such places. In Orange County, Calif., similar to Gwinnett County in both its growth patterns and demographics, consumer confidence consistently ranked much higher than in the rest of the country during the 1980s, according to an annual survey conducted by Mr. Baldassare. But in recent surveys, confidence is just as low as elsewhere. In Orange County and places like it, "the expectations were unrealistic. People were far too optimistic," he says.

In Gwinnett, real estate was the cornerstone of many families' dreams. For those who were thinking of remaining in the Atlanta area, the progression was laid out clearly: start in a place like Pony Run, with a rustic house that has small bedrooms and a stained-wood exterior. Then trade up to a "five-four and a door" in Peachtree Station: a two-story brick Colonial with five windows upstairs and four downstairs. And hope to wind up in an $800,000 tract mansion in St. Ives or Country Club of the South, where Jacuzzis, circular driveways and Tara-inspired Greek columns are standard.

Appreciation seemed such a sure bet in Gwinnett that families staked their entire futures on it. To take full advantage of housing inflation—which ran 1% a month at times—buyers stretched to get the most expensive house possible. Frequently, they kept their walls and carpets off-white to be able to sell at a moment's notice. Families raced to be the first ones into brand-new, treeless subdivisions, putting up with all the noise, dirt and construction just so they could ride the neighborhood's appreciation as each subsequent house sold for a higher price.

Then, in 1989, the game of musical houses stopped.

Jeffrey and Corrine Marcantonio's house on Gold Mine Road was to be the nest egg that would send them to Florida. The Marcantonios, both 37, had moved every four years since college, making a tidy profit on each house, which they used to buy a better house. They had planned to make one or two more moves and end up in Florida with a $30,000 to $40,000 nest egg. Mr. Marcantonio, an electrical engineer, had never been able to put much money away for savings and thought of the house as, eventually, the retirement fund.

They bought one of the first houses in their subdivision and waited for it to appreciate. But when the real-estate market slowed, builders began putting up cheaper houses nearby, many of them built on smaller lots and without porches or bay windows. When the Marcantonios tried to refinance their home recently, it was assessed for $14,000 less than they had paid for it. "It made me sick to my stomach, but there's not a damn thing I can do," says Mr. Marcantonio. "It means we're stuck here," his wife adds.

Gwinnett's real-estate bust has been aggravated by the sins of its past. George Barbee, an Army Corps of Engineers veteran who manages rental houses in Gwinnett, says he is already starting to see the casualties of fast growth: creaking floors, cracking walls, termites and paint that's peeling off window and door trim because nobody bothered to prime the wood first. "They were throwing these houses together," he says. "I'm talking about homes in the $160,000 to $190,000 price range that are literally falling apart after five or six years."

Moreover, the constant supply of new home buyers that was fueling the flow from Pony Run to St. Ives dried up. Instead of the baby boom, it's the baby bust that's now approaching home-buying age. So, during the 1990s, the Atlanta area is expected to gain just one adult under the age of 35 for every eight it gained in the previous decade, according to the University of North Carolina's Kenan Institute of Private Enterprise.

Among the victims are Ron and Dottie Darr, who had so much trouble trying to sell their house that Mr. Darr had to give up a job transfer back to the Midwest. The couple moved here in 1987 because they heard the local economy was hot. Now they're sick of it. Mr. Darr, who repairs industrial motors, wants to raise his daughters, ages 2 and 7, in a small town where people actually know each other, where "you can go to a basketball game and half the town will be there," he says. In Gwinnett, he never even sees the same person twice at the meat counter. "We want to move while our children are young enough not to remember this place," Mr. Darr says. As if the real-estate downturn weren't bad enough, corporate mobility has stalled, too. Gwinnett, with low land prices and aggressive self-promotion, had become host to a cluster of high-technology and defense companies. But many of those companies, like Scientific-Atlanta Inc. and Rockwell International Corp., have scaled back operations amid prolonged industry slumps. Some of the businesses that fed off the local real-estate boom, like law offices and engineering firms, haven't survived the long building drought. And Gwinnett's largest employers, like American Telephone & Telegraph Co., have trimmed middle-management ranks.

That has been a shock for people like 32-year-old Jeffrey Waychoff, who was on what appeared to be a rapid climb up the corporate ladder. Mr. Waychoff, who sells industrial tools for Black & Decker Corp., was transferred here from Arkansas two years ago, expecting to wait only a few years before the next transfer; his previous stint in Little Rock had been two years shorter than he and his wife, Kit, were told to expect. Gwinnett was a "stepping stone," recalls Ms. Waychoff, also 32. But the management job Mr. Waychoff would normally be stepping into has been eliminated. He says transfers are harder to get than before, and people have to negotiate for relocation packages now.

To be sure, there are still people moving into Gwinnett County. But fewer of them are white-collar professionals like Mr. Waychoff, and more of them are blue-collar or service workers like Willie Shannon and David Niblett. Mr. Shannon, who is 26, moved into an apartment here to be closer to his job driving a forklift in Gwinnett. Mr. Niblett, 29, moved to Gwinnett last month from Roanoke, Va., looking for opportunity, and promptly landed a night-shift job at a Wendy's. He is fairly confident he'll make the $200 he needs to pay the half-price first month's rent at the Cherrywood Square apartment complex, but "when the full price kicks in, I couldn't tell you," he says. Indeed, Gwinnett school officials say they're seeing more families that move around the area chasing rent specials.

They can afford to move in because in places like Peachtree Corners, a neighborhood that tries hard to be upscale, the apartments are offering lower rents. On Holcomb Bridge Road, one can find a restaurant that serves "Le Breakfast, Le Lunch, Le Dinner" and a beauty salon called Eugenie's Pampering Palace. But a few blocks away, at the Springs Village apartments, the balconies are rusting, the wood stain is fading, and the tennis nets are sagging. Victims of overbuilding and a weak economy, many such complexes have been taken over by lenders. Several, including Cherrywood Square, have invited police to occupy rooms to help chase out drug dealers.

Changes like these bother many of Gwinnett's better-heeled residents and make them feel that much more trapped. Deborah Valentine, a transplant from Decatur, Ill., who lives in a neighborhood of $220,000 Colonials on a fish pond less than a mile from Springs Village, is watching the developments nervously. She says her son's high school football team, for the first time, is having trouble keeping players eligible. She doesn't want her kids to attend a school where "all the kids drive BMWs," but she fears disadvantaged children will swing the balance the other way. "The more of those you get, the less the focus is going to be on kids like your kids," she says. And that makes Ms. Valentine, who's 43, worry that her neighborhood will take a nose dive. "Everybody's afraid to be the last to make a decision to sell out," she says. Moving isn't an option for many Gwinnett residents, though. So, instead, some are trying to change their attitude toward the place.

Laurence McCullough, pastor of Simpsonwood United Methodist Church, says he has noticed people focusing less on moving out and more on one another. His church is organizing monthly four-family dinner groups, so that participants can have conversations deeper than "Hi, how are you?" he says.

The transition toward traditional community is strained at best. Gwinnett residents come from a wide variety of backgrounds. Their subdivisions don't join together and have no sidewalks, making it hard even to jog around the neighborhood without fighting thoroughfare traffic. One boosterish guidebook was able to find just two places to go dancing in Gwinnett: a Marriott hotel and a steak house.

But in other ways the change is inevitable. The baby boomers who populate this place are approaching the age for settling down, even if they had been expecting to do it somewhere else. The Waychoffs didn't bother to make friends when they first moved to Gwinnett, since they thought they'd be leaving soon. But now they're making an effort. Ms. Waychoff recently agreed to serve as Greenfield Estates' hospitality chairwoman, greeting newly arrived neighbors with maps, a newsletter and a party, and Mr. Waychoff joined a neighborhood board. They are helping to start a church close to their home. After avoiding any "funky" touches that might hurt their home's resale value, Ms. Waychoff finally broke down and painted part of the kitchen green. And she and her husband are thinking about doing something more permanent with the backyard, which is still bare except for a swing set that can be removed to the next home. "Next year, my child will be in kindergarten. I'll become a den mom and all those things, I'm sure," says Ms. Waychoff, watching her oldest son play on the swings. "If you don't settle, it's your children who suffer," she adds. "I just realized I had to get out of the poor-pitiful-me attitude, and had to make the best of it."

# 10

# MEMO TO JUDGE: BEWARE IF TURNER BUYS TELEVISION RIGHTS TO THE TRIAL

*December 2, 1991*

ATLANTA—Thomas M. Machlay, a World Championship Wrestling referee who says his 20-year career ended when a wrestler sent him plunging headlong into the ropes, is suing the wrestler for not following the script. The lawsuit seeks . . .

Wait. Back up. The "script"? Surely Mr. Machlay isn't suggesting that all the helicopter spins, leapfrogs and body-slamming "suplexes" we see on televised wrestling are choreographed in advance?

Well, maybe. Mr. Machlay, whose stage name was Tommy Young, claims there was a script for the WCW match he adjudicated two years ago between Wild Fire Tommy Rich and Mike Rotunda. The script called for Wild Fire, a.k.a. Thomas Richardson, to push the referee out of the way "so that his attention would be diverted from the wrestlers, whereupon the other wrestler would throw Richardson from the ring," according to the lawsuit, filed Nov. 22 in state court in Atlanta.

Instead, in an unfortunate combination of mishaps, Mr. Rich tripped Mr. Machlay just as the lights in the arena went dim, and the referee struck his forehead on the ropes, causing serious spinal injury, the suit alleges. The wrestlers fought on until somebody realized that Mr. Machlay wasn't moving and might really be injured, says his attorney, David Cole.

Yes, but a script? Say it ain't so.

It ain't, says Barry Norman, publicist for World Championship Wrestling, which is owned by Turner Broadcasting System Inc. "In almost two years I've worked here, I've never, ever, ever seen a script," says Mr. Norman, who contends wrestlers really do fight and really do get injured. Dave Meltzer, who publishes the *Wrestling Observer Newsletter* from Campbell, Calif., isn't so sure. He's never seen a written script, but says that doesn't mean wrestlers don't get together before a match and let each other know what's coming. "It's kind of like, 'You lead, I'll follow,' " he says.

Mr. Rich, who couldn't be reached for comment on the suit, had a good-guy persona before recently transforming himself into a Wall Street–style villain. He now dresses in a three-piece suit for interviews, calls himself Thomas instead of Tommy, gets advice from a ringside computer during matches, and is routinely booed by fans. His motto: "Money makes the world go round."

Oh, yes: Mr. Machlay is seeking damages of more than $25,000.

# 11

# BASINGER BACKLASH BEGINS A-BREWIN' IN BURG OF BRASELTON

## Folks in the Town That Kim Bought Now Want Her to Pay Them Some Mind

*March 7, 1991*

BRASELTON, Ga.—This old cotton-trading town, owned by the same family for more than a century, went breathless when it was adopted by actress Kim Basinger.

After the Hollywood siren announced two years ago she would buy the town for $20 million, some folks rushed out to rent her movies so they would recognize her when she strolled into the Braselton Bros. Super Market. Others waited eagerly for her to open a movie studio, restore the old blacksmith shop and gristmill, and start tempting tourists from nearby Interstate Highway 85. Some people even thought the 37-year-old star of "Batman" and "9½ Weeks" would build herself a mansion in their one-stoplight town.

But so far, there is little sign of change in Braselton, population 500. And to make matters worse, there is no sign of Kim.

Ms. Basinger, in partnership with the pension fund of Ameritech Corp., the Chicago-based telecommunications company, closed the real-estate deal in January of 1990 in an Atlanta hotel. (The fund's share is undisclosed.) Since then, the part she has played has been that of an absentee landlady with increasingly testy tenants. The actress had to be replaced on the board of the $5.5-million Braselton Banking Co. because she wasn't attending meetings, and Mayor Henry Edward Braselton, whose family sold her the bank and most of the real estate in town, is still waiting to bestow the traditional municipal honors.

"We've got a key all ready for her," he says. "We just haven't been able to get her out here to pick it up."

"She's pretty," adds David Higgins, who lives with his mother, grandmother and eight cats in a Basinger-owned house (rent: $70 a month). "But she ain't done much for people around here." Braselton, to borrow a real-estate euphemism, is a fixer-upper with lots of potential. In 1887, the original Braselton boys opened a tiny general store here, about 45 miles northeast of Atlanta. Over the decades, the town grew into a bustling center for cotton trading, corn and wheat milling and—if the Braseltons weren't looking—occasional moonshining.

But the descendants of the original clan grew old, and their businesses and buildings began to decay. Today, three brick storefronts— Braselton Hardware, Braselton Furniture & Appliances and the supermarket—are still intact. But the rest of the town is a cross between "Gone With the Wind" and "The Grapes of Wrath": Two stately mansions stand beside homes with crumbling porches and sagging roofs.

Ms. Basinger entered the picture in 1987, after Braselton family members put their holdings up for sale. The deal included 18 rented homes, about 30 other buildings and some vacant land. (The town government provides municipal services.) The actress, who grew up in nearby Athens and whose parents are still there, has been fuzzy about her reasons for buying "God's little 2,800 acres," as she described it to *Movieline* magazine. (It's actually 1,700 acres.) An early Basinger press release said Braselton would let her rekindle childhood memories of "small-town warmth, inviting lazy summer afternoons and . . . binding friendships."

Ms. Basinger's only public appearance in Braselton came in 1989, soon after she agreed to buy the town, when she made an unannounced, 90-minute tour of the local Mitsubishi TV and telephone plant, signing autographs and chatting with dumbstruck workers. Mitsubishi isn't one of her tenants. Since then, the closest she has come to making contact with the town's residents is mailing autographed black-and-white photos to a few people. Terry Kitchens, 35, who has an auto-repair shop in a Basinger-owned building, has one with the inscription: "The best-looking mechanic in Braselton," supplied by her representative. But the mechanic has never met the actress.

More common are various "Kim sightings." One report has Ms. Basinger dropping in by helicopter to dine privately at a nearby winery. Another has her riding through town in a Chevy Suburban. The Barretts, who live on Route 53, swear the starlet pulled up to their house last summer in a white limousine and had her chauffeur step out and buy a cantaloupe. That made the local paper.

Townspeople have gamely tried to snare the real Kim, reasoning that her family lives just 20 miles away in Athens. But Jackson County Elementary School couldn't get her to address departing eighth graders, and Sam Sloan, manager of the Braselton Inn, can't get her to take part in a five-kilometer charity run.

"I would schedule it anytime to fit her convenience," says the still-hopeful Mr. Sloan, who keeps a "Welcome Kim Basinger" sign on his marquee.

Ms. Basinger's defenders, including one of the mayor's daughters and the real-estate agent who handled the sale, point out that the actress has a busy schedule, what with two albums and three movies in the works, plus pantyhose ads and promotional appearances. (Ms. Basinger's representatives didn't make the actress available for comment.) So Ms. Basinger leaves most details of developing Braselton to Mick Basinger, her brother and spokesman.

At a recent press conference in Braselton, Mr. Basinger said a soft real-estate market and an overloaded town sewer system—not lack of interest by his sister—are holding up plans to develop the town. He said she hopes eventually to put in shops, restaurants, a recording studio and maybe a theme park or golf course, or both. Mr. Basinger insists that his sister has been here many times, to meet with bankers and developers. But the visits aren't publicized, he says, to avoid chaos.

"You have to understand from Kim's perspective," Mr. Basinger says. "It's uncomfortable. She works her tail off to get to the position she's in, and then she has to wear sunglasses to disguise herself."

The explanations, however, do little to mollify residents. Indeed, a sort of "Basinger backlash" has been brewing here, where many residents already had their suspicions about her for reportedly dating Prince, the black rock star, and undeniably posing nude for *Playboy*. Upon learning of her spread in *Playboy*, one old-timer, who runs a local business, says he was so incensed he withdrew his money from Braselton Bank. The city council, controlled by the Braselton family, recently blocked the Basinger group from demolishing two decaying buildings pending a historical and architectural study. And even 11-year-old Chris

Howard now frets that "Batman's" co-star may turn his home into Gotham City.

"I like Braselton the way it is," he says. "You can go outside and not worry about being kidnapped or anything. If she gets all these people from Hollywood to come in, we'll have to worry about that stuff."

With each passing month, the Hollywood star and her staid little Georgia town seem to drift farther apart. December: Ms. Basinger is reported to have sold her $1 million Hollywood Hills cottage because she almost never used it; Braselton drafts a $90,700 annual budget. January: Ms. Basinger denies a magazine report that she threw temper tantrums on a movie set and demanded to fly to Brazil to see a psychic; Kit Braselton travels to Albany, Ga., to have his neck examined by his doctor nephew. February: Ms. Basinger tells *Cosmopolitan* magazine, "I don't really live in a time zone. I don't abide by the rules here on Earth"; Braselton's Lions Club, over fried chicken, coleslaw and blueberries, hears plans for a membership telethon.

Still, Ms. Basinger can probably expect a warm reception here if she returns. Consider Mr. Kitchens, who runs the auto shop. He gets giddy at the thought of being face-to-face with the blonde screen temptress who apparently considers him the best-looking mechanic in Braselton. "I want to meet her, but I don't know if I could handle it," Mr. Kitchens confides. "If I was a racing engine, I'd probably get over-revved and blow up."

# PART TWO

# *I Hope Gabriel Likes My Music*

Danny Pearl was always a music man, from country to bluegrass to jazz to soul. When he played bluegrass, he called himself a fiddler. When he played classical, he was a violinist. He played the guitar. He took salsa lessons. He wrote music. He listened to music.

Boy, did he listen to music. Danny was obsessive about music. For someone so forgetful—he left his cherished wedding album on a colleague's chair in Washington, then forgot where he'd left it—Danny was highly structured. Especially when it came to music.

"Danny had an idiosyncratic system for organizing his CD collection that had multiple axes and was based somehow—God knows how—on how the music sounded," says Jesse Pesta, a *Journal* reporter also stationed in India. "One day I was at his apartment in Bombay and he kept mentioning how he had just reorganized his CDs, and wasn't I interested to see how he had done it?"

"Unfortunately, I wasn't interested. But each time he walked by his CD shelf he would say something like, 'What did you say you wanted to listen to?' Then he would name some random band. Wellllllll, that should be . . . Right here!!!!' "

Danny was the laid-back musician at the ultimate corporate newspaper. "I loved to hear Danny write," says Alan Murray, Danny's boss in Washington. He would work and work on crafting the perfect sentence. "Nah, it doesn't sing yet," he once told a coworker in Atlanta.

If his stories about transportation or telecommunications were like music, his stories about music were a joy to read. And he found them everywhere. In Georgia, covering air cargo, of all things, Danny slipped in a story about Elvis Presley's head.

In Washington, covering telecommunications, Danny wrote a story about a missing violin. The lede character could have been a clone of Danny himself:

David Margetts still doesn't know if he left the borrowed Stradivarius on the roof of his car and drove off, or if it was stolen from the unlocked vehicle while he bought groceries.

Danny wasn't supposed to do that story. He was a Washington transportation reporter, and sometimes the *Journal* can be pretty territorial about beats. But Danny came across the idea in a music store and sweet-talked Washington bureau chief Alan Murray into sending him to Los Angeles to work on the story. It wasn't until he was on the airplane that he realized he could get into a turf battle with the *Journal*'s L.A. bureau for stealing into their backyard, recalls his mom, Ruth Pearl, who helped report the story. When the Los Angeles bureau chief asked him why a transportation reporter from Washington was writing about music from L.A., he replied: "Didn't the owner drive his car with the Stradivarius on the roof?"

Danny used to say his harshest critic was his mom. But after working with him on the story, including spending two hours in the library while Danny dug up information on the Duke of Alcantara (and found very little), Mrs. Pearl read what her son had written. "I thought it was beautiful," she says.

Danny found rock-and-roll in Tehran, and songs that will make you weep in Qatar. Both stories ran on page one and technically were on his beat at the time—the Middle East. But they are unlike any other Middle East story.

His love of music permeated his life, too. Once, during a two-day bike trip up the Potomac River, his friend Tom Jennings asked about his belief in an afterlife. "I don't know," Danny replied. "I don't have answers, mainly just questions." Then he added: "But I sure hope Gabriel likes my music."

After Danny died, Tom was going through his friend's vinyl collection (Dvořák, Liszt, Miles Davis, REM) and stumbled across this album: Stuff Smith and the Onyx Club Orchestra. "Danny loved Stuff Smith—a great jazz violinist," Tom says. "Here on side A, track 3, I found this: Stuff Smith playing 'I Hope Gabriel Likes My Music.' "

"That was Danny—full of oblique references," Tom says. "Sometimes I didn't know what the hell he was talking about."

Here's to Danny's music.

—H.C.

# 12

# BEHIND THE MUSIC: ROCK ROLLS ONCE MORE IN IRAN AS HARD-LINERS BACK A POP REVIVAL

## New Genre Speaks of Love in Veiled Terms, but You Still Can't Dance to It

### Mr. Assar's Mystical Persona

*June 2, 2000*

TEHRAN, Iran—In a basement studio here, Iranian pop singer Alireza Assar and his crew are mixing their latest rock ballad. Mr. Assar's strong solo voice rings out in Farsi, singing, "We should find love in the rain." As the music swells, an electric guitar begins to wail, and women's voices take up the song.

If Iran's political hard-liners ever heard this, there'd be hell to pay, right?

Wrong. In fact, the conservatives sponsor Mr. Assar. They own this digital recording studio, they promote his $5-a-ticket concerts, and they approve each of his songs before its release.

Pop music, prohibited for most of the Islamic Republic of Iran's two decades of existence, has made a comeback in the past two years. And its revival owes more to the nation's conservatives than to its reformists. Iranian TV, a hard-liner stronghold, gave most of the new popular-music stars their start. A related record label is the nation's biggest producer of pop. Iran's most original recording, critics say, is Mr. Assar's 1999 debut album, which was conceived by an arts center aligned with the hard-liners.

On the surface, this nation's hard-liners are doing all they can to prevent cultural change, but the reality is more complex. These days, the real political struggles here are over the pace of change—and who gets the spoils. That shows in the hard-liner's strategy of championing the new home-grown pop, which they hope will preempt the unruly Western variety.

Pop music is a good window into Iran's all-consuming politics. Most developments in the industry trace back to one faction or the other: a guitar is shown on TV (conservatives), a book of translated Pink Floyd lyrics appears in a city-run bookstore in Tehran (reformists), a young crowd gathers to hear a local rock band play the Dire Straits hit "Sultans of Swing" (conservatives), and Googoosh, a reclusive prerevolution star, hints she will soon return to the stage (reformists).

"Music has always been in the service" of the state, says Fouad Hejazi, Mr. Assar's 29-year-old composer. Mr. Hejazi doesn't mind. He gets what he wants: seven days in the studio to polish each song and free rein in arranging the music.

What the government wants is a bulwark against the "cultural invasion of the West." For their part, the hard-liners used the judiciary recently to shut down 15 newspapers, some of which they decried as "bases of the enemy." And they tried without success to derail Sunday's installation of a new parliament that favors greater freedoms for Iran's youth.

Conservatives fret about the Madonna and Michael Jackson songs blaring illegally from car stereos in Tehran, but they worry even more about the Iranian artists in exile who record in Farsi in Los Angeles, evoking prerevolutionary nostalgia and new social freedoms. That music seeps into Iran via smuggled cassettes, hidden satellite dishes and the Internet. A hard-line judge recently decriminalized the private use of such music, but selling it is still against the law. "With your sexy moves, you provoke me," goes a typical L.A. song. Young Iranians laugh with embarrassment at the suggestive lyrics but find the fast six-count rhythm perfect for co-ed dancing.

Iran's Islamic government doesn't condone dancing or dating, however. So, led by the conservatives, it came up with a plan to co-opt the forbidden pop. It put Tehran pop on the airwaves, with singers who could match the voices and melodies of the popular L.A. acts, but with slower rhythms and ambiguous lyrics. One example: "I wish it were possible, for the spring of my dreams, with you, to come true."

Is this poem about God or a girl? It's hard to tell, and that's why it lends itself so well to the new Iranian pop scene.

Now, the Shandaz Nights restaurant can present live cover bands, under the watchful eye of government inspectors. If diners request a song by Iranian exile Dariush, they often get one from Khashayar Etemadi, who has the same rasp in his voice. Mr. Etemadi's career was launched by the conservatives, but the singer, who typically sports a goatee and suspenders, recently formed his own record company and wrote a song for Iran's reformist president, Mohammed Khatami—"In the age of coin and gunpowder, come and believe in humanity."

In the Permitted Music store in a downtown alley here, shoppers asking for an under-the-counter tape of L.A.-based singer Ebi may end up with Tehran teen idol Shadmehr Aghili, with his silky voice, slick hair and showy violin solos. His songs have jazz, funk and Latin influences. "You know that life is hard without you, but how easily your eyes take death from my heart," Mr. Aghili sings in a track titled "Skylike."

The strategy works, according to those who deal in contraband tunes. One such merchant, who goes by the name Akbar, has operated downtown for the past eight years, approaching passersby with the whispered offer of "new tapes." Akbar says his business is off 50% since the Iranian pop cassettes became available.

As the novelty wears off, however, sales of sanctioned pop are slipping, too. "You feel that they want to talk about earthly love, but they have to talk about love for God. They should say whatever they want to say, frankly," says Morteza, 24, as his clandestine date nods. Shabnam Assadi, a 20-year-old management student, says the seven or eight Iranian pop tapes she owns aren't suitable for dancing, but "for listening to them once, they're not bad."

Iran's music industry is trying to break new ground. Mr. Etemadi's coming album features a samba tune called "Wow." People who have heard the bootleg versions of Mr. Aghili's next release say it has words that are clearly about girls. Mr. Assar's next effort features "lambada and rap" rhythms, says his composer. Saxophones, Spanish guitar, techno-electronic beats and lush string arrangements are all being squeezed behind Iranian pop's typically oriental melodies. Still, most of the music has the same 1970s-film-soundtrack style that Iran's pop musicians used before the 1979 Islamic Revolution.

For centuries here, music was restricted to Islamic mystics who played only for themselves, or motrebi singers, who provided the royal court with cheap entertainment. The once-disdained motrebis moved into downtown cabarets in the 1970s, and some became super-stars, with the aid of the shah's government, which subsidized record producers.

The Islamic Revolution initially banned all but traditional and classi-cal music and barred women from singing in public. Most of the top performers fled to the West.

In 1990, Mr. Khatami, then minister of culture, tried to liberalize the arts. Mr. Assar, for example, recalls playing in a three-month blues show called "Victory of Chicago." But the establishment rebelled, and Mr. Khatami lost his job. Mr. Assar resorted to giving piano lessons. Many people cite Mr. Khatami's 1997 election as president as the beginning of Iran's musical reform. Actually, it began a few years earlier with Iran's supreme leader, Ayatollah Ali Khamenei. A champion of the hard-liners, he is also a shrewd politician who knows a bit about music; he plays the dotar, a traditional stringed instrument. His cultural advisers convinced him that if Iran didn't produce its own pop, music from abroad would corrupt Iran's youth and undermine Islamic values.

Ayatollah Khamenei quietly sought the approval of top Islamic scholars. "He told them he would look for classical poems and military themes," says one adviser.

One tool he used was the Islamic Arts Center in Tehran, which was set up at the beginning of the revolution to help spread Islamic culture. The center put aside its traditional-music projects and learned to rock. It installed a modern studio on its tree-lined campus, and in 1997 started a one-year search for musicians.

Television was there to help. Iran's five TV channels are all run by Is-lamic Republic of Iran Broadcasting, whose politics are clear from the portraits hanging in the studio's lobby: Ayatollah Khamenei's, not Presi-dent Khatami's. IRIB's music director is a close friend of the ayatollah. The conservatives introduced pop to Iran in gradual doses, to let reli-gious hard-liners get used to it. IRIB started Radio Payam, which aired instrumentals by such acts as the Gipsy Kings. Some songs featuring drums and guitar were played on TV. Soroush Distribution, an affiliate of IRIB, issued a pop tape two years ago, a compilation of patriotic songs tied to the soccer World Cup. "Iran, Iran, ey-mahd-e daliran. Iran, Iran, eftekhar-e dowran," one singer intones over a discolike beat.

("Iran, Iran, the land of the brave. Iran, Iran, the honor of the era.") IRIB polled young people about their preferences and auditioned singers.

Mr. Assar and Mr. Hejazi, his composer, seemed unlikely material. The two musicians had grown up together listening to progressive rock. But Mr. Hejazi had a friend at IRIB and went to Mr. Assar's apartment one day to persuade him to audition. Their recording, with Mr. Assar singing a classical text by the poet Hafez, aired on TV over a nature film.

An Islamic Arts Center producer heard Mr. Assar and signed him up. Arts center officials interpreted classical poems with him. Looking for "thoughtful" music, the center encouraged the singer to emphasize the words through careful articulation, like Canadian superstar Celine Dion. Mr. Assar says he isn't "into politics" and has warned his backers he would withdraw if they used him to pursue a right-wing agenda. He has, however, developed an interest in Islamic mysticism, and the image that goes with it. The singer grew a beard, started wearing a black robe, and avoided parties where men and women mixed or alcohol was served. The sleeve of Mr. Assar's first album, "Kooch," which means migration, shows his profile in blue light, with liner notes citing his lineage to the prophet Mohammed and asking God's help "not to fall out of the honest path." The album, with its tense, syncopated tunes, sold an estimated 300,000 copies, producing a windfall for the arts center.

Meanwhile, the reformists were establishing their own pop empire, centered on the Ministry of Culture and Islamic Guidance, whose approval is needed to release an album. The ministry is under Mr. Khatami's control, but that doesn't mean it lets artists do what they want.

On a recent day, Farid Salmanian of the ministry's Music Council sits in his office and listens to a demo tape, with a clipboard that holds marked-up lyrics of a soft-rock song about traveling. The ministry's Lyrics Council has changed the words: "It's the start of the hard road of the hot weather of the West" becomes "It's the demands of the long road." Mr. Salmanian says the tape will be rejected anyway because the singer is out of tune.

The Ministry of Culture gives some record labels financial aid and advice on music and packaging, and labels close to the ministry have recruited some of the TV-launched singers. In November, the ministry shocked the music industry when a Khatami appointee overruled the Music Council by approving a Shadmehr Aghili album that included songs with a fast, six-count rhythm. The album has sold more than a million copies.

The musical battles between the two camps have escalated. Iranian TV shows only singers who have stayed on its own record label. Several pop singers appeared at a rally for a proreform political party before the February parliamentary elections. Conservatives and reformists have vied for control of civic centers where many concerts are held.

The reformists may hold the ultimate pop weapon: Googoosh, the sensuous empress of 1970s Iranian pop. Iranian expatriates still adore her, and sometimes portray her as a silenced prisoner of the Islamic regime. These days, women are allowed to sing solos only before female audiences, and they can perform for mixed audiences or on recordings only as part of a chorus. Googoosh was in the first row recently at a women-only pop festival sponsored by the Ministry of Culture. And she may well perform at the next festival, in October, says the head of Revelations of Dawn, a record label with connections to the singer. If Googoosh returned to the stage, the regime would score a propaganda coup and, music-industry insiders say, the reformists would get the credit.

# 13

# THESE SONGS BRING TEARS TO YOUR EYES, OR SOMETHING WORSE

## In Persian Gulf, Some Say Vocalists May Be Blinded by Pearl-Diving Spirituals

*May 14, 1996*

*My eye is crying all the time*
*Until my eye gets sick.*
*My eyes. My eyes.*
*This is my fate.*
*I have to wait for it.*
*I can't do anything about it.*

DOHA, Qatar—American blues can make you sad. Russian work songs can make you suffer. The fervent belief of many in the Persian Gulf is that pearl-diving songs can make you go blind.

The songs are undergoing a revival, a half-century after crowded pearl boats plied the shallow Gulf waters for the last time. As a new generation in the Gulf rediscovers the wailing old spirituals, they are also rediscovering the special pain of singing them.

"Sometimes I feel like my head is going to explode," 37-year-old soloist Omar Busaqar says after recently singing a few pearling songs with the Qatar National Folkloric Troupe in Doha. "I get migraines," says another soloist, Monssour Al-Mahannadi, 24. After singing for six years, he concedes, he has gone a bit farsighted and wears glasses. "Ah, you're going to go blind," Mr. Busaqar taunts.

He wouldn't be the first. Soloists, or nahams, were notorious for going blind in decades past, according to Aldulrahman Al-Mannai, a Qatari folklorist. Researchers who recorded the remaining nahams in the 1970s and 1980s say the best ones had poor vision, or none at all: Al Allan, Bahrain's most famous naham, was blind. So was Kuwait's Abu-

Mussa'ed, according to one researcher. Rashed Al-Mass, a Qatari singer whose voice was so sweet his nickname was "The Sugar," stopped singing certain songs in the early 1980s after his eyesight deteriorated. The chief culprit seems to be the fjeri, a haunting type of song filled with wailing improvisation and accompanied by a crescendo of drums and low droning hums. Fjeris were often sung during restful moments and the words are mostly about crying and missing home. The fjeri never made it to Dubai, where pearl divers stuck to more upbeat work songs for raising the boat's anchor, jib or mainsail. "People were more business-oriented here," singer Omar Sabt Ashoor says after performing with his turban-clad troupe at the Dubai Shopping Festival.

Ethnomusicologists haven't been able to trace the fjeri's origins, except to record a curious tale told by many old pearl-diving hands. One day, according to the story, some sailors looking for a quiet place to sing stumbled upon some half-man, half-donkey genies. They were singing a mesmerizing song, which they taught the sailors, but only after warning them that singing the songs in public would make the singer go blind or die. The songs proved too beautiful to keep bottled up.

The emotion involved in singing these songs makes nahams go blind, contends Khalif Bin Salah Al Mannai, a septuagenarian Qatari naham who learned to sing as a pearl diver in the 1940s and whose eyesight is now starting to fade. "If you really get involved, you get deeply sad, deeply hurt," he says, but if you stop singing the songs you feel even worse. The beginning part of a fjeri is even called jarhan, or "hurt." The hurt can get physical, says Feisal Atmimi, the Qatari Troupe's leader. As evidence, he recalls the autopsy of one naham: "His chest was herniated, because he sang with such deep feeling."

It wasn't the emotion, it was the volume of the singing that made nahams go blind, says Nasser Al-Hamadi, a Qatari musician and marine biologist. "The bass drum, it's working, the clapping, the humming—he has to put his voice first. He has to shout to be the clearest one," Mr. Al-Mahadi says, motioning to a pearl-diving video playing in the Qatar National Museum. "Now there's no need to shout. With just a small mike you can reach 3,000 people."

In truth, it wasn't the volume, it was the sun that made nahams go blind, say doctors at Qatar's Hamad Hospital. Nahams spent the whole day in the sun while divers plunged in and out of the water. Long exposure to the sun's rays can cause cataracts. Those nahams who also dove faced another problem: fast pressure changes can hurt the eyes as well.

Everybody agrees that pearl diving, which dates back hundreds of years, was a brutal way to make a living. Historians and divers say that even up to the 1930s, the job required men to dive all day without oxygen tanks, with only the briefest of air breaks. They got one meal of rice and dates a day for four months at sea. The boat was cramped, and sharks and jellyfish were never far away. A diver who contracted a communicable disease was left on an island to die. And divers got sharecropper's pay that depended on the season's take.

Nahams were paid better. "He was the main figure. He was sort of the maestro on the ship," says Scheherazade Q. Hassan, a researcher who helped to record a troupe with a partially blind naham in 1987. A good naham could attract workers to a boat, keep them motivated by singing through the day, and help them beg Allah for protection, Ms. Hassan says.

Cultured pearls, developed in Japan in the 1890s, and oil, discovered in the Gulf in the 1930s, combined to kill off pearl diving and leave the songs in obscurity. But in the 1970s, Gulf countries started rediscovering their folklore. Pictures of pearls started appearing on business logos, and a statue of a giant pearl was built on Doha's beach walk. Singing troupes sprouted to perform pearl-diving songs at weddings and official state functions. Several compact disks hit the market, and troupes traveled as far as the U.S. and Australia to perform.

Some singers scoff at the tales of blindness. Muhammad Jassim Harban, a young naham in Bahrain, counts seven active groups in that small country, including his own troupe, which includes his four brothers and father. And he doesn't know of a single naham who went blind. True, there was Al Allan, but "he lost his eyes a long time ago, not when he was singing," Mr. Harban says.

Which suggests another theory: maybe blindness actually made the nahams better singers. As an Arab researcher once wrote, "Isn't it said, that if a nightingale's eyes are popped, its singing will improve?"

# 14

# MISSING VIOLIN'S CASE: THE FINDER FIDDLES WHILE LOSERS SUE

## 'Alcantara' Stradivarius, Lost 27 Years Ago, Resurfaces but New Owner Plays Coy

*October 17, 1994*

LOS ANGELES—David Margetts still doesn't know if he left the borrowed Stradivarius on the roof of his car and drove off, or if it was stolen from the unlocked vehicle while he bought groceries.

That was in August 1967. Mr. Margetts, then a second violinist with a string quartet at the University of California at Los Angeles, sent notices to pawn shops and violin stores and took out classified ads. He spent the next 27 years worrying that the "Duke of Alcantara" Stradivarius, made in 1732, was gone forever.

It wasn't. Officials of UCLA, to which the instrument had been donated, say the same violin reappeared this January. But the tale doesn't end there. University officials have discovered that once somebody is smitten with the love of a Stradivarius, taking it away is like wresting a baby from its mother's arms.

Antonio Stradivari of Cremona, Italy, made about 1,200 violins, half of which still survive. After his death in 1737, factories churned out hundreds of thousands of copies. And every day, people bring violins with Stradivarius labels to appraisers, thinking they have bought the genuine article for a song. To break the bad news to such would-be millionaires, Los Angeles violin dealer Robert Cauer shows them a 1909 Sears Roebuck catalog advertising a Stradivarius copy for $1.95.

But Joseph Grubaugh, a violin dealer in Petaluma, Calif., says that when a violin teacher showed him a student's instrument bearing a Stradivarius label one day in January, he thought he was looking at the real thing. The slight ruggedness of the scroll, the spontaneity of the "purfling," and the "ropiness" of the Bosnian maple backside suggested that only the Italian master could have made the instrument.

He opened his copy of the *Iconography of Antonio Stradivari* and found a photograph of a violin with similar scratch marks on the back. It was the Duke of Alcantara. A bigger shock came a week later when the violin teacher picked up the repaired fiddle. Mr. Grubaugh flipped through a violin registry and saw the instrument listed as stolen from UCLA.

The student was amateur violinist Teresa Salvato, who says she got the violin as part of a divorce settlement last year. She says her husband received the violin around 1979 from his aunt, who helped run a music store and kept the double-violin case in a closet for years before her death. (The case also contained another violin that had been reported as missing at the same time.) Where the aunt got the violin case isn't known, Ms. Salvato says, but one piece of family lore had her picking it up beside a freeway on-ramp after mistaking the canvas-covered case for a baby.

Ms. Salvato contacted UCLA, but over the next 10 months declined the university's pleas to surrender the violin. Also, Ms. Salvato didn't appreciate the unannounced visit to her home in May by two campus police officers who, she says, threatened to arrest her and told neighbors she was a theft suspect. When they reappeared last week to serve civil court papers, Ms. Salvato wouldn't leave her locked car. She now is staying in a hotel.

And the Alcantara is in hiding. UCLA lawyers tried to get an injunction Friday in Superior Court in Los Angeles to force Ms. Salvato to disclose the location. Instead, university officials settled for Ms. Salvato's offer to bring the violin today to a museum, where it will stay unplayed while the court decides who owns it.

All the fuss is over a violin that by one estimate is valued at $800,000—a quarter of what the best Strads fetch. Antonio Stradivari would have been 88 years old when he built the Alcantara, and his sons Omobono and Francesco probably cut the F-holes. Experts who have seen the violin say its varnish was later touched up clumsily.

Besides, the violin wasn't played by anybody famous, unless one counts the concertmaster of the Detroit Symphony. The original owner was an obscure Spanish nobleman described in archives only as an "aide-de-camp of King Don Carlos, assassinated in Lisbon," according to Charles Beare, a Stradivarius expert and dealer in London.

Still, even a mediocre Stradivarius can be inspirational. Violinist W. Thomas Marrocco, who played the Alcantara in the 1960s, wrote a novel whose main character was the violin. Of the Alcantara, he says: "It's sweet, it's mellow, it's strong, it responds to every notion one has." Violinists can have sticky fingers with such instruments. One New York violinist waited until he was on his deathbed in 1985 to reveal that the instrument he played for years was a Stradivarius stolen from Carnegie Hall nearly a half-century earlier. And David Sarser is losing hope of playing another Bach partita on his 1735 "ex-Zimbalist" Stradivarius, which disappeared three decades ago. Mr. Sarser says the violin has been photographed in Japan, but nobody will tell him who has it. "I have no desire to play any other instrument," he says. "It became part of me, and I became part of it."

Ms. Salvato played her mystery violin for the first time in January. It was "heavenly," she says, "smooth and gorgeous." It even helped her play in tune. "There are things I can't do on the violin, but I can execute them on that violin," she said.

During a recent telephone conversation with Robert Portillo, a musical curator for UCLA, Ms. Salvato asked if less-accomplished musicians might be allowed to play the violin. And she wondered "if there is any possible legal way I could keep it."

There isn't, says Carla Shapreau, a violin maker and lawyer retained by the university. If the Duke of Alcantara was stolen, "You can't get good title from a thief," and if it was found, the finder would have had to try to locate the owner.

But Ms. Salvato notes in a court filing that she wasn't the finder, and that several lawyers have told her she might have a claim to the violin. Attorney Allen Hyman, who represented her in Friday's hearing, said later that the violin could have been stolen centuries before UCLA ever got it.

"Can they trace it back to the Duke?" he asked with a grin. "Maybe we have to get in touch with the Duke's relatives."

Ms. Salvato insists she only wants what is right for the instrument. The university "lost it once," she says. "They're really not careful."

Mr. Portillo—who complains that Ms. Salvato is taking the university "for a ride"—says UCLA will be extremely mindful of the instrument if it is returned. One faculty member who is likely to play it is Alexander Treger, concertmaster of the Los Angeles Philharmonic Orchestra, who already plays an orchestra-owned 1711 Stradivarius. On tour, Mr. Treger says, "I don't leave the violin even if I have to go to the bathroom."

# 15

# THIS MAY MAKE MILLI VANILLI GLAD THEY GOT OUT WHEN THEY DID

*January 2, 1991*

What really happened to Elvis Presley? Never mind that. A Los Angeles disc jockey is having enough trouble figuring out what happened to Elvis's head.

All 1,200 pounds of it, that is, made of steel, wire, fiberglass, flowers and birdseed. The 10-foot-high head rode on Mississippi's float in last January's Tournament of Roses Parade in Pasadena, Calif., alongside flowery facsimiles of fellow Mississippi musicians Tammy Wynette, Leontyne Price and B. B. King.

Tammy, Leontyne and B. B. were dismantled after the parade. But Elvis found his way home. Two morning disc jockeys at KLOS-FM in Los Angeles drove the head on a flatbed truck to Graceland, the late singer's mansion in Memphis, Tenn. Elvis later turned up at a shopping mall and a restaurant in Jackson, Miss., then languished in a Jackson scrapyard.

Last month, the head became a hot property. The sculptors who built it offered to buy it. The *Jackson Clarion–Ledger* reported that KLOS wanted it for a new promotion. Graceland said it would buy the head to destroy it and thus snuff out its humorous appeal. But that offer only alerted another disc jockey—Magic Matt Alan of KIIS-FM in Los Angeles—who started phoning the Mississippi scrapyard, on the air, to inquire about the head.

The publicity-shy scrapyard isn't telling anybody if it still has Elvis, including Mr. Alan, who has offered $500 and 100 pounds of extra crispy Kentucky Fried Chicken for the King's crown. (Mr. Alan has said he wants Elvis for his yard in Encino, a Los Angeles suburb. "Encino is Elvis, and Elvis is Encino," he tells listeners.)

At last sighting, the head wasn't doing very well. "All the seeds were gone because the birds were feeding on it," says J. Malcolm White, a Jackson restaurateur who baby-sat the head briefly in an abortive plan to make it an "Elvis was Irish" entry in a local St. Patrick's Day parade. "It didn't really resemble Elvis at all."

The suspicious minds at Graceland had an inkling such tomfoolery would result if it allowed an Elvis float. "I told them, 'We know from experience that if you make a 10-foot-high head of Elvis Presley, it won't disappear after the Rose Parade,' " says Jack Soden, Graceland's executive director. Mr. Soden says the sponsors promised him the head would be destroyed. The state's parade committee wasn't taking any chances with rock icons yesterday. Its Tournament of Roses entry honored the International Ballet Competition.

# PART THREE

# Mr. Precis

Danny Pearl walked around the office without shoes, his head cocked to one side, and a black planner-book balanced on one arm. The absence of shoes revealed the laid-back, forgetful Danny—he lost the notes for a deadlined page-one story about black cops' stress and frustration following the Rodney King verdict. But the omnipresent black planner showed the other side of Danny: obsessively organized and thorough. He owned not one, but two Palm Pilots. He was the best Microsoft Outlook "power user" ever. He freaked out colleagues by looking up stuff they did two years ago—written in his old planners—and then calling to remind them.

At *The Wall Street Journal,* there is an arcane tradition: story proposals. Any story that isn't a deadline story has to be proposed first. Danny hated proposals just like every other reporter. He came up with the idea—way back early in his *Journal* career, when he was in Atlanta—of writing what he called a precis that he put on the top of each proposal. It was his way of mocking himself and the *Journal* as well. Danny's precis—later picked up by other reporters—said what his story would be about. He actually titled his precis "Precis," just in case the page-one editors didn't recognize the precis when they saw it.

When he got to India, he took his precis to new organizational highs, or lows, as the case may be. As the new South Asia bureau chief, he decided to create massive, interactive, all-encompassing Microsoft Word documents, containing every single fact, contact and news burp on every conceivable beat. He mockingly called these "dossiers," says *Journal* reporter Jesse Pesta, who was in Delhi while Danny was in Bombay. "Each of us was supposed to read six newspapers a day," Jesse says. "Then, we undertook an elaborate daily ballet of faxing clips back and forth between Delhi and Bombay, so each of us could update our dossiers by typing a 'precis' for each story."

"I spent hours on this every day, until finally my contributions to the dossiers dwindled into irrelevance—I was exhausted by lunch just typing up my precis," Jesse says. "Danny, of course, kept at it." Today they are masterful beat compendiums for reporters in the region.

Here's an excerpt of Danny's "Power Industry" of India dossier:

> Scientists at Indian Institute of Science developed new solar cell, which doesn't require silicon; can be worn like a sari. (*Press Trust of India*, 1/5/01)

Solar panels you can wear like a sari. Like, wow.

Danny was dogged, once even enlisting his baby sister, Michelle Pearl, in reporting about booming—and medically harmful—sales of illicit pharmaceuticals in India. "He wanted to know whether some of the drugs that were being hyped in India, particularly for women's reproductive health, were harmful," says Michelle, an expert in epidemics. "I was honored that my brother thought of me as an epidemiologist, rather than just a little sister, albeit for only 15 minutes."

"He would continue reporting a story virtually up until the moment it appeared in the paper," says *Journal* reporter Steve Stecklow, who worked with Danny on that Aug. 16, 2001, page-one story. "I was confident after a week of reporting in Bombay that we had completed most of our reporting. But Danny told me he wanted to go with Mariane out to a rural area to do further research." Steve didn't think the long trip would deliver more than an extra paragraph or two. Danny went anyway. He got four paragraphs, including this:

> On a busy recent Sunday afternoon at the Shree Samarth Medical Store in the western India agricultural town of Dinduri, owner Bapusaheb Patil was openly selling prescription drugs without prescriptions, including anti-inflammatory pills, ulcer tablets and antituberculosis drugs. . . . He said he sells vials of injectable medicines to the area's village doctors. As in much of rural India, few of them have formal training in Western medi-

cine or are even licensed by the Indian government to practice conventional medicine.

Danny's obsessive streak surfaced in another joint reporting venture—a March 12, 2001, piece with investigative editor Alix Freedman about a drug company's decision to offer inexpensive AIDS drugs in the developing world.

He talked to the story's protagonist endlessly, Alix recalls. "He buttonholed an ever-lengthening list of the subject's colleagues and competitors, friends and detractors. All the while, Danny kept sifting through the avalanche of facts, figures and opinions, applying an ever-more-finely calibrated scale to weigh and reweigh his own conclusions."

Danny had two fights with Alix during their weekslong collaboration.

The first was over Danny's insistence that Alix get a byline on the story, even though editors at the *Journal* typically remain anonymous. The second was over Danny's insistence that he interview prostitutes in Bombay. He wanted to gauge their reaction to the prospect of affordable AIDS drugs. Alix argued that this was a waste of time.

"Danny said little, but I left with the definite impression that he had capitulated on both points," Alix recalls. "Then, I read our story in the paper—and discovered two new names. Mine—and that of a Bombay streetwalker named Sumiti."

Here are some stories that result from obsessive reporting.

—H.C.

# 16

# AFGHAN CONNECTION:
# TALIBAN BANNED TV BUT COLLECTED
# PROFITS ON SMUGGLED SONYS

## Big Manufacturers Decry Illicit Traffic to Pakistan but
## Do Little to Stop It

### Mr. Khan's Trips to Karkhano

*This article written with Steve Stecklow*

*January 9, 2002*

PESHAWAR, Pakistan—During their five years in power in Afghanistan, the Taliban raged against modern culture and values. But the regime profited from traffic in Sony televisions, Gillette shaving cream and Marlboro cigarettes, among other products.

None of these consumer goods from the West and Asia are made in Afghanistan, and under the Taliban government, they didn't have much of a market there. Watching television, for instance, was banned.

But for decades, whoever has run Afghanistan has exacted tolls on smugglers who ship foreign-made goods through the country and then illegally move the merchandise over the border to Pakistan. The products end up in places such as Peshawar's sprawling Karkhano market, where vendors' shelves are packed with cartons of smuggled Marlboro and Dunhill cigarettes and sidewalk carts offer bright Korean fabrics. Stacks of mud-stained cartons of Sony Trinitron televisions line courtyard after courtyard.

By smuggling these items through Afghanistan, traders evade Pakistan's stiff taxes and duties on foreign goods. This allows consumers at Karkhano and other markets to enjoy large discounts compared to legally imported products.

Smuggling also effectively boosts Western and Asian manufacturers' sales volume by allowing goods to be retailed at lower prices in Pakistan, a poor nation overall, but one with 140 million inhabitants and a substantial consumer class. The manufacturers all condemn smuggling but say they can't stop it once products leave their direct control. But a close look at the behavior of one major manufacturer, Sony Corp., reveals that some company representatives appear to have tolerated smuggling as part of Sony's marketing strategy in the region.

The fees the Taliban collected on shipments of goods manufactured by Sony and other foreign companies provided one of that harsh regime's biggest sources of earnings. A United Nations study released last year estimated that "unofficial" exports from Afghanistan to Pakistan in 2000 totaled $941 million, with merchandise worth another $139 million moving illegally from Afghanistan to Iran. The U.N. estimated the Taliban's annual take at $36 million. The World Bank, in a 1999 report, said it was $75 million.

The prospect of exacting similar tolls on the smuggling business helps explain why the Taliban's successors are now wrestling for control over Kandahar, Jalalabad and other cities that are important transit points on smuggling routes. U.S. bombing and poor security have discouraged smuggling for the last three months, but it is expected to resume as relative calm returns. Beyond providing potential revenue to those in charge, smuggling offers employment to poor inhabitants of tribal areas along the Afghan border. That is one reason Pakistan— eager for stability in that area—has made only feeble attempts to compel vendors at Karkhano to pay taxes.

Smuggling economics are simple: A smuggled 21-inch Sony Wega TV typically costs the equivalent of about $400 in Pakistan. The same legally imported television costs the equivalent of $440, after duties and taxes. Sony receives the same payment—about $220—from the distributor either way. Manufacturers thus have little financial incentive to crack down on smuggling.

During most of the 1990s, Sony imported few TVs through legal channels into Pakistan and assembled no sets locally, according to Sony Gulf FZE, Sony Corp.'s wholly-owned subsidiary and sales office in Dubai, United Arab Emirates. But that doesn't mean Sonys were unavailable. The Pakistan Electronics Manufacturers Association, a trade group that includes local TV assemblers hurt by sales of smuggled goods, found in a 1996 survey that 500,000 televisions were smuggled into the country that year. At least 70%, or 350,000, of them were Sonys, the survey found.

Today, Sony TVs remain one of the most prominent consumer-electronics products in Pakistani smuggled-goods markets. Sony Gulf's authorized distributor in Dubai sells sets to traders who often ship them to the Iranian port of Bandar Abbas. From there, some of the goods head northeast to the Afghan border near Herat, then southeast on the highway to Kandahar, on to Jalalabad, and then typically enter Pakistan illegally along the Khyber Pass near Peshawar. Twice a month, Khalid M. Khan, a manager with Sony Gulf, visits the Karkhano market in Peshawar, which is widely known as a major retail center for smuggled goods. He says he makes the trips merely to see which models are popular and should be supplied legally by the local assembly plant in Pakistan that Sony opened in 1999. Mr. Khan acknowledges, though, that none of the locally made Sonys are sold in Karkhano. All of the TVs he sees changing hands here have been smuggled from Afghanistan, he says.

Dealers in the Karkhano market who acknowledge they sell smuggled TVs say that for years they have routinely ordered Sony products from the traders in Dubai who obtain the goods from the authorized Sony distributor there, Jumbo Electronics Co. One of the Karkhano dealers, Abdul Basir Khan, manager of Muslim Electronics, says Sony Gulf's Khalid Khan (no relation) "doesn't come here to book orders, but he gives ideas." For instance, the Sony Gulf man points out that " 'such-and-such model is available,' " Abdul Basir Khan says. The Muslim Electronics shop is filled with Sony Trinitron TVs and has a large Sony sign above the door. "Khalid usually presses us hard to dispose [of inventory] as quickly as possible," Abdul Basir Khan says.

For his part, Khalid Khan makes no apology for telling black-market dealers here that certain Sony models are available in Dubai or Singapore. "There is no harm" in this encouragement, he says. "They are making our brand popular in the country."

But he denies promoting smuggling in any way. He says that when Sony Gulf discovers traders selling through unauthorized channels, it threatens to punish them. The company has fined one trader and briefly cut off another one, he says. Smuggling hurts sales of the Sony televisions assembled in Pakistan, he says. But, he adds, smuggling is "beyond our control."

Ram Modak, a spokesman for Sony Gulf, also denies his company has knowingly shipped any goods intended for Pakistan through Afghanistan. He says, "Sony Gulf is not aware of the routes the [Dubai-based traders] use for their shipments to Pakistan." Kei Sakaguchi, a spokesman at Sony's headquarters in Tokyo, says the parent corporation has nothing to add to Mr. Modak's comments.

Vishesh L. Bhatia, director of Jumbo Electronics, says his company isn't allowed by Sony Gulf to sell goods directly in Pakistan, and it often can't control what traders do. "Duty barriers always encourage smuggling," he notes.

Minoru Kubota, Japan's ambassador to Pakistan from 1997 through early 2000, says he heard complaints from Pakistani businessmen during that period about the smuggling of Japanese goods. But he says the smuggling issue "is a business matter," not a concern of governments. "If trade shrinks, it will not benefit anyone," he adds.

Smugglers have operated across the Afghan-Pakistani border since Pakistan became independent in 1947. In the 1980s, huge amounts of U.S. money flooded the region, as the Central Intelligence Agency used Pakistani proxies to fund the mujahedeen resistance to Afghanistan's Soviet-backed government. Smuggling of electronics, tires, crockery and textiles gave some mujahedeen commanders a way to enrich themselves and keep supporters employed. For its part, "the government of Pakistan encouraged people to invest in this business," even supplying telephone and electricity connections for the Karkhano market, recalls Rafique Shinwari, a longtime distributor of smuggled goods in Peshawar who says he now imports only legally. In 1994, after the Soviets had left Afghanistan and the country was divided among rival commanders, Abdul Haq, an ex-mujahedeen Afghan leader living in Peshawar, approached Sony Gulf about distributing TVs in Afghanistan. Sony Gulf's Khalid Khan says he negotiated a deal under which Mr. Haq's company, Khyber-Afghan International, began sending televisions by his family's airline from Dubai to Jalalabad, in eastern Afghanistan. "Whatever he did [with the TVs] inside Afghanistan, we don't know," Mr. Khan says.

Black-market dealers in Pakistan say Mr. Haq's family was prominent in the cross-border television trade in the mid-1990s. Mr. Haq was killed in October [2001] trying to organize anti-Taliban forces. His nephew, Abdulrahim Zalmai, says, "The family itself was not involved by any means," in smuggling. But he says that traders in Jalalabad who bought TVs from his uncle may have smuggled them into Pakistan.

Pakistani officials say they haven't cracked down aggressively on smuggling markets such as Karkhano. "We have been working over the last two or three years to start curtailing smuggling," says Abdul Razak Dawood, Pakistan's commerce minister, but "through economic means rather than coercion."

Pakistan has been reducing import duties to diminish the price advantage of smuggled products. It has also ended duty-free access through the Pakistani port of Karachi for Afghanistan-bound goods, such as TVs, that often end up being smuggled back into Pakistan. Smugglers responded to the new obstacle in Karachi, however, simply by shipping through Iran and then across Afghanistan.

Traversing Afghanistan is by no means a simple trip. During the country's civil war in the early 1990s, various mujahedeen set up more than a dozen checkpoints along the country's major roads. Truckers had to pay small fees at each stop, and sometimes had their whole cargo expropriated by fighters or roving bandits.

The Taliban first gained prominence in Afghanistan in 1994 by eliminating most of the highway checkpoints and robberies. Afghan traders based in Dubai and Singapore poured money into the Taliban's coffers, as the regime extended its control from Herat to Jalalabad and enforced more orderly transportation, according to Pakistani officials who were also assisting the Taliban at the time.

After conquering Kabul in 1996, the Taliban simplified the fees for passage through Afghanistan, exacting a single payment determined by weight and other factors. For example, the Taliban sometimes imposed fees equivalent to roughly five-to-10 cents a kilogram, regardless of the merchandise, says one Dubai-based freight forwarder. "These guys didn't want to use calculators," he says. The 1999 World Bank study estimated that televisions valued at $367 million were smuggled into Pakistan from Afghanistan in 1997.

Traders say they quickly adjusted to the Taliban's spiritually motivated rules. To get around the ban on packages with depictions of humans or living animals, traders put boxes in larger, blank cartons or simply reminded Taliban authorities that the packages were moving on to Pakistan. The smuggling of American-made goods was hindered in July 1999, when former president Clinton signed an antiterrorism executive order prohibiting U.S. companies from exporting any goods, except for humanitarian aid, to Afghanistan. But Pakistani traders say they still could obtain products smuggled from Afghanistan—such as Gillette shaving cream, Head & Shoulders shampoo and Marlboro cigarettes— if the goods came from distributors outside of the U.S. Manufacturers of these goods say they discourage any smuggling but can't always control it in distant lands. "It is obviously something we don't sponsor or endorse," says Eric Kraus, a spokesman for Gillette Co. Linda Ulrey, a spokeswoman for Procter & Gamble Co., maker of Head & Shoulders, says the company lacks specific information about smuggling through Afghanistan.

A spokesman for Philip Morris Cos., which makes Marlboros, says the company can't comment because it doesn't do any business in Afghanistan. British American Tobacco PLC, maker of Dunhill cigarettes, says in a written statement that it doesn't condone or encourage smuggling. Dubai's emergence as a major trading hub has helped fuel the expansion of smuggling through Afghanistan. In the mid-1990s, many large U.S., Japanese and European consumer-goods manufacturers opened operations that brought products through the duty-free zone of Jebel Ali, along the Dubai coast. Official Dubai customs records show that such "re-exports" from Dubai to Afghanistan jumped 79%, to $819 million, in 1996, the year the Taliban took over, compared with 1995.

Much of this trading relies on the illegal hawala currency-exchange system. (Hawala means "change" in Arabic.) Black-market consumer-electronics dealers in Pakistan say that after they place orders with traders in Dubai, they pay for the goods by giving Pakistani rupees to a hawala dealer in Peshawar. The hawala dealer telephones a counterpart in Dubai, who hands over United Arab Emirates dirhams to a consumer-electronics trader in Dubai. The hawala dealers settle their accounts later, splitting the commission.

Most of the victims of Afghan smuggling receive benefits as well.

The Pakistani government has lost tax revenues, but border tribes engaged in smuggling are less likely to resort to kidnapping or drug-running. Authorized Pakistani dealers of foreign goods lose sales to black-market competition, but in the capital of Islamabad, many such dealers stock smuggled and legally imported goods on the same shelves.

The biggest losers have been local manufacturers that have assembled TVs but found their products consistently undercut by smuggled goods. Several local-assembly factories stopped production in the mid-1990s.

These difficulties prompted the Pakistan Electronics Manufacturers Association to conduct its 1996 survey. The trade group found that for every TV legally imported or assembled locally, more than two were smuggled in.

Sarfrazuddin, the association's chairman, who goes by one name, says he subsequently showed Sony officials and Japanese diplomats copies of documents indicating that in 1997 Sony Gulf was promoting service guarantees that retailers could offer to buyers in Pakistan. Since at the time Sony TVs were "neither being manufactured in Pakistan nor being imported" legally, "we wonder how the guarantees" could be offered, he wrote in a July 1997 letter to the Japanese Embassy in Islamabad, Pakistan.

Faiz Rahim Khan, chief executive of Data Electronics, a Lahore, Pakistan–based company that provided service under Sony gulf's guarantees in Pakistan until 1999, says the Sony unit routinely reimbursed his firm for repairs on TVs sold in the Middle East and used in Pakistan. "How it got there was not our concern," he says.

Sony Gulfs Mr. Modak confirms the company had an agreement in the 1990s with Data Electronics to repair Sony products in Pakistan. He also says Sony Gulf's authorized Dubai distributor, Jumbo Electronics, has offered warranties on Sony products that are good in Pakistan. He adds that Sony Gulf didn't make the Pakistan warranties available to Dubai-based traders who bought products from Jumbo.

In 1999, Sony began assembling televisions in Pakistan, contracting with a Pakistani-Korean joint-venture company. Tahir Arshad, the venture's finance manager, says smuggling of Sony TVs has been reduced in recent years. Still, the local-assembly plant is running at only half capacity, and the venture's officials are worried about whether their contract will be renewed this year. Sony Gulf declines to comment on whether it will renew the contract.

Televisions are legal again in Afghanistan, and if Sony closes down local production in Pakistan, it "can still sell" in Afghanistan, says Mr. Arshad. In fact, the late Abdul Haq's brother, Haji Abdul Qadir, is back in power in Jalalabad as provincial governor, and he is trying to revive the family's Dubai-Jalalabad air-cargo service.

Khalid Khan of Sony Gulf says he has begun scouting for authorized Sony dealers to operate in Afghanistan. One place he intends to recruit is in Peshawar, although he says that any TVs imported into Afghanistan would be sold to Afghan buyers, not smuggled into neighboring countries. Mr. Modak, the Sony Gulf spokesman, says it hasn't authorized Mr. Khan to do this recruiting.

Some dealers of smuggled goods in Karkhano say they are eager to be recruited. "If we manage to work from Afghanistan, we can export to Russia, to Iran, to other neighboring countries"—if possible, without paying taxes and duties, says Muslim Electronics's Abdul Basir Khan. "We will have a much greater market."

*—Peter Landers in Tokyo
contributed to this article.*

# 17

# UNDERGROUND TRADE: MUCH-SMUGGLED GEM CALLED TANZANITE HELPS BIN LADEN SUPPORTERS

## Bought and Sold by Militants Near Mine, Stones Often End Up at Mideast Souks

### Deal-Making at the Mosque

*This article written with Robert Block*

*November 16, 2001*

MERERANI, Tanzania—In the shadow of Mount Kilimanjaro, miners with flashlights tied to their heads crawl hundreds of feet beneath the East African plain, searching for a purple-brown crystal that will turn into a blue gem called tanzanite.

Many of the rare stones chipped off by the spacemen, as the miners are called, find their way to display cases at Zales, QVC or Tiffany. But it's a long way from these dusty plains to U.S. jewelry stores, and the stones pass through many hands on their journey. Some of those hands, it is increasingly clear, belong to active supporters of Osama bin Laden.

A trade group called the Tanzanian Mineral Dealers Association denies that Mr. bin Laden's al Qaeda has any role in the tanzanite trade. But in the bars and cafés that dot the streets of Tanzania's mining community, the radical connections are no secret. According to miners and local residents, Muslim extremists loyal to Mr. bin Laden buy stones from miners and middlemen, smuggling them out of Tanzania to free-trade havens such as Dubai and Hong Kong. "Yes, people here are trading for Osama. Just look around and you will find serious Muslims who believe in him and work for him," says Musa Abdallah, a Kenyan who has worked as a tanzanite miner for six years.

Many details of the trade remain murky, such as whether its main role is to earn money for the militants or simply to help them move funds secretly about the world. Still, William Wechsler, a former National Security Council member in charge of counterterrorism under President Clinton, says there is little doubt that Mr. bin Laden's links to gemstones, including tanzanite, have been used at times to help fund his terror activities. Al Qaeda's dealings in tanzanite in the 1990s were detailed at length during the recent federal trial that convicted four bin Laden men in connection with the U.S. embassy bombings in Tanzania and Kenya.

Alex Magyane, a Tanzanian government official actively investigating the tanzanite trade, says he has recently traced bin Laden–linked smuggling of rough stones through Kenya to bazaars in the Middle East. "Beyond any doubt, I am 100% sure that these Muslim gem traders are connected to Osama bin Laden," the official says.

Tanzanite is so rare it is mined in only one place on earth, a five-square-mile patch of graphite rock here in northeastern Tanzania. Legend has it that Masai tribesmen discovered the gem when a bolt of lightning set fire to the plains and some crystals on the ground turned blue. In 1967 an Indian geologist identified the stone as a rare form of the mineral zoisite and determined that it turned a velvety blue when heated to 400 degrees Celsius. Tiffany & Co. named it "tanzanite" and promoted it as "the most important gemological discovery in 2,000 years." Tanzanite became a U.S. marketing phenomenon, second in popularity only to sapphire among colored stones.

Its popularity soared when movie fans learned that the sapphire heart-shaped pendant Kate Winslet hurled into the sea in the movie "Titanic" was actually tanzanite. By then, the U.S. was selling $380 million of tanzanite jewelry a year.

Yet Tanzania's official exports of uncut tanzanite crystal totaled a mere $16 million last year. Rampant smuggling spirits as much as 90% of the production out of the country, Tanzanian government statistics show. Local traders often buy plastic bags full of rough stones, paying cash and exchanging none of the paperwork that would trigger a 3% export duty. And in faraway places where the rough tanzanite is cooked, cut and polished, such as the Indian city of Jaipur, dealers say they don't question suppliers closely about sources.

Mererani, which is a 30-minute drive from the mines along a treacherous dirt road, is reminiscent of a Gold Rush town, with shacks, bars, brothels and hordes of young men hoping for a strike. Besides a few big mechanized mining operations, hundreds of individuals hold tiny, 50-yard-square claims that they mine as best they can. Working with the "spacemen" who descend the tunnels are "snakes," the term for boys who sift piles of grit on the surface and sometimes wriggle into the crevices too small for adults. Restaurants play on the dreams of prosperity, taking names like New York and The Big Apple. But alongside the dreams and the decadence, a religious radicalism is brewing.

Tanzania's Muslims, who make up about 40% of the populace, have long practiced a "soft" Islam, tolerant of drinking, revealing dress and their many Christian neighbors. But Muslim radicalism began to rise in the early 1990s, fueled by poverty and financial support from Islamic charities abroad. It included the al Qaeda cell that bombed the U.S. embassy in Tanzania three years ago.

In Mererani, a new mosque called Taqwa has brought an openly radical Muslim presence to the tanzanite district. Taqwa's imam, Sheik Omari, has issued edicts that Muslims miners should sell their stones only to fellow Muslims. The diktats breed resentment. "The fundamentalists have established a mafia to dominate the trade," says Mr. Abdallah, the Kenyan spaceman. "Even if non-Muslims offer better prices for our stones, we are harassed by the fundamentalists not to sell to anyone but them. Many Muslim miners obey because they are scared of them."

The Taqwa mosque is still under construction on a dusty side street. Inside a temporary prayer hall of wood and corrugated metal, miners are taught the importance of avenging the "arrogance" of America and defending Afghanistan from "U.S. oppression." Support for Mr. bin Laden is a duty, miners are told. The faithful of Taqwa often address one another as Jahidini, a Swahili word that means Muslim militant. Some routinely greet one another as "Osama."

After prayers, the mosque's courtyard becomes an open-air gem-dealing space, where Sheik Omari and other mosque leaders trade tanzanite with small-time miners. In between haggling, the elders preach the virtues of suicide attacks as a way to defend their faith.

"Remember, Islam teaches us that your body is a weapon," Sheik Omari tells a group of young men in Swahili. "But if you die, you should take as many of your enemy with you as you can. This will be your ticket to paradise."

Asked if he works with or belongs to al Qaeda, Sheik Omari gives a vague answer, as do others at the mosque. " 'Al Qaeda' means 'base.' I don't know any base. But Islam says we must support our brothers and sisters and those who defend Islam from its enemies," Sheik Omari says. The mosque traders, who aren't licensed as dealers but act as informal middlemen, make clear the gem business must serve their militant brand of Islam. "We as Muslims must unite in dealing in gemstones to help one another and to generate funds to defend Islam from those who want to destroy it," says Aman Mustafa, a Kenyan gem broker and teacher at the mosque, who says he has studied Islamic law in Sudan.

U.S. investigators of al Qaeda's business say that it is designed to create self-sustaining networks and cells. Here in Mererani, some proceeds from the tanzanite trade are plowed back into expanding Taqwa's influence. "This mosque is being built with tanzanite," Sheik Omari says. "Our Islam is stronger with our efforts to create a Muslim force in this gemstone."

Mr. Magyane, whose government title is regional mine officer, says some of the stones bought by the Muslim militants are smuggled through "rat routes" to the Kenyan city of Mombasa. That city is a stronghold of al Qaeda sympathizers and was a base for the 1998 embassy bombings. Throughout the embassy-bomber trial this year in New York, several bin Laden associates or former ones, both state witnesses and defendants, referred to dealings in tanzanite in the mid-1990s. Testimony described how the stones moved through Kenya to Hong Kong via one of two al Qaeda companies, Tanzanite King or Black Giant, set up by defendant Wadih el Hage, a gem dealer and former personal secretary to Mr. bin Laden. Mr. el Hage is serving a life sentence for his role as the bombers' financial facilitator.

Bin Laden supporters trading tanzanite today face no interference from Tanzanian authorities. "We have no proof they are involved in terrorist activities," says the mining area's regional governor, Daniel Ole Njoolay.

Adadi Rajabu, head of Tanzania's counterterrorism police, adds that "before 1998, we never knew there were people smuggling gemstones on behalf of a terrorist group. But it is not an area we have looked at carefully. Most of our attention since 1998 has been focused on operatives who were likely to be engaged in activities like bombings, not business."

Sheik Omari and Mr. Mustafa say they sell their stones to a prominent local dealer, Abdulhakim Mulla, who Mr. Mustafa says sends some of the gems on to Dubai. The dealer denies the Dubai connection. In any event, on a recent day Sheik Omari could be overheard telling miners to bring perfect stones to the mosque, because "our market in Dubai only wants perfect stones."

To Westerners in the gem business, mention of Dubai raises alarms. For one thing, the emirate is known as a center of money laundering and the underground cash-transfer system known as hawala much favored by Mr. bin Laden. Dubai also has no gem-cutting industry. It lies far outside normal channels for the trade in rough gemstones, most of which go to Jaipur, to Bangkok or to a few other traditional centers of cutting and polishing.

"Dubai is the kind of place that should throw up a flag that something is definitely askew," says Cap R. Beesley, president of American Gemological Laboratories in New York, which tests colored stones. "When you see any rechanneling through nontraditional destinations like Dubai, it means someone is finding some financial incentive not to play by the book."

U.S. law-enforcement officials have identified Dubai as a haven for al Qaeda business interests. The FBI and the Treasury Department are currently trying to help the United Arab Emirates, of which Dubai is a part, to crack down on the abuse of Dubai's free-trade zones by terrorists and criminals. While this effort mainly focuses on gold smuggling, the U.S. also has reports that al Qaeda uses tanzanite as a way to move funds around the world, says a U.S. government investigator familiar with Dubai.

Out of more than 12,000 pounds of official tanzanite exports from Tanzania last year, a mere 13 pounds were sold to Dubai dealers. But Mr. Magyane estimates that a hundred times that amount actually made its way to Dubai, through smuggling.

In Dubai, on a strip of small jewel shops along a creek, Africans often go door-to-door trying to sell plastic bags full of unrefined gold and sometimes uncut gemstones for cash. D. B. Siroya, an Indian dealer based in Dubai for two decades, says he has sometimes acquired rough tanzanite in Dubai on behalf of Indian friends, buying from sellers he knows.

The cash element is part of what makes the gem trade attractive to al Qaeda, according to Mr. Wechsler, the former U.S. counterterrorism official. He says the gem business is also attractive because it is tiered, with many layers of brokers, traders, cutters, polishers and wholesalers between miner and consumer.

A U.S. government–funded report last year for Tanzania's mining industry noted that the country's gem industry was "subject to abuse by money launderers, arms and drug dealers." Afgem Ltd., a South African mining company, has been trying to change that. It advocates branding tanzanite stones with tiny laser-etched logos and bar codes, plus other regulations to discourage smuggling. But its plan last year ignited clashes with small miners, who, Tanzanian intelligence claims, were funded by foreigners with a stake in the current loose system. The many tiers in the business make it possible for unsavory players to get in and out without leaving much of a trace. In the U.S. jewelry industry, which consumes nearly 80% of tanzanite gems, many participants say they have heard industry reports of tanzanite links to al Qaeda only recently, and tend to discount them.

QVC Inc. says it has met with its seven tanzanite vendors to make sure they comply with its ethics code, which says QVC won't knowingly deal in gemstones "that originate from a group or a country which engages in illegal, inhumane or terrorist activities." Darlene Daggett, executive vice president of merchandising, says that if tanzanite "definitively can be linked to terrorist activities, we will not continue to sell it."

Zale Corp. says it has heard "bits and pieces" about such a link, but not enough to know if it needs to change procedures. "It comes down to knowing who we do business with and knowing where they get their stones," says spokeswoman Sue Davidson. "But all we really know is what they're telling us. Without some kind of gemstone authorization, certification and tracking system in place, we cannot guarantee that no stone has been smuggled."

Zale CEO Robert DiNicola adds: "If it came to light that there is a problem with tanzanite, we wouldn't deal with it."

Jewelers of America, a retail jewelers' trade group, says it has been focusing on the "far more significant consequences to human life" of "blood" diamonds, those whose sale helps to fuel African conflicts. "I'm not suggesting we are not willing to look at other connections," but "we need more information," says the group's chief executive, Matthew Runci.

—*Ann Zimmerman*
*contributed to this article.*

# -18-

# PUSHING PILLS: DRUG FIRMS' INCENTIVES TO PHARMACISTS IN INDIA FUEL MOUNTING ABUSE

### Gifts, 'Bonus Schemes' Boost Illicit and Harmful Sales of Prescription Medicines

#### Win a Free Trip to Nepal

*This article written with Steve Stecklow*

*August 16, 2001*

BOMBAY, India—Pharmacy owner Ranjit Ranawat smiles as he recalls how he surprised his wife one day with a new 29-inch color television, courtesy of GlaxoSmithKline PLC's India unit. How did he get it? He ordered 600 vials of Fortum, an antibiotic, and 100 boxes of Ceftum, a drug for urinary-tract and respiratory infections. That's about 10 times as much as he normally would stock.

Incentives to buy large quantities of prescription drugs have become commonplace in India, where thousands of drug manufacturers compete for shelf space and the country's half-million pharmacists wield an unusual amount of clout.

Pharmacists in the U.S. and other developed countries have little influence over the volume of prescription-drug sales. There, the marketing push usually targets doctors, the main legal conduit for prescription drugs. In India, many patients are too poor or too busy to see a doctor and often rely on local pharmacists for medical advice. As a result, powerful drugs are routinely, and illegally, sold over-the-counter.

The strange contours of India's medicines market arise partly from the country's success in fostering wide-open competition, which has lowered prices, made drugs widely available and served as a model for

89

other developing countries. But the incentive system poses dangers for customers and raises ethical issues for drug makers and pharmacists. And with an estimated 20,000 pharmaceutical companies fighting over $3 billion in annual sales amid little regulation, the Indian model has taken competition to a questionable extreme.

"It's a war out there. You have to get maximum business," says Deepak Arora, group product manager for Bombay-based Glenmark Pharmaceuticals Ltd. and a former Glaxo salesman. The pharmacist, he adds, is "a powerful person in the decision chain."

To boost prescription-drug sales, pharmaceutical companies—many of them local outfits making knockoffs of Western drugs—try to woo Indian pharmacists with gifts and other incentives. The most popular incentive, often called a "bonus scheme," offers a free foil-and-plastic strip of prescription pills for every, say, 10 strips a druggist orders.

A study by the Bombay market-research firm Interlink Healthcare Consultancy found that all but one of the top 25 drug companies in India offer such discounting deals at least once a month. A recent letter to pharmacists from Blue Cross Laboratories Ltd., a Bombay company with no connection to Blue Cross & Blue Shield of the U.S., outlines a deal that offers druggists up to a 103% profit margin on a variety of prescription drugs.

For pharmaceutical companies, offering profit incentives to pharmacies serves a variety of purposes: to introduce a new brand, to liquidate a slow-moving batch of drugs, to book more sales at the end of a financial quarter, or to push competing brands off the shelves. The incentives change so often and there are so many new ones that just keeping track is a chore for drug wholesalers. Janak J. Kothari, director of R. J. Distributors Pvt. Ltd. near Bombay, created a special function for his computerized database to monitor the deals available.

Some of the prescription drugs being promoted by pharmaceutical companies are mild cough medications or skin creams. But many of the more lucrative incentive plans promote a powerful array of antibiotics, anti-inflammatories, sedatives and painkillers, some of which must be injected.

Moreover, some of the medications have been banned in other countries because of potential serious side effects. One of Aventis SA's Indian units, Hoechst Marion Roussel Ltd., has been promoting Baralgan-M (buy 19 packs, get one free) and Novalgin (buy 24, get one free). These are painkillers that contain metamizole (also known as dipyrone and Analgin), which has been banned in the U.S. and some other countries because it can cause a rare but fatal blood disorder. Aventis, based in Strasbourg, France, said in a statement, "We believe that the safety and efficacy of metamizole have been well-established in its more than 75 years of clinical use" and noted that the drug "is currently approved and marketed in more than 100 countries."

Many companies also use bonus deals to market cough syrups containing phenylpropanolamine. Last fall, the U.S. Food and Drug Administration asked drug companies to discontinue marketing any drug products that contained the ingredient after a study showed it can increase the risk of stroke.

Health experts say the drug companies' incentives have helped foster a marketplace in India rife with abuse, encouraging pharmacists to sell prescription drugs that may not be appropriate and to do so illegally. "It's the tipping of the market toward the clinically irrational," says Dr. Dennis Ross-Degan, an associate professor at Harvard Medical School who specializes in health care in developing countries. To benefit from the discount deals, which are based on volume sales, pharmacies "have to push the product," he says.

That can be dangerous. Hospitals say they get a steady flow of patients who suffer gastric bleeding and kidney complications shortly after taking prescription pain medications without a doctor's supervision. One such patient is 34-year-old Vipul Shah, a Bombay businessman. He says when he had leg pain, three different pharmacies in Bombay sold him Dicloran pills even though he had no prescription. He also says he was given no instructions on how the drug should be taken. Dicloran is an Indian brand name for diclofenac sodium, a prescription arthritis drug. It is marketed to druggists by Bombay-based J. B. Chemicals & Pharmaceuticals Ltd. under a buy-nine-get-one-free scheme.

After taking two tablets a day for a month, Mr. Shah started feeling lower-back pain and saw a doctor, Bharat Shah, at Bombay's Hinduja Hospital. Dr. Shah (no relation to the patient) found permanent kidney damage and believes the drug aggravated an existing condition. Patients with serious kidney problems normally are advised to use diclofenac with great caution. J. B. Chemicals didn't respond to repeated requests for comment.

The bonus deals worry health advocates for other reasons. By giving extra profits to the pharmacist instead of reducing the retail price, they say, manufacturers are keeping medicine prices higher than necessary for Indian patients. In addition, nearly half of all bonus deals feature antibiotics, which are overused and misused in India, according to health experts. "For any condition, a patient gets antibiotics over-the-counter," says Sujeet K. Bhattacharya, director of the National Institute of Cholera and Enteric Diseases in Calcutta.

Frequently, those patients don't complete the full course of treatment, he adds. That has led to a number of serious diseases in India, including cholera, typhoid and gonorrhea, growing resistant to common antibiotics in recent years.

The offers of televisions and other prizes to pharmacists would raise ethical questions in Western countries. Officials at two large U.S. drugstore chains, CVS Corp. and Walgreen Co., say their pharmacists are prohibited from accepting any gifts from vendors.

Local and foreign drug companies in India defend the incentives, and say they aren't designed to boost sales without a prescription. They say the main purpose is to persuade pharmacists to substitute their brand over competing brands when a prescription is written—or "to defend our own prescriptions," as Glaxo India's director of pharmaceuticals, Kal Sundaram, puts it. He says that for every two Glaxo prescriptions written, only one Glaxo drug ends up being sold because druggists often substitute a competing medication. Glaxo, the world's No. 2 drug maker after Pfizer Inc., says it decided to award TV sets to druggists buying high volumes of Ceftum and Fortum in late 1999 after a rash of substitutions of other brands. The company says trade promotions represent less than 1% of Glaxo's sales in India, which totaled $198.5 million last year.

Aventis says it offers incentives on a "need basis only," to make sure patients "get what they ask for."

"For certain drugs, bonus schemes have to be given," adds Rashmi Pai, a Bombay-based product manager with Wyeth Lederle Ltd., an Indian unit of American Home Products Corp., Madison, N.J. Some drugs in India are available in as many as 100 different brands, she says.

Pharmacists weren't always so powerful in India. Until the 1970s, foreign companies such as Britain's Glaxo and New York–based Pfizer dominated the market, and most drugs had only a single manufacturer, so pharmacists had little choice over what brands to stock. Some manufacturers gave retailers margins below 4% on certain drugs and refused to issue cash refunds on medicines that expired.

The balance of power started changing in 1972, when India passed a new patent law allowing companies to duplicate any foreign drug under patent as long as they altered the manufacturing process, even slightly. (International trade rules require India to enact a tough patent law by 2005.) Thousands of manufacturers sprang up, producing more than 60,000 brands of drugs. When Eli Lilly & Co. of Indianapolis introduced Prozac in 1986, nearly two dozen copycat products appeared within two years.

Marketing also changed. As in the U.S., pharmaceutical companies had long courted Indian doctors with gifts and junkets. But as the number of Indian companies proliferated and their representatives began descending on doctors' offices in droves, they often were given scant time to promote their products. So the drug makers began paying more attention to pharmacists. To increase their leverage over drug companies, pharmacy owners banded together into trade associations. The associations launched boycotts against drug companies to win higher profit margins. The associations also began demanding that drug companies obtain a "no-objection letter" from each state trade association before a new drug could be sold there. Otherwise it would be excluded from the pharmacists' stock lists. For each new drug, the trade groups usually solicit a cash donation.

Dilip Mehta, president of the All India Organization of Chemists and Druggists, which represents 500,000 Indian pharmacists, boasts of how his association also has forced drug companies to sign "memorandums of understanding" in which they agree to increase profit margins to pharmacies.

"They have to surrender," Mr. Mehta says, speaking from his tiny office at the rear of a wholesale apparel center in Bombay. The chemists association, he says, is like "a parallel government."

Mr. Mehta doesn't dispute that his members often dispense medicines without prescriptions. He argues that they are performing a public service by doing so. "We cannot allow a person to die without medicine," he says.

On a busy recent Sunday afternoon at the Shree Samarth Medical Store in the western India agricultural town of Dinduri, owner Bapusaheb Patil was openly selling prescription drugs without prescriptions, including anti-inflammatory pills, ulcer tables and anti-tuberculosis drugs. He used a notebook to keep track of his regular customers' favorite medicines, in case they forgot the name or remembered only the color.

Mr. Patil also didn't disguise his motivation for recommending certain brands. "The ultimate decision is based on what the margins are," he said. For fevers, he usually recommended a generic version of the antibiotic ciprofloxacin; a recent incentive deal from an Indian manufacturer offered him a 250% profit margin and a chance to win a motorcycle. Mr. Patil said he needed the extra profit because many of his customers are poor villagers who buy on credit and sometimes fail to pay up.

He said he sells vials of injectable medicines to the area's village doctors. As in much of rural India, few of them have formal training in Western medicine or are even licensed by the Indian government to practice conventional medicine. Mr. Patil also lets his customers return any unused pills. "I tell them to stop after a few pills if they have side effects," said Mr. Patil, who has a degree in pharmacology. He said he won't recommend drugs he believes are hazardous. At least Mr. Patil's customers get advice from someone with an education. Despite Indian regulations that require a licensed pharmacist to dispense all prescription drugs, untrained counter assistants often perform that role. And even when pharmacists are on hand, they often don't provide printed information about a drug's possible adverse reactions or explain the proper dosage.

To overcome competition from multinationals, Indian companies usually offer the retailer significantly higher profit margins. India's leading home-grown drug maker, New Delhi–based Ranbaxy Laboratories Ltd., recently offered pharmacy owners eight free vials of injectable ciprofloxacin for every seven they bought. Ranbaxy says most of those sales go to hospitals. Some companies have become creative. German Remedies Ltd., an Indian company that manufactures products under license from GlaxoSmithKline's SmithKline Beecham unit and Schering AG of Berlin, among others, recently offered a promotion dubbed "Mega Merchants: Sell and Enjoy." In exchange for buying three boxes of Primolut-N, a Schering hormone prescribed for menstrual irregularities, and several other drugs, a retailer received a free box of the antibiotic amoxycillin and a ticket for a drawing for 124 vacations in Germany, Nepal and several Indian destinations.

Makarand Deshpande, general manager of sales and marketing for German Remedies, says the four-month promotion was a "moderate success." It boosted sales of some slow-selling drugs by $1 million, while the trips cost the company only about $100,000. He acknowledges that some of Primolut-N's sales in general are over-the-counter, but he says the promotion wasn't aimed at encouraging that.

Schering spokesman Oliver Renner says that because German Remedies is a licensee, "all the promotion they do for the product is their sole responsibility."

Gynecologists say Indian women frequently buy Primolut-N without a prescription and use it to delay menstruation during religious holidays. The practice can increase chances of birth defects if the woman has just become pregnant, gynecologists warn.

Drawing the winning tickets for the "Mega Merchants" promotion was Mr. Mehta, the pharmacists' association president and an unabashed fan of promotions. "Who doesn't like schemes?" he asks.

Some multinational drug companies don't. "It's a mugger's game," says Vinod Topa, director of sales and marketing for the Indian subsidiary of Abbott Laboratories, of Abbott Park, Ill. He says when he joined the company in December, it was saddled with huge amounts of expired medicines returned by pharmacies that had bought them under incentive programs but failed to sell them. He notified distributors that there would be no more bonus plans after July 31, but he says pharmacies immediately responded by reducing purchases of Abbott drugs. "I am facing the music now," he says.

# 19

# THE CATALYST: BEHIND CIPLA'S OFFER OF CHEAP AIDS DRUGS: POTENT MIX OF MOTIVES

## Altruism, Local Politics and the Bottom Line Intersect at Indian Generics Firm

### Waiting for Government Call

*This article written with Alix Freedman*

*March 12, 2001*

BOMBAY, India—Yusuf K. Hamied is a man with impressive humanitarian credentials. His pharmaceuticals company, Cipla Ltd., runs a free cancer-care hospital in India. His apartment near London's Hyde Park boasts a series of paintings of Mother Teresa that bear her signature. When a devastating earthquake recently struck India's Gujarat state, Dr. Hamied ordered his company's warehouses opened, on a holiday, to supply free medicine.

And yet, even Dr. Hamied's friends say it wasn't simply compassion that drove the generic-drug pioneer to make his attention-grabbing offer last month to sell AIDS drugs at deep discounts, a move that has set off an extraordinary price war for supplying the life-saving medicines to Africa and developing nations elsewhere. The developing world is home to the vast majority of the globe's 35 million people infected with HIV, the virus that causes AIDS.

One friend, Bombay patent lawyer Narendra Zaveri, says Dr. Hamied's offer was "very much a business deal" designed to build Cipla's brand name outside India. Others say Dr. Hamied wanted to impress Indian government officials with his ability to cut prices, as part of an effort to preserve the legal rights of India's generic-drug companies to make and market copies of newly developed drugs.

Regardless, Cipla's offer to sell a triple-combination of "antiretroviral" AIDS drugs to the international aid group Doctors Without Borders at less than $1 a day per patient is transforming the debate over how to provide critical medicines to poor nations.

For the first time, companies like Cipla that copy drugs still under patent in other countries are being taken seriously by the United Nations. That is making them important players in a new plan U.N. officials are drafting for supplying much-needed medicines to Africa.

Multinational pharmaceuticals companies dismiss Cipla and its peers as patent "pirates." But the big multinationals are nonetheless responding with discounts for developing nations that the drug giants themselves would have labeled impossible just a few months ago. And other Indian generic-drug makers are fueling the pricing battle as they try to outdo Cipla.

Health-care advocates in the U.S. are paying attention, too. Cipla's price, $350 a year per patient for one three-drug cocktail known to extend the lives of AIDS patients, is ⅟₃₀ of the treatment's cost in the U.S. Paul Davis of the AIDS activist organization Act Up/Philadephia says his group has decided to lobby against big drug companies' patent extensions in the U.S., in order to pressure them to sell drugs cheaply in Africa.

"Whatever you may say, what we have started has been a crusade," says the mercurial 64-year-old Dr. Hamied. "It has unwittingly developed into this."

Cipla, whose name was largely unknown in the West until recently, is keeping up the pressure, too. Later this month, Dr. Hamied is scheduled to meet with officials of the U.N.'s World Health Organization to talk about ways to administer international sales of generic AIDS drugs. Just last week, the company filed a request in South Africa for a license to sell cheap versions of patented AIDS drugs there. That request may bolster the South African government's defense of a controversial law that allows it to authorize imports of low-cost generics, even as 39 major drug makers attack the law in a South African court.

How much the crusade will help AIDS patients is still unclear. Cipla's offer to Paris-based Doctors Without Borders so far seems largely symbolic, since the group lacks the resources, infrastructure or desire to be a global drug distributor. Doctors Without Borders is unsure whether it will be able to get the funding to buy Cipla's drugs. If it does, the group says it plans to set up only small pilot projects to dispense them.

Campaigns to get cheap drugs into African nations also face legal and logistical hurdles as well as questions about who will verify that the knockoffs work like the originals. Dr. Hamied hasn't extended the $350-a-year offer to governments, which might buy large volumes of drugs, but he says he is willing to sell them the three-drug regimen for $600 a patient per year. That price appears to be comfortably profitable for the Indian drug maker, whose overall AIDS-drug sales have been paltry thus far.

Last May, five large drug companies pledged to provide their AIDS drugs to people in sub–Sahara Africa at about 80% off the prices they charge in the U.S. and Europe. But because prices were still far above most Africans' reach that effort received a limited response. Last week, in an effort to encourage African nations and international donors to begin buying or subsidizing the drugs, but also partly in response to Cipla and its Indian rivals, Merck & Co. slashed its prices by an additional 50%. New price cuts from other big companies are expected to follow.

But, as with the large drug companies' offers, many wonder if Cipla's proposals will have impact beyond their publicity value. "That's the question we all have," says Denis Broun, a former U.N. pharmaceuticals specialist who has advised Dr. Hamied over the past year. Saving lives with the AIDS drugs requires specially trained doctors and nurses and careful tracking of patient dosages, says Dr. Broun, who now works for Management Sciences for Health, a nonprofit consulting group based in Boston. Dr. Hamied, he believes, is mostly concerned with influencing patent laws in India.

"He is pretty cleverly using the AIDS issue to push his views, and show their validity," says Dr. Broun. "He is pursuing, internationally, an Indian objective."

Dr. Hamied says that his sole motive for offering to supply cheap AIDS drugs is simply "my social obligation to society."

In India, Cipla's agenda hasn't always been to push down drug prices. It and other big generic companies recently asked the government to slap 35% import duties on lamivudine, an AIDS drug known as 3TC, that Dr. Hamied's company also makes. And Cipla is engaged in a bitter dispute with the Indian government over India's price-control regulations. When the government ordered Cipla to reduce prices of certain drugs, the company went to court instead. It could have to cough up $20 million should the government win.

Yogin Majmudar, an Indian generic-drug executive close to Dr. Hamied, says the case may have influenced Cipla to make an international splash on AIDS-drug pricing. "Hamied is trying to get his due recognition from the government," he says.

Every day, on his way to work, Dr. Hamied drives his Lexus past Dr. K. A. Hamied Square, named after his father, an Indian nationalist who started Cipla in 1935. Guards salute Dr. Hamied as he rolls down the driveway of Cipla's midtown Bombay headquarters. In his office, Dr. Hamied shows visitors photos of himself with his Bombay childhood playmate, the conductor Zubin Mehta.

Cipla's chairman is a true cosmopolitan. His father was a Muslim and his mother a Lithuanian Jew. Dr. Hamied's accent is more European than Indian. He spends much of the year in London and the Indian Ocean island of Mauritius, and claims "nonresident Indian" status. In Bombay, he stays in shape by walking around the pool at the European-controlled Breach Candy Swimming Trust, which once barred Indians and now limits their memberships. Still, Dr. Hamied's eyes sharpen as he recounts how foreign companies overcharged India for medicines in the 1960s, when he went to work for Cipla after returning from Cambridge University with a doctorate in chemistry.

It was, in part, a foreign patent holder's attempts to stop Cipla from making Propranolol, a heart-disease drug, that spurred the company to political action 30 years ago. Cipla went to then Prime Minister Indira Gandhi, according to later testimony by Dr. Hamied, and asked: "Should millions of Indians be denied the use of a life-saving drug just because the originator doesn't like the color of our skin?"

With the prime minister's support, India enacted a new patent law in 1972 that protected only the process for making a drug, leaving the product itself fair game for copying.

Within India's growing community of drug duplicators, Dr. Hamied remained a hard-liner. He pulled Cipla out of a trade group he had helped create, because the group was starting to issue some joint statements with foreign drug companies. Dr. Hamied showed a special brilliance for decoding the foreign companies' newly invented drugs. Colleagues in the industry recall seeing him scribble from memory all the steps needed to synthesize a particular molecule. "I'm a scientist, not a businessman," he likes to say. Still, Cipla is now the No. 3 Indian generic-drug company in terms of sales, and it earns some of the highest operating profits in the business: 26% in the quarter ended December 31.

Cipla is "a company with a sustainable competitive advantage," its promotional video proclaims. But by 2005, that competitive advantage could end. International trade rules require India to put a strong pharmaceuticals patent law in place by then. To get ready, some Indian companies have moved aggressively into research. Meanwhile, Cipla has been duplicating foreign drugs at a furious pace. (The new patent law probably won't cover drugs patented before 1995, as long as generic versions are already on the market.)

With family and friends, Dr. Hamied controls 41% of Cipla's shares, valued at a total of $530 million. Some industry officials say he has entertained offers to sell the company. Dr. Hamied denies that he has done so.

Fielding calls at his office, Dr. Hamied seems very much a businessman. "I'd love to do business with Oxfam," the British charity, he tells Cipla's agent in Argentina, and then starts dickering over AIDS drugs. "The lowest price I can give you for Stavudine is $1,500 a kilo," or about $682 a pound, he says. He is referring to the active ingredients in Bristol-Myers Squibb Co.'s patented AIDS drug Zerit.

Such bulk ingredients are created in thickly insulated glass vats, in a series of reactions that can take a month. By refining the process, generic-drug companies typically drive costs down over time. It is a competitive business, with regular requests for bids from buyers in Brazil and Argentina. But Cipla set itself apart in India by forming the ingredients into actual pills, as well, and putting them on pharmacy shelves under its own brand names, such as Stavir.

Its AIDS pills are too valuable to keep on the shelves at Riddhi Siddhi, a Cipla distributor in Bombay's industrial district. Co-owner Priti Mayani says she keeps Cipla AIDS medicines such as nevirapine, patented by Germany's Boehringer-Ingelheim GmbH, under her desk for safekeeping, because they're the most expensive of 500 Cipla products she sells. Cipla is the market leader in AIDS drugs in India, which has an estimated HIV-positive population of 3.7 million. It sells the drugs at a cost of $1,090 a year for a typical combination treatment.

Yet, AIDS therapy isn't a thriving business for Cipla. Ever since it began synthesizing AIDS drugs a decade ago, selling them in India has been an uphill battle. Dr. Alla V. Ramarao, former director of a government lab who helped Cipla concoct the drugs, says he had to plead with Dr. Hamied to carry on after early batches of the AIDS drug AZT passed their expiration dates without being sold.

Even now, after years of rival seminars for doctors sponsored by Cipla and by Glaxo PLC (now part of GlaxoSmithKline PLC), the entire Indian market for antiretrovirals barely amounts to $3 million, according to Bombay market-data provider Org-Marg Research Ltd. Glaxo estimates that no more than one in 300 HIV-positive Indians is on antiretroviral drugs.

The reasons are many. Indian doctors often suggest herbal remedies and diet improvements before turning to Western drugs. Some hospitals still won't admit AIDS patients, and many AIDS patients are reluctant to visit doctors. Prafulta Against AIDS, a church-funded organization that works with Bombay's well-organized prostitutes, held meetings with them for a year before trying to persuade them to take AIDS tests.

One 26-year-old streetwalker, who goes by the name Sumiti, says nobody trusts local doctors to keep a prostitute's condition secret from her clients or her profession secret from her relatives. Anyhow, Sumiti, who earns enough to buy her husband alcohol and send her daughter to private school, says she wouldn't spend even $1 a day to save her life if she tested positive for AIDS. Fifty cents, maybe.

Most Indians don't have the choice, since a year's supply of the cheapest antiretroviral combination available costs more than India's average per capita annual income. And the hidden costs are even higher. Shahrukh Irani, a wine salesman in the city of Pune, shows a February bill for his HIV-positive 12-year-old daughter: $110 for a two-drug combination, $170 for a liver test, blood tests, urea test and viral-load test to keep track of the drug's effects and side effects, and another $130 for doctor's bills and incidental expenses. A Zoroastrian charity pays those bills. Cipla has tried to persuade the Indian government to start funding AIDS treatment. But India is a country that hasn't eradicated leprosy, and thousands of people die there each year for lack of such basic necessities as clean water. Its health officials, who have only $45 million a year to spend on fighting AIDS, aren't convinced it is worth shifting funds from prevention to care. Export markets pose other problems for Cipla. For the past two years it has tried to sell the AIDS drugs to South Africa. It has a 40-person office there and took a small booth at last year's AIDS conference in South Africa. One analyst estimated Cipla could take in $100 million if it could get into South Africa. But few markets have patent laws as lax as India's.

In August, Cipla canceled a shipment of its Combivir AIDS drug to Ghana after getting a letter from GlaxoSmithKline warning that the product was under patent. Ghanian authorities disagreed, and even Glaxo officials now concede they were in error. Even so, Cipla decided not to stay and fight.

It was a loose alliance of Americans who handed Cipla the idea for a new export strategy. The group's leader was Jamie Love, 51, of Consumer Project on Technology, a Washington, D.C–based activist group associated with Ralph Nader. In August, as part of his campaign to break the hold of the multinationals on AIDS drugs, Mr. Love's team began looking for ways to get lower-priced versions of the medicines into sub-Sahara Africa. He met with William F. Haddad, a pharmaceuticals entrepreneur who helped found the Peace Corps and is credited with helping foster legislation that has boosted the generic-drug industry in the U.S.

Mr. Haddad says he left the meeting with a piece of paper on which he had drawn four boxes, each containing a question mark. Each was a raw material. For advice on where to get them, he turned to Agnes Varis, a New Jersey drug maker, who told him simply: "Yusuf Hamied of Cipla."

"Who's that?" Mr. Haddad replied.

"An iconoclast," and somebody who wasn't afraid of big drug companies, Ms. Varis said.

Within days, Mr. Haddad and the Naderites flew to London to meet Dr. Hamied in his spacious flat. Dr. Hamied impressed the others with his offhand recitation of the costs of making AIDS drugs. Asked about AZT, he said, "Talk to the Koreans, they're cheaper than the Indians."

Mr. Love says he asked Dr. Hamied what it would cost for Cipla's three-drug combination if the buyer picked up the drugs at the factory door. The answer: $350 per patient a year.

Eager to publicize the "true" cost of making AIDS drugs, generic-drug industry officials helped secure Dr. Hamied a slot at a September 28 European Commission meeting on AIDS and other diseases. Dr. Hamied says he worked for days on his speech, which he delivered in Brussels to African health ministers, international organizations and big drug companies.

"Friends, I represent the Third World," he began. There should be "no monopolies for vital, life-saving and essential drugs," he said. Then he listed Cipla's wholesale prices for AIDS drugs and said the company would give governments a special rate of $1,000 per year per patient—maybe even $800, for one particular three-drug combination. A buzz went through the room.

"I was hoping if the meeting went on two more days he could go to $200," recalls Jonathan Quick, a WHO official.

Actually, reducing prices for governments made good business sense. Other generic-drug companies in India say they avoid Indian excise tax, wholesale and retail markups, and fancy packaging by selling to foreign governments. That allows the drug makers to reduce prices 40% and keep the same profit. Selling to governments also means fewer problems with defaults, and possibly even with patents.

The scheme of selling AIDS drugs to a nongovernmental health organization was more of a political statement. At the Brussels meeting, Dr. Hamied met Bernard Pecoul of Doctors Without Borders. The aid group needed a supply of medicine to launch some small programs for treating AIDS patients. But AIDS had also become an emotional issue within the organization. Physicians working on other diseases were distressed to see how many of the organization's nurses, doctors and drivers in Africa were succumbing to the AIDS virus. And Doctors Without Borders was frustrated by the slow response from big drug companies and the U.N.

"Our objective is to create the pressure," Dr. Pecoul now explains.

Mr. Love, the Nader activist, had the same goal. On December 11, he came to India to discuss with a group of pharmaceuticals executives how trade rules allowed countries to write laws, like those in South Africa, that could force drug-patent owners to give licenses to generic companies. Drug-company executives in India were expecting government officials to present a new patent law to India's parliament within weeks. With Mr. Love's encouragement, Cipla soon sent letters to four companies holding patents on the AIDS drugs Cipla made, offering to pay a 5% royalty in exchange for a license to make the drugs.

At the same time, Mr. Love was bent on showing how low AIDS-drug prices could go. While in Geneva on January 19 for the World Health Assembly executive board meeting, he says he went to a dinner party thrown by Dr. Pecoul of Doctors Without Borders and announced to his incredulous host, "I guarantee I can get you $350."

Meanwhile, by e-mail, Mr. Love pushed Dr. Hamied to offer that price. "Cipla could call it a donation or whatever it needs to," Mr. Love said in one such message. "This will be a very closely watched price quote, and will go directly to the question of whether or not Africa should pursue a generics strategy, or negotiate endlessly with the big pharma players."

Dr. Hamied says it was the devastating January 26 earthquake in Gujarat that finally persuaded him to act. He told one friend that he started thinking about the unavoidable deaths, and then about all the AIDS deaths that could be avoided in Africa. During a February 6 conference call with Doctors Without Borders, to iron out technical issues involved in purchases of other drugs, Dr. Hamied turned the subject to the AIDS drugs and said, "I'm thinking of offering a $350 price to subsidize your distribution costs," Doctors Without Borders officials recall.

Cipla sent the organization a faxed confirmation letter the next day, offering the $350 price, so long as the drugs were distributed free of charge. Mr. Love made sure the news became public. A week later, Dr. Hamied had a thick stack of press clippings on his desk, and a fax from Unaids asking him to speak at a U.N. Special Assembly session on AIDS in June. But the following week he found himself frustrated with the U.N's response to his $350 offer. Rather than rushing to embrace his overture, U.N. agencies were just asking for further details about the offer, like how long Cipla would supply drugs at that price. The U.N. was "only working with the multinationals, so good luck to them," Dr.

Hamied concluded. As for the Indian government, health officials were waiting for Cipla to contact them; Dr. Hamied was waiting for them to contact him.

Doctors Without Borders soon learned that negotiating with Cipla wasn't like negotiating with a multinational. Daniel Berman, an essential-medicines specialist with the group, recalls that when he showed up at Bristol-Myers last year for talks on an AIDS-drug distribution plan, the company's negotiating team included five public-relations staffers and two drug specialists. At Cipla's headquarters, however, Mr. Berman and an associate met with Dr. Hamied, the company's managing director and its marketing director, Dr. Hamied's younger brother. The company didn't even have a public-relations department or a foundation set up to deal with nonprofit organizations.

That actually posed a problem. Dr. Hamied told Mr. Berman about a telephone call he had received the previous day from a Kenyan orphanage asking for $350-a-year AIDS drugs. He said he asked the orphanage to go through Doctors Without Borders, because he couldn't be expected to field such requests himself. But Doctors Without Borders didn't want the role of deciding what organizations got AIDS drugs. Neither Cipla nor Doctors Without Borders wanted to have to study the patent laws of each country. Nor did Doctors Without Borders want to start a big drug-distribution project in India, as Dr. Hamied suggested.

The two sides did make progress, however. Mr. Berman says he convinced Dr. Hamied that the queries from the U.N. were actually a good sign, and Cipla agreed to work with the World Health Organization. One issue Dr. Hamied wants the WHO to work on is quality assurance. Two other Indian companies, Hetero Drugs Ltd. and Aurobindo Pharma Ltd., are pushing to export AIDS drugs through governments and international organizations. Hetero says Cipla has a problem because its AIDS drugs haven't been fully tested on human beings to show they are equivalent to the patented originals. Cipla says the other companies have a problem because their drug factories don't have full international quality checks.

"Fly-by-night" companies should be kept out of international AIDS-drug supply, Dr. Hamied says one morning. By evening, though, he says, "I genuinely believe there's room for everyone" because Cipla can't possibly supply enough drugs by itself for the millions of AIDS patients in Africa.

Whether for charitable or business purposes, Cipla slashed its AIDS-drug prices in India by 35% on February 27. That night, he predicted the government of India would surely have to respond. But in the nearly two weeks since then, the government still hasn't contacted him.

# 20

# PERSIAN GULF: IN IRAN'S HOLY CITY, ISLAMIC FACTIONS FIGHT FOR SOUL OF A NATION

## Student Unrest Emboldens Qom's Reformers to Test Resolve of Hard-Liners

### 'Coal Burning Under Ashes'

*August 11, 1999*

QOM, Iran—If Iran is locked in a struggle between Islamic clerics and secular reformers, there should be little doubt which side this holy city is on.

At seminaries here, 30,000 students train themselves to be tomorrow's mullahs, or religious scholars. Bookstores have little else but Islamic-studies titles—a few stores are even devoted to a single scholar. Women cover themselves thoroughly. And from tiny offices in alleyways, gray-bearded ayatollahs, the top religious experts for the Shiite Muslims who dominate Iran, issue pronouncements that can prompt government officials to drive two hours southwest through the desert from Tehran to explain themselves.

But Iran's Islamic conservatives do have something to worry about: Here in this Shiite power center, a growing number of clerics are trying to break the hard-liners' control.

"Qom, as a whole, has become hostile" to the hard-liners, maintains Abolhasan Bani Sadr, Iran's former president, from his exile home in Versailles, France. It's a hidden hostility, "like coal burning under ashes," says a businessman in Qom. "They're waiting for a way to show, 'We're with you.'"

Some leftist mullahs are openly campaigning against the long house arrest of top religious figures who criticized the country's conservative religious leadership. Two ayatollahs boldly say that a recent police raid on a student dormitory in Tehran was worse than anything the shah did before the Islamic revolution ousted him in 1979. The hard-liners are fighting back. A parade of left-wing clerics who oppose the hard-liners have been beaten, jailed or hauled into court in recent months.

Though the protests that recently rocked Iran were widely described as a rebellion by youth against the clerical establishment, the truth is that Iran is embroiled in a struggle between two factions of clerics.

Iranians know them as the "Yat" and the "Youn," and their rift goes back two decades. The conservative Jameh Rouhaniyat Mobarez ("militant clergy association") has great influence with Iran's unelected supreme leader, Ayatollah Ali Khamenei. The Majma-e Rouhaniyoun-e Mobarez ("militant clergy society") backs the reformist President Mohammed Khatami. The Rouhaniyoun controlled the newspaper whose closure prompted last month's bloody student riots, and are shouting as loudly as anybody in Iran for free speech, rule of law and greater presidential power.

"We can't be photocopies of each other," says Ayatollah Assadollah Bayat of the clergy. Ayatollah Bayat, one of the Rouhaniyoun's founders, was prosecuted by the hard-line judiciary in December for alleged financial improprieties, but later released. "Plato did not always agree with Aristotle, and Republicans don't always agree with Democrats," he says.

The mullahs' power struggle helps explain Iran's turbulence, but also suggests its limits. No mullahs, and probably few Iranians, want to topple the government. Leaders of both clerical factions have made private assurances they'll join hands if a new revolution is in the air. For now, the Rouhaniyoun are keeping up the pressure. They're encouraging President Khatami to investigate the authorities who ordered the recent raid on a student dormitory that led to bloody protests. They say they will relaunch their pro-Khatami newspaper, *Salaam.* And pro-Khatami mullahs plan to run a full slate of 270 candidates in crucial parliamentary elections this February, virtually daring the hard-liners who control the electoral process to risk street demonstrations by disqualifying them.

The proreform mullahs also are trying to stir things up in Qom itself, with a new group that brings lecturers from Tehran. Hard-liners have tried to muzzle the group, and fist-throwing vigilantes ended two lectures this year. "If anything, I'd say it seems they have more tolerance toward nonclerical political opponents," Tehran University professor Sadeq Zibakalam says of Iran's right wing.

There's a reason for that. Newscasters still call Qom the "city of blood and revolt," because a June 1962 police attack on the Faizieh Theological School started Ayatollah Ruhollah Khomeini's rebellion against the shah. Going to prison under the shah or taking political jobs after he fled was a badge of honor for the clergy.

Now, clerics fill barely one-tenth of the seats in Iran's parliament—a postrevolution low. A growing minority of ayatollahs argue that the clergy should shun government service and stay in Qom because Iran's government is giving Islam a bad name, just as they say Israel is harming the reputation of Jews.

Qom is a dreary city, enlivened somewhat by the smell of pistachio brittle and the sight of robed clerics on motorbikes. Students spend up to two decades studying Islamic philosophy or law in Qom's seminaries, scraping by on $30-a-month stipends from senior ayatollahs. Sitting in low-ceilinged rooms, or walking around the quadrangle of the Faizieh Theological School, students and teachers discuss questions such as whether God created the soul or the body first.

Scholars who stay out of politics have a lot of freedom. Take Ayatollah Ibrahim Jannaati, an energetic, red-bearded man who can discuss the 72 sects of Shiite Islam but has trouble remembering the name of Iran's president. Reaching into a briefcase, Ayatollah Jannaati pulls out his 100-page proof that music with clean lyrics is permitted, his treatise proving that a woman could serve as president, his "Theory of Absolute Cleanness of All Human Beings." "It has to be based on reason," he says, but "you can say anything."

The trouble has more to do with political factions within the clergy dating to the revolution. One faction comprised traditionalists with ties to Iranian businessmen. The other group was made up of leftists, proud of their advocacy of Iran's poor, their intimacy with Ayatollah Khomeini, and their seizure of the U.S. Embassy. The leftists included a gang of radical mullahs who organized Islamist guerrillas in Lebanon, and were known for their zeal in executing political prisoners in the early 1980s.

Now, some of the same mullahs are the backers of Mr. Khatami's "open society" and "dialogue of civilizations." They explain the change by noting that Iran is more stable in the 1990s than it was in the 1980s. But some skeptics wonder if the leftists, who lost power in a 1992 purge, simply adopted the language of political have-nots.

"The background of some of them is not that much different than the right-wingers," says Ali Noorizadeh of the Centre for Arab and Iranian Studies in London. "God knows, if they come back, what they will do."

By 1997, tired of political exile, the Rouhaniyoun sought an audience with the country's powerful supreme leader, Ayatollah Khamenei. Though he is often described in the West as a "hard-liner," he is also a seasoned politician who recently has been appointing moderates to top positions in an apparent attempt to reduce his reliance on hard-line clerics.

Ayatollah Khamenei told the Rouhaniyoun to choose a candidate, and assured his support if the candidate won the presidency, one cleric who attended the meeting recalls. Mr. Khatami, a gentle Qom-trained scholar and former minister of culture, accepted the challenge, and attracted the support of Tehran's intellectuals, but clergy were the muscle in his campaign. The Rouhaniyoun's daily newspaper, *Salaam*, defended the candidate against right-wing attacks, and the organization assembled 3,000 clerics to tout Mr. Khatami around the country in Friday-prayer speeches.

Mr. Khatami's May 1997 election victory emboldened the Rouhaniyoun. Some members were frustrated that it didn't increase their power in Qom, where big institutions remain in the hands of the rival Rouhaniyat. The right-wingers "felt their exclusive sovereignty in danger," and started sacking left-wing mullahs from their jobs as Friday prayer leaders, says Rouhaniyoun spokesman Rasoul Montajabnia, in his office above a West Tehran mosque.

And the right-wing judiciary started building files on Rouhaniyoun clerics, says Mr. Montajabnia, who says he was recently hauled to court for criticizing the police in a university speech last year. Rouhaniyoun members believed it was a right-wing effort to find excuses to keep them off the ballot in next year's parliamentary elections.

This year, tired of reading hard-line announcements from the Qom Seminary Teachers Association, leftists joined with sympathetic student groups and brought lecturers to Qom who believed Islam had to adapt itself to the modern world.

One reformer was the Ayatollah Khamenei's younger brother, Hadi. When he tried to speak at a mosque in Qom in February, thugs charged at him, fists flying, and sent him to the hospital, witnesses say. A Tehran-based cleric who helped organize the lectures was jailed by a special clerical court after writing a book suggesting the supreme leader's powers be limited.

Winning real influence in Qom will require going to the top. Shiite Muslims believe that until the 12th imam reappears on Earth, they must take religious guidance from one of the most learned scholars. There are seven or eight of these elite ayatollahs, called marjas, in Qom. They collect religious donations and dispense advice to both the powerful and the powerless. "The support and approval of one marja for Khatami would have a great effect," says one clerical adviser to Mr. Khatami, who made two trips to Qom to meet with the marjas.

Mr. Khatami did get one marja's support, but it backfired. Ayatollah Hussein Ali Montazeri, a squeaky-voiced scholar who once was in line to be Iran's leader, started a small riot in Qom in November 1997 with a taped diatribe calling on Mr. Khatami to demand more presidential power. The police put the ayatollah under house arrest. President Khatami kept his distance. This year, leftist clerics have been agitating to spring the dissident cleric free. Sources in Tehran and Qom say the Khatami-led National Security Council recently tried to lift the ban on Ayatollah Montazeri. Police still block anybody but immediate family from the ayatollah's home, but a newspaper run by one cleric close to the president recently printed one of Ayatollah Montazeri's announcements.

Some students also believe top ayatollahs had an unusually moderate response to the student riots that followed the deadly July 9 dormitory raid. Student leaders reached out to friendly clerics, taking them on a three-hour tour of the dormitory, with its smashed furniture and ransacked bookshelves. A team of students drove to Qom to show photographs of beaten students. One ayatollah broke down in tears, meeting participants say.

And Mr. Khatami kept the pressure on, saying he blamed the theorists behind violence more than those who commit it. It seemed to be a clear reference to a hard-line Qom ayatollah who had just explained that violence is permitted against enemies of Islam.

But in Qom, some leftists aren't ready to take on their adversaries publicly. When the Rouhaniyoun were in power, Mohammed Abai-Khorasani ran the Islamic Propagation Office in Qom, which has a staff of 700 researchers and publishes 12 Islamic journals. Now, he runs a one-man research center, in the basement of his home across the street from a bike shop. Returning from noon prayers at a hard-line ayatollah's mosque, the diminutive Ayatollah Khorasani serves sweetened water and is asked whom he thought Mr. Khatami was referring to in the speech.

"I cannot name those people," he says. "Maybe I'm scared. Maybe I don't know them."

# 21

# TODAY'S POP QUIZ: WHERE IS COCA-COLA NOT THE REAL THING?

## In Iran, Where Coke Bottles Contain Something Else: A Court in Tehran Mulls

*This article was written with Nikhil Deogun*

*July 10, 1998*

TEHRAN, Iran—In a soda factory here, a circular machine injects a familiar brown liquid into familiar old Coke bottles. The bottles go into red "Coca-Cola" crates. Upstairs, the factory's marketing manager sits at a desk etched with a huge "Coca-Cola" logo and declares: "We have nothing to do with Coca-Cola."

In 1995, when President Clinton prohibited U.S. companies from doing business with Iran, Noushab Manufacturing Co. suddenly became a Coke-free Coke bottler. It no longer gets concentrate from Coca-Cola, using local sources instead.

Now, Coca-Cola wants an Iranian judge to stop Noushab from using Coke bottles. And Noushab is suing Coke for cutting off shipments of concentrate and stopping its investment in the Noushab plant. Noushab wants as much as $72 million.

"Basically, Noushab is suing us for following U.S.-government-imposed sanctions," says Randal Donaldson, a Coca-Cola vice president.

That might sound strange in Atlanta, but this is Tehran, and a commercial court is taking the suit seriously. It recently assigned three experts to study contract documents and assess possible damages. The sanctions are "not my client's fault," argues Noushab's lawyer, Akbar Hendizadeh. He concedes his client would have trouble collecting any damages from Coke, but says a judgment would spell trouble for Coke should it ever enter Iran again.

"We know some other U.S. companies provide materials and spare parts" to Iran, says Mr. Hendizadeh. "This Coca-Cola is the only one that said they cannot."

Iran certainly is full of U.S. products. McGraw Hill Cos. had one of the biggest booths at the Tehran International Book Fair in May. Nearby, Microsoft Corp. software lined a wall of the Information Technology Fair. Black & Decker Corp. kitchen appliances take an entire row of Tehran's Shahrevand department store; the warranty cards have Farsi lettering, and list an address "In the GM Building" in Tehran.

Some companies, including McGraw Hill, enjoy an exemption for information products. Also, foreign subsidiaries sometimes can sell legally in Iran: Black & Decker says its Dubai subsidiary handles Iran. In other cases, Iranian merchants say they order American goods from retailers in Dubai. Microsoft says any of its products displayed in Tehran more likely come from software pirates in Bulgaria.

In March, a Pepsi bottler in Dubai told reporters it was "invading new markets such as Iran." But PepsiCo says the bottler was referring to its non-Pepsi products, like mineral water. A Pepsi bottler in Iran recently started producing plastic bottles of "Pepsi" with a small disclaimer on the label that the ingredients are actually Iranian. "If someone is locally producing what they're calling Pepsi, it's an infringement of our trademark, and we're going to look into it," said Brad Shaw, a spokesman for PepsiCo, in Purchase, N.Y.

Coke says it asked U.S. officials if it could supply Iran from third countries, and was told no. But Noushab lawyers say Coke did supply a bottler in eastern Iran that way. In court, Noushab produced a letter purportedly from Coca-Cola Atlantic in Ireland to the bottler, called Khoshgovar, saying Coke will increase "the number of units sold to you." It has the stamp of Iran's Ministry of Industry, which approves importers' requests for hard currency, and is dated September 22, 1995—four months after sanctions took effect. How did Noushab get the letter? "It's Tehran, you can get anything," says Hamid Sabi, a Noushab lawyer.

Coke categorically denies shipping concentrate to Khoshgovar after the sanctions took effect, and says the letter is bogus. In any case, both sides agree that Coke stopped supplying Noushab when the sanctions took effect. Noushab turned to Fariborz Sarmad, a food technician and Coca-Cola admirer who has been trying to replicate Coke's taste since the last U.S. embargo, in 1980. Back then, Dr. Sarmad, whose Tehran office is decorated with Coke bottles, brewed caramel in an open kettle in his backyard and combed books for supposed ingredients of Coca-Cola. His early batches of concentrate were so bad soft-drink plants turned them down. Now, says Dr. Sarmad, "We buy from the very sources Pepsi-Cola and Coca-Cola use: citrus oils, orange and lemon." A quick test of his handiwork: Twelve men, including construction workers and actors, were given glasses filled with Noushab, real Coca-Cola smuggled in from Russia and the United Kingdom, and Iran's Coulack Cola (slogan: "Drink Coulack"), which also buys concentrate from Dr. Sarmad. Only four picked out The Real Thing.

Still, "nongenuine product" in genuine bottles damages Coke's "image and goodwill," says Gregory Kearney, a Coca-Cola Co. lawyer in Windsor, England. Mr. Sabi says another Coke official was more blunt, telling him, "I will not allow our bottles to go around with junk cola." Coke demanded that Noushab retire the Coca-Cola bottles. But Noushab, which is financed by a Saudi sheik and Iranian investors, said it would cost $3.5 million to replace them.

And so, to court. Tehran's Public Court granted an injunction allowing Noushab to keep its bottles; Coke has appealed. Meanwhile, Noushab sued Coke, blaming it for the fact that Noushab still has only one production line, even as Tehran faces summertime soda shortages. (Iranians don't take cola breaks, but they are increasingly using soda instead of yogurt to wash down their meat-heavy meals.)

Tehran's courts have some sympathy for the American company. The judge in the bottle case ordered Noushab to remove the Coke label from trucks and bottle caps, and to place ads telling consumers that its "Coke" bottles don't really contain Coke. Noushab, which no longer has a bottling contract with Coke, repainted its red delivery trucks with big smiley faces. "With time, we'll probably replace the bottles. We're working on a design," says marketing director Sassan Jahan.

For now, Noushab retrieves, washes and reuses as many of its bottles as it can. In Mohsen Lotfi's Tehran grocery store, some of the "Coca-Cola" bottles look a bit worse for wear. One has a fingernail-size chip in the glass. Mr. Lotfi will sell Parsi Cola or Zam Zam cola to take away, but he insists the contents of any "Coca-Cola" bottle be consumed on the premises. If a single bottle breaks or is missing, he explains, Noushab cuts his allotment.

Mr. Lotfi, whose shop still has a red Coca-Cola awning, thinks Noushab's strict policy may have something to do with the Coke name. That baffles him. "If you make a good cola, you can call it what you like," he says. "I personally prefer Zam Zam."

# PART FOUR

# *Poisoning the Well*

"Did you know you can buy leather in India?"

The question came out of the blue. A few months into his posting to Bombay, Danny was visiting the U.S. and having drinks with me. Like many of his questions, this one came from nowhere and didn't really require a response. He had been peddling a precis around the *Journal* for months—even before he was sent to India—and had become convinced that it was a big story just waiting to be done.

The cow, Danny had decided, was no sacred cow in India. He loved counterintuitive stories. He loved reading them; he loved writing them. A few years back, I'd written a story that said the tobacco industry didn't account for many jobs in North Carolina. Danny gave it his highest form of praise: "I guess you poisoned that well," he said.

Danny specialized in debunking conventional wisdom: Iraq's planes, supposedly being bombed by the U.S., were actually all safe and sound in Iran. Many Muslims aren't sure when Ramadan really starts. The British tabloids were all telling the truth about Charles and Diana.

On December 31, 1999, he and fellow reporter Bobby Block wrote a story challenging the notion that the Serbs were guilty of genocide:

> In Kosovo last spring, Yugoslav forces did heinous things. They expelled hundreds of thousands of ethnic Albanians, burning houses and committing summary executions. It may well be enough to justify the North Atlantic Treaty Organization bombing campaign and the war-crimes indictment of Yugoslav president Slobodan Milosevic.
>
> But other allegations—indiscriminate mass murder, rape camps, crematoriums, mutilation of the dead—haven't been borne out in the six months since NATO troops entered Kosovo.

119

Ethnic-Albanian militants, humanitarian organizations, NATO and the news media fed off each other to give genocide rumors credibility. Now, a different picture is emerging.

Danny and Bobby were intrigued when they noticed that the number of dead Kosovars being uncovered by international forensic investigators didn't match the rhetoric of genocide during the war, even when allowing for grave tampering by Serb forces. They didn't want to focus on the numbers, so Danny suggested tracking down stories of some of the worst massacres in Kosovo, including a tale of bodies being dumped down mineshafts. Danny worked Kosovo to find the mythmakers, while Bobby worked Serbia to get the Serb side of the story.

"The fallout was huge," Bobby says. "Danny and I found ourselves in the uncomfortable position of being embraced by Serb nationalists and denounced by the U.S. State Department. Danny's response was to laugh and go on vacation with Mariane to Cuba, leaving me to debate various angry American officials on radio and television by myself."

Counterintuitive stories must be overreported. They are subjected to a far more rigorous editing process than most stories. They are greeted with skepticism by reporters, editors and the public, so they have to be nailed down hard.

Danny nailed them.

The *pièce de résistance* of this genre was Danny's piece questioning the U.S. government's evidence that a Sudanese factory it bombed was involved in terrorism. It still offers a simple lesson to all reporters: Question everything.

"It was vintage Danny—a determined effort, under taxing, difficult-to-report circumstances," recalls Ken Wells, the page-one editor assigned to the story. Danny got American intelligence sources to admit that, in the wake of an earlier terrorist bombing of the U.S. Embassy in Kenya, they needed to get retaliatory targets fast.

The full truth of El Shifa, wrapped in the divisive politics of antiterrorism, may never be known. The hardest evidence is a scoop of soil, taken near the plant and judged by the U.S. to contain a chemical used to make nerve gas. But other evidence becomes murkier the closer you look.

Editing such stories can be contentious, Ken says. "Good reporters necessarily become advocates of their own stories, especially in a case like this one, where Danny had invested a huge amount of time and energy." Editors play the skeptics. The story became what *Journal* insiders call a "group grope"—for reporters, the worst possible editing experience. Everybody has two cents to put in. "But Danny was the kind of reporter who never turned editing into a battle," Ken says.

Even though Danny got a lot of respect after that story, it couldn't surmount the skepticism he encountered when he turned to India's sacred cows. He spent months trying to interest various *Journal* editors. Page one turned him down, unenthused by a proposed story saying Indians were sneaking around making leather and eating beef. Danny pressed on. He interviewed "just about every single person in India who ever had anything to do with a cow," says Bill Spindle, deputy foreign editor. Most turned out to be Muslim, not Hindu, a point Danny noted. It appeared, finally, on July 18, 2001, on the Marketplace page:

> With a population that is an estimated 80% Hindu, India slaughters 14 million cattle a year, making it the world's fifth most active cattle killer, according to the United Nations Food and Agriculture Organization.

Here are some stories that puncture conventional wisdom.

—H.C.

# 22

# HOW MANY WAYS CAN YOU SKIN A COW? IN HINDU INDIA, PLENTY

## Thriving Leather Industry Relies on Muslims, 'Fallen' Cattle; Next, a Bovine Pension Plan?

*July 19, 2001*

ERODE, India—To Western companies operating in India, the cow is a sacred cow.

McDonald's avoids selling beef here. Berlitz International warns its cross-cultural training clients to avoid giving Indians leather gifts, because most Indians are Hindu and Hindus revere cows. But nothing is so straightforward in India. On a Sunday morning at the Perunderai market, in the southern state of Tamil Nadu, traders haggle as bloody hides of freshly slaughtered cows are slapped onto a cement slab and unfolded like Persian rugs. "The quality depends on the wounds and the germs," explains R. Raja, a veteran hide-buyer who is Hindu, like many traders here. (He and other southerners in India often use single names, sometimes with an initial.)

India is actually a major producer and consumer of leather, and only some of it comes from goat, sheep and buffalo. With a population that is an estimated 80% Hindu, India slaughters 14 million cattle a year, making it the world's fifth most active cattle killer, according to the United Nations Food and Agriculture Organization. Government tax breaks have helped make leather of all kinds one of India's biggest exports.

But it takes some effort to accommodate business and religion when it comes to cowhide, though. The Hindu religion forbids eating beef and slaughtering cows, but permits taking the hide of a "fallen" cow, or one that has died naturally. Muslims, who can slaughter cows, work in slaughterhouses and butcher shops. But in the case of "fallen" cows, a low-caste Hindu does the work, because it is against Islamic belief to skin an animal that has died naturally.

Higher-caste Hindus run leather-shoe factories and the government's Central Leather Research Institute in Madras. The institute's Brahmin executive director, T. Ramasami, has a wall of plaques from local leather-promotion boards and meets regularly with the top Hindu religious authority in Tamil Nadu. He estimates 10,000 cows are slaughtered in India each day. "We're able to link the rural farmer from a decentralized village to the best fashion in the world," he says.

Dr. Ramasami says leather is just a by-product of cows that are slaughtered for meat. "The leather industry is not the main provider of value to a slaughtered animal," he says. Economics are a big reason cows became sacred, he says. Once, one cow would provide milk for an entire village. Economics change faster than religious beliefs, he says. And Mohandas Gandhi himself promoted "nonviolent" leather, from fallen cows, as a way to help India's poor, he says.

Animal-rights activists are forcing the industry to take a closer look. People for the Ethical Treatment of Animals (PETA) produced a videotape of bleeding, emaciated cattle on a "death march" across India's state lines. It sent the tape to companies such as Gap Inc., of San Francisco, and Liz Claiborne Inc., of New York. Last year, the companies stopped buying clothes made from Indian leather, acknowledging the animals' treatment as a reason. "We would hope to re-enter this market at such a time that the industry has been reformed," a Liz Claiborne spokeswoman says in an e-mail.

Distance and middlemen separate India's leather magnates from slaughtered cows and raw cow skins. Typically, cows are sent to West Bengal and Kerala, two communist-influenced states where cow slaughtering is legal. From there, agents bring the raw hides to cowhide centers like Erode, where dozens of factories turn them into "wet-blue"—a defleshed, dehaired hide that smells decent and won't rot. More agents truck the wet-blue 250 miles east to tanners in and around Madras.

By the time the resulting leather is polished and stitched, a factory owner may have just a hazy idea of how the hide came off the cow. Snehdep Aggarwal, managing director of Bhartiya International, a big leather-coat exporter in New Delhi, tells people the company makes its jackets from animals that die naturally. It's a guess. "It's not possible that they could slaughter so many cows," he says. "A Hindu population exists in every village."

P.S. Rajagopal Naidu, a Hindu octogenarian whose company sells domestic and foreign hides, says Mr. Aggarwal is deluding himself. "The moment the animal is dead, the worms get him. Putrefaction, insects boring holes in it—how can you get a garment out of it?" he says. Cow slaughter isn't a secret in Erode, but farmers hold onto plausible deniability. In the past, they would simply wait for cows to die, then call in a low-caste hide-skinner. Now, many hide-skinners have government jobs or live in the cities.

Enter traders like Guruvan, a 30-year-old Hindu who used to be a sari weaver. Now, he scours the region for cows that don't provide milk or good luck anymore. He makes the farmer an offer, perhaps $100 a cow. The cow's fate isn't discussed.

Some farmers sell cows while they still give milk, leaving open the possibility that they're being sold for milk. Guruvan brings the cows to a local butcher during the night. Cow-killing is illegal in Tamil Nadu, but butchers here say they avoid trouble by staying out of Hindu-nationalist neighborhoods. By the time the butcher hangs the meat for sale, Guruvan has left with the hide. "I'm not doing any killing," he says.

Some farmers give aging cows to Hindu temples. At the Vedanaiki Solisvaran Temple, near the cow market, prayer leader Dharmasivan says temple leaders are too busy with day jobs to care for the donated cows. So the temple sells them in the market. Dharmasivan has seen a cow being slaughtered there. "We know it's wrong," he says. "We can't stop it."

Some leather-industry leaders are trying to concoct a bovine pension plan, under which part of a cow's milk earnings would go into a fund to feed the cow from retirement until its natural death. The scheme could be politically difficult, though. At a Madras cow shelter—run by the Jain religious community, which believes in protecting all animals—straw, cattle feed and grass cost 47 cents a day per cow. The average Indian human spends 32 cents a day on food, beverage and tobacco.

# 23

# BODY COUNT: WAR IN KOSOVO WAS CRUEL, BITTER, SAVAGE; GENOCIDE IT WASN'T

## Tales of Mass Atrocity Arose and Were Passed Along, Often With Little Proof

### No Corpses in the Mine Shaft

*This article written with Robert Block*

*December 31, 1999*

TREPCA, Yugoslavia—When the blanket-covered trucks rolled toward the mining complex near this northern Kosovo town in April, Bexhet Kurti didn't give them much thought. The Yugoslav army had a military base there, after all.

It was in July, after the fighting ended and Mr. Kurti returned to battle-scarred Trepca, that the young house painter started hearing the whispers. "Did you hear there are 700 bodies in the mine?" asked one acquaintance in the hilltop café above the mine-shaft tower. "No, not in the mine, but in the furnace" on the other side of the mountain, said another.

By late summer, stories about a Nazi-like body-disposal facility were so widespread that investigators sent a three-man French gendarmerie team spelunking half a mile down the mine to search for bodies. They found none. Another team analyzed ashes in the furnace. They found no teeth or other signs of burnt bodies.

In Kosovo last spring, Yugoslav forces did heinous things. They expelled hundreds of thousands of ethnic Albanians, burning houses and committing summary executions. It may well be enough to justify the North Atlantic Treaty Organization bombing campaign and the war-crimes indictment of Yugoslav president Slobodan Milosevic.

But other allegations—indiscriminate mass murder, rape camps, crematoriums, mutilation of the dead—haven't been borne out in the

125

six months since NATO troops entered Kosovo. Ethnic-Albanian militants, humanitarian organizations, NATO and the news media fed off each other to give genocide rumors credibility. Now, a different picture is emerging.

"Rwanda was a true genocide. Kosovo was ethnic cleansing light," says Emilio Perez Pujol, a Spanish pathologist who exhumed bodies after both conflicts. In his sector of western Kosovo, he says, the United Nations told him to expect as many as 2,000 victims. His team found 187 corpses, none of which showed evidence to confirm local accounts of mutilations.

Some human-rights researchers now say that most killings and burnings occurred in areas where the separatist Kosovo Liberation Army had been active, or in urban streets that backed into rural areas where KLA fighters could infiltrate. They say the Serbs were trying to clear out areas of KLA support, using selective terror, robberies and sporadic killings.

"We believed NATO was using the KLA as its invasion force," says retired Gen. Radovan Radinovic, a former chief strategist for the Yugoslav Army who advised military planners during the war with NATO. Gen. Radinovic says individuals may have committed abuses, while killing "thousands" of KLA guerrillas. (A successor organization to the KLA says it lost 2,400 dead over two years.)

British and American officials still maintain that 10,000 or more ethnic-Albanian civilians died at Serb hands during the fighting in Kosovo. The U.N.'s International Criminal Tribunal for the former Yugoslavia has accused Serbs of covering up war crimes by moving bodies. It has begun its own military analysis of the Serb offensive.

But the number of bodies discovered so far is much lower—2,108 as of November, and not all of them necessarily war-crimes victims. While more than 300 reported grave sites remain to be investigated, the tribunal has checked the largest reported sites first, and found most to contain no more than five bodies, suggesting intimate acts of barbarity rather than mass murder.

The KLA helped form the West's wartime image of Kosovo. International human-rights groups say officials of the guerrilla force served on the Kosovo-based Council for the Defense of Human Rights and Freedoms, whose activists were often the first to interview refugees arriving in Macedonia. Journalists later cited the council's missing-persons list to support theories about how many people died in Kosovo, and the State Department this month echoed the council's recent estimate of 10,000 missing. But the number has to be taken on faith: Western investigators say the council won't share its list of missing persons.

Even more closely connected to the KLA was Radio Free Kosova, set up in January as outsiders were cut off from Kosovo hot spots. A former correspondent for the radio station, Qemail Aliu, says he and five other journalists holed up with the KLA in central Kosovo mountains, using satellite phones to take reports from KLA regional commanders. The radio broadcasts were just strong enough to reach the provincial capital, Pristina, where a correspondent translated the reports into English for the KLA's Kosova Press Internet site.

When the guerrilla encampment had electricity, Mr. Aliu watched NATO briefings on TV. "Many times we saw Jamie Shea talking about the number of people killed, and many times they were the numbers from Kosova Press," he says.

NATO says Mr. Shea, its spokesman, didn't get information directly from Kosova Press. But officials acknowledge that NATO's member governments had little independent information about what was happening on the ground. "We were all hamstrung," a NATO official says. As the war dragged on, he says, NATO saw a fatigued press corps drifting toward the contrarian story: civilians killed by NATO's bombs. NATO stepped up its claims about Serb "killing fields."

Human-rights groups fed the information chain directly. As human-rights researchers assembled in neighboring Macedonia and Albania to interview refugees, State Department officials handed them proposed survey forms, trying to get everybody to ask standard questions about violence to aid war-crimes cases. Among the groups cooperating was Physicians for Human Rights, which had long been calling for a ground force to protect ethnic Albanians.

Kosovo was a "genocide to come," warned Holly Burkhalter, Washington director of Physicians for Human Rights, in a National Public Radio commentary in April. "I was wrong," she says now. "But if you wait until it's proved to you six ways to Sunday, you haven't prevented it, have you?"

Human-rights groups at least used some scientific rigor, asking refugees what they personally saw. The news media's standards were more mixed. Many journalists had experience in Bosnia, where the mass slaughter of an estimated 7,000 men from the "safe area" at Srebrenica in 1995 was a warning not to be too skeptical about reports of Serb atrocities. Bosnia yielded three Pulitzer Prizes for reporters who proved atrocities. When Kosovo was finally opened to the foreign press in June, "fixers" cruising through the lobby of Pristina's Grand Hotel offered to take correspondents to burial sites.

An example of the mass-grave obsession is Ljubenic, a poor western Kosovo village of 200-odd homes below the Cursed Mountains, which KLA fighters had used as a supply route. On the morning of April 1, Serb forces surrounded the town, villagers say, and three heavily armed militiamen walked up the village's main dirt road. They say the Serbs corralled village men at a crossroads, questioning them about weapons and the KLA. Two villagers who spoke up were shot. One of the Serbs then said, "The KLA killed my brother," and the Serbs started mowing down the men with machine guns, survivors say.

Eleven wounded men later staggered away in two groups, says survivor Sadik Jahmurataj, who adds that his group found a KLA hospital in the hills a day later. When a KLA commander asked how many were killed, "the others were in a panic and said '150 to 200.' I said, 'No, that can't be. One hundred at the most.' "

Over the next weeks, Mr. Jahmurataj and others told their stories to investigators from several human-rights groups. And after the war, returning villagers, who found 12 bodies scattered around Ljubenic, told Italian peacekeeping troops that 350 people were still missing from Ljubenic and the surrounding hamlets. One villager told of seeing worms coming from the ground in a field where the grass was unusually short.

On July 9, after getting an "operations report" from the Italians, Dutch Army Maj. Jan Joosten mentioned during a regular press briefing in Pristina that a suspected grave had been found, and there could be as many as 350 bodies. He says journalists started packing their bags for Ljubenic before he even finished. "Biggest grave site holds 350 victims," London's Independent newspaper proclaimed the next day. Concern Worldwide, a charity working in Ljubenic, claimed that three-fourths of the families lost their main wage-earner.

In fact, investigators found no bodies in the field. It now appears that the number killed in Ljubenic was about 65. That is how many names are listed in KLA-printed memorial posters. Mr. Jahmurataj, sitting on the lawn beside the Concern Worldwide tent, says villagers who weren't there distorted the story. When a U.N. van pulls up, Mr. Jahmurataj trots over to greet Alistair Graham, a war-crimes-tribunal official who had interviewed him in an Albanian refugee camp. Mr. Graham is just dropping off candy for children, but Mr. Jahmurataj pleads with him to continue the investigation.

"If other people exaggerated, that's bad," Mr. Jahmurataj says. "But everything I told you was exactly true." Mr. Graham says the tribunal will return in the spring.

Kosovo would be easier to investigate if it had the huge killing fields some investigators were led to expect. Instead, the pattern is of scattered killings. Many cases defy simple explanation: two blanket-covered bodies pulled out of a farmer's yard in a village where nobody was missing; a body that a child discovered by chance along a river; a semiclad torture victim.

Human-rights groups didn't give so much attention to the small killings. From Macedonia, a researcher for Human Rights Watch, Benjamin Ward, wrote a report about the slaying of two youths during a Serb-ordered exodus from the southeast Kosovo village of Malisevo. Townspeople say Serb gunmen forced 20 or so young men to lie facedown in a field, fired a machine gun inches from their heads demanding information about KLA fighters, and killed two teenagers who trotted up the road from a nearby village. But Mr. Ward's report never left his computer; he says, "It wasn't compelling" when reports of bigger massacres arrived.

Meanwhile, the Yugoslav government in Belgrade is pursuing its own investigations and war-crimes trials, which skeptics regard as either an effort to deflect blame from President Milosevic or a warning to disaffected Serbian reservists to stay in line lest they be accused.

In one trial, Serbian police reservist Boban Petkovic is accused of murdering four ethnic Albanians in the western Kosovo village of Rija on May 9, and policeman Djordje Simic is charged as an accomplice. The prosecution's documents charge that Mr. Petkovic, during a battle with the KLA, saw an ethnic Albanian running toward the forest and being grabbed by a Yugoslav soldier.

"Petkovic, believing the man to be a captured terrorist, approached the prisoner, took a sidearm from Mr. Simic, and shot the man in the head," the documents charge. They say Mr. Petkovic later heard voices from a house, and, "believing they were terrorists, Petkovic took his machine gun and killed all three people inside." The prosecution says the victims were "obviously civilians."

Mr. Petkovic's defense is that he was in battle, and that the chronic stress from being under attack by KLA terrorists affected his judgment. Mr. Simic says his gun was used without his permission.

Though brutal, these incidents don't have the impact of accounts of Serbs rounding up Albanian men and dumping their corpses down a mine shaft. The world may owe that image to Halit Berani, head of a branch of the Council for the Defense of Human Rights and Freedoms in the city of Mitrovica. Mr. Berani is a former actor with a Karl Marx beard who summarizes Serb war crimes by showing a photo of a baby with a smashed skull.

Mr. Berani spent the war moving from village to village with his manual typewriter, calling in reports to foreign radio services and diplomats with his daily allotment of three minutes on a KLA satellite phone. He says he heard from villagers near Trepca that trucks were rolling in full and rolling out empty, and that a strange smell was coming from the mine complex. He phoned in a report in early April suggesting that the mines had become a body-disposal site, and Deutsche Welle, a German-based radio service, carried the report in Albanian.

The story spread. In June, Kosova Press's Internet site quoted a U.S. embassy official in Athens as saying there are "witnesses and still photos" of trucks carrying bodies. Western journalists phoned the embassy, but a spokeswoman said she couldn't find the supposed source. London's *Observer* ran a similar story, citing a KLA commander, a girl who got a call from an elderly resident, and a Kosovar who heard the story from refugees. A Pentagon spokesman, quizzed about Trepca at the time, said, "There have been several reports throughout the last 10 weeks of bodies being burned in former industrial sites in Kosovo." Some commentators stated the theory as fact.

When French troops took over the mines, they reported to the tribunal that they had found well-scrubbed vats and piles of clothing. Tribunal investigators weren't impressed: Clothes are found everywhere in trash-strewn Kosovo, and why would the Serbs clean vats but not burn clothes? After the fruitless search, "we don't see any need to do further investigation at this point," a tribunal official says.

Mr. Berani doesn't completely stand by his story. "I told everybody it was supposition, it was not confirmed information," he says. But he adds, "For the Serbs, everything is possible."

# 24

# AFTER THE BOMBINGS: THE DIFFICULT SEARCH FOR 'TRUTH'

## Blasting Flap: In Sudanese Bombing, 'Evidence' Depends on Who Is Viewing It

## Dissident Fans Terror Links, but Factory Owner Says the U.S. Got It Wrong

## Worm Medicine in the Rubble

*October 28, 1998*

KHARTOUM, Sudan—Salah Idris, a Sudanese investor, has a few problems: His factory is in ruins, his account with a U.S. bank is frozen, and he has been fingered by U.S. intelligence authorities as a presumed front man for Islamic fundamentalist terrorist Osama bin Laden.

If the last is true—and Mr. Idris says emphatically that it isn't—you might think it helps explain why American cruise missiles last August 20 blew up the El Shifa Pharmaceutical Industries Co. plant here, in retaliation for terrorist bombings at U.S. embassies in Africa. In fact, at the time the missiles flew from American warships, U.S. intelligence officials admit they knew little about Mr. Idris, and didn't know he had acquired El Shifa a few months before. Yet, since the bombing, sources old and new have provided them information about Mr. Idris to bolster the case that El Shifa was linked to Osama bin Laden and his alleged chemical-weapons aspirations. Some U.S. allies and Washington officials still doubt the U.S. hit a legitimate target, and the full truth of El Shifa, wrapped in the divisive politics of antiterrorism, may never be known. The hardest evidence is a scoop of soil, taken near the plant and judged by the U.S. to contain a chemical used to make nerve gas. But other evidence becomes murkier the closer you look.

El Shifa had a tangled past, and Mr. Idris, a fortune-charmed millionaire of the kind the Middle East often produces, was a seemingly rash investor, agreeing to buy the factory in March after only a cursory examination. He can't categorically say that El Shifa was never used to make chemical-weapons ingredients, because he was still doing a thorough study of the factory when the U.S. destroyed it. Some of his Sudan deals put him in business with people who had past contact with Mr. bin Laden or his companies, though Mr. Idris says the links are inconsequential. He says he intended to recapitalize El Shifa to compete in African and Middle East pharmaceutical markets.

The U.S. had reasons to believe Sudan would want chemical weapons. It is fighting a civil war against U.S.-supported rebels, has little money to buy conventional arms, and hasn't signed on to a global anti-chemical-weapons treaty. And because the country has given refuge to terrorists in the past, the U.S. says it had to take seriously reports that Mr. bin Laden and Iraq were helping Sudan make chemical weapons.

U.S. officials say the main argument for making El Shifa a target was and remains a soil sample, obtained in January, which they say was taken "a stone's throw" from El Shifa, by a CIA-trained agent as another agent looked on. The officials say three separate tests on the soil turned up strong "hits" for a substance known as EMPTA, which can easily be turned into deadly VX nerve gas.

Still, other links in the chain of evidence outlined by U.S. officials are weaker than past reports have suggested. The U.S. has repeatedly said the plant was part of a complex run by the Sudanese government's weapons-making arm, the Military Industries Corp. But asked how investigators knew that, a U.S. intelligence official says they assumed any chemical-weapons plant in Sudan would be run by the government. Also, despite media reports that the U.S. intercepted conversations between the plant and Iraq, a U.S. intelligence official says that what the U.S. actually discovered were records indicating El Shifa officials started paying visits to Iraq last year.

U.S. officials assume the discussions were about chemical weapons because they took place in a pharmaceutical plant overseen by a key figure in Iraq's VX nerve-gas program, Emad Ani. But El Shifa officials say they had routine talks about a manufacturing alliance, and never met that man. And the United Nations weapons inspector who dealt most closely with the Iraqi plant says Mr. Ani actually is a high-ranking manager for the plant's state-owned parent company and has never been directly associated with the factory itself.

Asked about the U.S. strike, Mr. Idris says, "I think it's something done by mistake." But asked about some of the allegations that have dogged him since the bombing, he says, "It's Mubarak." He means Mubarak Fadl Al Mahdi, a Sudanese opposition figure who has been feuding with Mr. Idris for more than a year over conflicting political allegiances. Mr. Mahdi acknowledges collecting information on the plant after learning in May that Mr. Idris had bought it. And five days after the cruise-missile attack, he issued a communique, released on the letterhead of the National Democratic Alliance, an umbrella dissidents' group, denouncing Mr. Idris as an investor in a Sudanese military project—a claim U.S. officials would later echo. He also took direct aim at El Shifa, saying it was staffed with "Iraqi scientists and technicians" and contending that most pharmaceutical plants in Sudan aren't "manned by foreign experts."

But Mr. Mahdi denies sharing these concerns with anyone before the bombing and U.S. intelligence officials deny relying on anyone with an ax to grind in fingering El Shifa, and then Mr. Idris. Still, it's no secret that U.S. officials, who have no embassy in Khartoum to use as a listening post, had been seeking information on chemical weapons from dissidents, and that friendly governments such as Egypt also get information from Sudanese opposition members. Mr. Idris, citing his own ties to Sudanese dissidents, says he is hardly the kind of person that the government here would trust to take part in any sensitive military project. The lawyer he used on the El Shifa deal, for example, calls the incumbent regime a "dictatorship."

That said, Mr. Idris also acknowledges doing business with regime figures, including Abdul Baset Hamza, a former government engineer who says he once oversaw a road-construction project of an Osama bin Laden company during Mr. bin Laden's years of exile in Sudan. Mr. Hamza now builds military factories for Sudan's fundamentalist regime. He says he tried to get Mr. bin Laden to invest in a telephone company and a mortar-shell factory, but the fundamentalist declined to mix funds with the government. But Mr. Hamza later got Mr. Idris to invest in the telephone company, and to hire Mr. Hamza's firm to build a steel mill.

Mr. Idris's Washington lawyers are now trying to convince the Justice Department that he has no ties to Osama bin Laden, and that the government should lift its freeze on Mr. Idris's Bank America Corp. account. U.S. intelligence officials, however, aren't making that easy. They have said, in interviews, that they have found evidence that Mr. Idris may have accepted money from a member of Egyptian Islamic Jihad, a group tied to Mr. bin Laden. Mr. Idris denies that. Also, his advisers are quizzing former El Shifa workers and trying to line up independent laboratories to test the soil near the El Shifa site. Still, U.S. officials, and some chemical-weapons experts, say it isn't clear that EMPTA would survive the heat of a missile attack. The U.S., partly for that reason, is blocking investigation by the U.N. Security Council. El Shifa officials, meanwhile, say documents supporting their case were lost in the bombing.

Friends say the idea of Mr. Idris's fronting for hard-core fundamentalists is absurd because, though an observant Muslim, he doesn't share the puritanism of Mr. bin Laden. Mr. Idris, a connoisseur of Sudanese love songs, keeps an Arabian lute ready to strum on the couch in each of his homes in Cairo, Jeddah, Khartoum and London, and friends say he doesn't object if others drink alcohol at his parties. Two associates recall his refusing to put money in collection boxes outside mosques and explaining that he feared the money would buy weapons in Bosnia. And though his rise from a bank accountant to a millionaire has stirred suspicions here, his friends say there isn't much real mystery.

Mr. Idris is a protégé and sometimes business partner of two publicity-shy Saudi Arabian tycoons who by conservative estimates could buy Osama bin Laden 20 times over, even if the fundamentalist really has the $200 million he is reported to have inherited some years ago. One of the tycoons is Sheik Mohammed Hussein Al-Amoudi, a construction magnate with Ethiopian roots who just built a luxury Sheraton hotel in the Ethiopian capital. Another is Sheik Khalid Bin Mahfouz, a banking tycoon with Yemeni roots who is rebuilding Yemen's port at Aden.

Mr. Idris, a 46-year-old tailor's son, hails from a farming town in north Sudan. He moved to Saudi Arabia in 1976 and found work as an accountant at Sheik Khalid's National Commercial Bank. Eventually, he joined Sheik Khalid's circle of close advisers, where he could earn commissions by finding investments for his friends. One deal he signed onto early was Worldspace Corp., a Washington-based enterprise that has raised about $1 billion—it won't reveal how—and is to launch the first of three satellites today to beam radio programming to Africa and the Middle East.

Mr. Idris also impressed Sheik Khalid by helping get him and his bank disentangled from the Bank of Credit & Commerce International money-laundering scandal, intimates say. Mr. Idris worked behind the scenes, briefing Arab journalists and helping to negotiate a $442 million settlement with BCCI's liquidators. Mr. Idris lost some of his own money at a London branch of BCCI when the bank collapsed in 1991, but he later hired the former branch manager to help run his London businesses. "He's a good guy," Mr. Idris explains.

Mr. Idris says he does business with people tied to Sudan's ruling National Islamic Front, or NIF, because it's unavoidable. But the main reason for his investments in Sudan now is that when the government falls, "I'm here."

Mr. Idris says he thought about building a pharmaceutical factory for years. But El Shifa was a creation of Bashir Hassan Bashir, an NIF supporter. Using an American designer and a Chinese construction crew, Mr. Bashir says, he built El Shifa in 1993 with the aim of exporting most of its products, something no Sudanese drug plant did.

Sudan now praises El Shifa as a model factory, but it was actually poorly planned, workers say. Mr. Bashir wanted a veterinary-drugs factory, but built it too big, so he added human medicines. That meant expanding the plant further, over an unused road in the back, he says. To get the factory open, he had to offer a 40% stake to a Saudi family. Inexperienced managers bought the wrong-sized equipment; Sudanese authorities often rejected pills coming off El Shifa's production lines.

The plant's Sudanese general manager, Osman Salman, says El Shifa fell behind on payments to suppliers, and he even spent a few nights in prison for bouncing checks. So Mr. Salman sent a desperate fax to Mr. Idris asking him to buy El Shifa; he knew he had money and had been buying up a number of Sudanese companies. The two men say they met in Saudi Arabia, where Mr. Salman ran a food company before moving back to Sudan.

U.S. intelligence officials cite a link between Mr. Salman and Mr. bin Laden. Mr. Salman says a bin Laden construction company in 1992 rented his house in Khartoum. But the closest he came to the fundamentalist was standing in the dirt road outside and shouting at Mr. bin Laden's agent because the tenants had ripped out the house's Western-style toilets, he says.

Mr. Idris rushed to Khartoum within a few days of getting Mr. Salman's fax, which had mentioned that a Saudi conglomerate was also talking to El Shifa. Mr. Idris knew the factory's owner was intimate with the NIF, but also knew him as a drug importer who had had some regulatory scrapes with the government. Mr. Idris, having flipped through an El Shifa photo album, took a half-hour tour of the factory, signed an agreement on the spot to pay $12 million and assume $18 million of debt—and then left town, employees say.

The due diligence on the plant fell to his cousin, a pharmacology professor named Idris Babiker Eltayeb. Dr. Eltayeb quickly concluded that one-third of the staff could go, and that a pharmaceuticals specialist should replace Mr. Salman. This summer, Dr. Eltayeb says, a friend told him of dissidents' rumors that El Shifa was a chemical-weapons plant, but Dr. Eltayeb shrugged it off as absurd. How, he asks, could chemicals be made secretly at El Shifa? It was a small factory with no distilling equipment and it was so open to outside perusal that he wanted visits be restricted for hygiene's sake.

The plant's contacts with Iraq were no secret to Mr. Idris's team. In August 1997, Mr. Bashir and a sales executive say they rode into Baghdad with cartons of drug samples and found the Al Rasheed Hotel swamped with rival drug executives vying for contracts to supply Iraq under a U.N. program. The executives say they went to Iraq's Samarra Drug Industries to try to reach a manufacturing alliance. If Samarra could make certain drugs in Sudan, and El Shifa could make others in Iraq, each would cut costs and get a marketing edge. Dr. Eltayeb says he knew about the proposal, which neither company pursued, because he sat on a Sudanese pharmacy board that briefly reviewed it last year.

El Shifa had won a contract in January under the U.N. deal, to ship $199,000 worth of "Shifazole" animal-deworming fluid to Iraq. This summer, it still hadn't shipped a single bottle, citing technical difficulties. As proof that the plant was about to make a shipment, however, Dr. Eltayeb points to hundreds of white one-liter bottles labeled Shifazole that now lie atop a pile of rubble at the El Shifa site.

Mr. Idris was in London on August 20 when he learned U.S. cruise missiles had destroyed El Shifa. "I laughed," he says, thinking the missiles surely intended another target. Then he flew off to consult with Sudanese dissident friends in Cairo.

The feud between Mr. Idris and Mr. Mahdi is emblematic of their fractured country. Mr. Idris supports the Muslim-dominated, moderate Democratic Unionist Party, which is vying with the Muslim-dominated, moderate Umma party for future control of Sudan. Each party suspects the other of trying to cut a deal with the ruling regime.

Mubarak Fadl Al Mahdi, interior minister before a 1989 coup, is known as the Umma Party's organizer and fund-raiser. He and Mr. Idris have never met but have a healthy mutual mistrust. Mr. Idris says opposition figures like Mr. Mahdi are the reason Sudanese don't throw out the current government. Mr. Mahdi says the reason is businessmen like Mr. Idris, who he says is "guilty of collaboration" for importing wheat into impoverished Sudan. Supporting certain opposition parties is a way for Mr. Idris to "spread some confusion" about his true goals, he says. Early last year, with rebels facing a strong Sudanese counterattack along the eastern border, Mr. Mahdi went on an Arabic television show broadcast from London and laid out claims that a cargo company owned by a Saudi businessman from Sudan was shuttling weapons from Iran to Sudan. It was a clear reference to Trans Arabian Air Transport, a company owned by Mr. Idris, who says he discovered his airline had made an unauthorized shipment from Iran. He says it was police equipment, not army weapons, though he won't elaborate.

Still, Mr. Idris was furious that Mr. Mahdi hadn't approached him before going public, and he spurned efforts by two Sudanese journalists in London to arrange a peacemaking meeting. The night of the El Shifa bombing, Mr. Mahdi, reached at his Cairo home by a *Wall Street Journal* reporter for reaction, could tick off seemingly incriminating facts about Mr. Idris's factory. It was connected by a new, paved road to a nearby state military complex, he said. (The trip is two miles, part of that on a busy highway.) Mr. Idris's Saudi patron, Sheik Khalid, was married to the sister of Osama bin Laden, he said. (Even if that's true—and Saudi sources say it isn't—Mr. bin Laden and his family seem to be miles apart ideologically; the Defense Department recently hired the family construction company to build new housing for U.S. troops in Saudi Arabia.)

On August 25, Mr. Mahdi distributed a fax saying El Shifa had been built partly over government-confiscated land and, although nominally owned by Mr. Idris, was actually "owned by the NIF." Mr. Idris quickly met with the head of Mr. Mahdi's party in Cairo and threatened a lawsuit. Mr. Mahdi refused to back down.

In interviews, Mr. Mahdi said the ruling NIF was pushing into businesses, and Mr. Idris, "a bank clerk," was building factories all over Sudan. Mr. Mahdi said that Mr. Idris's seven-factory complex, known as Sariah, was part of Sudan's effort to find civilian factories that could be converted to military use. He also asserted that Mr. Idris's steel mill is located near a Military Industrial Corp. center that is "probably making poison gas."

Scoffing at such notions, Mr. Idris invited a reporter to tour the facilities. An inside view of the Sariah complex in southern Khartoum revealed nothing more military than car batteries and ankle-high men's boots. The steel mill, off a desert highway, was guarded by three unarmed youths in T-shirts.

Fellow dissidents find Mr. Mahdi persuasive on many issues, though they say he often makes charges without all the evidence in hand. "I have questioned the credibility of Mubarak," says opposition figure Sharif Harir over cappuccino at the American Cafe, unofficial gossip headquarters for the Sudanese opposition based in neighboring Eritrea. But Mr. Idris's rise was "too quick. On a clerk's salary, he wouldn't have money to invest in factories."

Some American officials are skeptical about the dissidents, too, but they still meet one another frequently in Asmara, the Eritrean capital. At one get-together in April, at the U.S. ambassador's residence, participants recall, a U.S. intelligence officer said the U.S. was concerned about chemical weapons in Sudan and welcomed any information. Dissidents say they gave the U.S. a list of suspected sites, but it didn't include El Shifa.

U.S. intelligence officials say they noticed El Shifa last year because of reports of high security during the construction. Then they detected the El Shifa officials' visit to Samarra. Intelligence officials say they knew El Shifa won an Iraqi contract but questioned why the Sudanese would negotiate through Samarra Drug.

Iraq doesn't exactly inspire trust when it comes to chemical weapons. It is one of the few countries to have used them. There have been unconfirmed reports Iraq farmed out its unconventional weapons to friendly states to avoid detection. And Iraq had been caught making VX gas, using the EMPTA process.

That, say U.S. intelligence officials, is why they decided to test for EMPTA along with other chemicals when they took soil samples from suspected sites in Sudan. El Shifa was the only "hit," U.S. intelligence officials say. The test results came back in the summer, they say, and investigators started planning a second round of soil samples around the site, to pinpoint where the EMPTA was coming from. But then came the August 7 embassy bombings. Authorities quickly decided Mr. bin Laden was behind them, and President Clinton needed a list of retaliation targets, fast.

One-hundred-percent confidence is impossible in intelligence work, says one U.S. official. El Shifa, the official says, may have reached the 80% range. But "we are at somewhat of a war" with Osama bin Laden. "It's not going to be a clean thing. It's going to be a messy thing, with messy choices and messy decisions," he adds.

# 25

# SAME OLD SONG: IRAQ'S BEST PLANES ARE MAINLY IN IRAN

## Flown There For Safekeeping During the 1991 Gulf War, They're Going Nowhere

*April 29, 1998*

TEHRAN, Iran—Iraq and Iran, sworn enemies, have had high-level meetings in recent weeks to discuss exchanging prisoners, opening the border and ending their state of war.

One other thing: Iraq would like to have its airplanes back.

As allied pilots began dropping smart bombs on Iraqi hangars in the 1991 Gulf War, Saddam Hussein ordered Iraqi pilots to fly 100-odd jets to three Iranian air bases near the border. Iranians say the planes were unexpected and unwelcome, and they won't return them.

The Iraqis are annoyed. Saddam Hussein, in a speech last year, referred to the episode as "the chapter of treachery and treason," saying Iranian officials encouraged Iraq to battle allied forces—and then withheld support. Iraq says Iran accepted the planes for safekeeping and should now fork them over. Iran doesn't deny the subject came up during the recent talks but says there is really nothing to discuss. Returning the planes would violate United Nations economic sanctions against Iraq, says Deputy Foreign Minister Javad Zarif, interviewed in Tehran. "We're constrained by the requirements of the sanctions," he says.

Besides, Iran has property claims of its own—against Iraq: The eight-year war Iraq started by invading Iran in 1980 caused damage estimated at $1 trillion. The planes now held by Iran were worth just a small fraction of that when they landed in Iran, and Mr. Zarif notes that Iran has incurred costs in warehousing them and in rolling out antiaircraft batteries during the Gulf War to protect them.

Saddam Hussein might have use for the planes now. U.S. forces are still at full strength in the Persian Gulf, and a new crisis may be brewing over Iraq's attempts to shake off economic sanctions; yesterday, the U.N. again refused to lift them. Iraq has another 300 or so fighters on its own soil, but they are believed to be the least of its air force.

On the other hand, if Iran truly has kept the best Iraqi planes parked for seven years, "the tires are going to go flat," says Michael Eisenstadt of the Washington Institute for Near East Policy, who has tried to make a study of the matter. "They may not even be able to start the engines up, or operate the hydraulics," he adds. "They're probably nonfunctional at this point."

Getting a fix on things isn't easy. Iranians understandably won't say where the planes are Mr. Zarif says the 100-plane figure is an exaggeration, particularly since some of the planes crash-landed in Iran, but he won't say how many intact planes there are. "We're not in the counting business," he says.

Wafiq al Samerrai, Saddam Hussein's intelligence chief during the Gulf War, says Iran at one point denied it had any planes at all when in fact Iraq sent 113 fighter jets, including MiG-15s and Mirages. Gen. Samerrai, who defected in 1994 and now lives in London, says that while sending the planes to Iran wasn't exactly a stroke of genius on the part of his former boss, Iran was hinting before the war that it would give Iraq indirect aid against the allies.

For one thing, after a trip to Tehran by Saddam's vice president, Iran agreed to give haven to more than 30 civilian planes, Gen. Samerrai says. (Iran denies that.) For another, Iranian officials agreed to return an Iraqi pilot who got lost and landed in Iran. They let him take the plane home, too.

By most accounts, Iran got no warning that the Iraqi war planes were headed its way in 1991. Indeed, Gen. Samerrai says he himself didn't know anything about it until the pilots started returning to Iraq. On landing in Iran, they had been taken straight to interrogation rooms on the bases and asked questions such as, "How many medals did you get from the Iran-Iraq war?" and, "What Iranian targets did you attack during the Iran-Iraq war?" Except for a few who defected, the Iraqi pilots were driven back to the border and allowed to go home. Gen. Samerrai says the interrogators' questions convinced him Iran wasn't going to help Iraq, but Saddam Hussein insisted on sending the rest of the planes anyway.

The tactic had worked before for Iraq. Ken Petrie of the Royal Institute for Strategic Studies in London says that while serving as a pilot in Britain's Royal Air Force, he saw Iraqi planes parked at a Saudi Arabian air base at the start of the Iran-Iraq war. The planes—painted in Iraqi airline colors, but with machine guns sticking out—stayed a few days and then returned to Iraq, he says. Today, Iraqis are saying that Islamic teachings call for its war planes to be similarly returned. On the sidelines of the Organization of the Islamic Conference summit here in December, members of the Iraqi delegation quoted a verse from the Koran to an Iranian journalist. The verse requires anybody who agrees to care for someone else's property to return it.

"The Koran also says anybody who kills one person kills all of humanity," observes Ayatollah Baqir Al-Hakeem, leader of the Supreme Council for Islamic Resistance, an Iraqi dissident group based here. "So what can you say about Saddam Hussein, who has killed millions of people and destroyed big cities?"

For the record, Iran denies that it has made use of any Iraqi fighter planes. Iran Air did repaint and reuse one civilian Iraqi jet after discovering that it was actually an Iranian jet that Iraq had captured and repainted during the Iran-Iraq war, says Ahmad Reza Kazemi, chairman of Iran Air. One diplomat says he saw a Boeing 747 parked near the main runway of Tehran's international airport, repainted white but with a touch of Iraqi green showing through. The rest of the civilian planes are scattered around different Iranian airports, including Shiraz and Esfahan. "All the planes are grounded," says Mr. Kazemi. "Don't worry about them. They are waiting for delivery at the appropriate time."

# 26

# MOON OVER MECCA: IT'S TOUGH TO PINPOINT START OF HOLY MONTH

## Muslims Argue Over Whether to Use New Technology For Fixing Ramadan Date

*January 7, 1997*

*"Whoever witnesses the crescent of the month, he must fast the month."*

—KORAN, AL BAQARAH 2:185

BIRMINGHAM, England—As they have for centuries, Muslims world-wide will start gazing at the sky tomorrow night to see whether a new moon appears. When it does, Ramadan will begin the next day, and Muslims will abstain from food and sex during daylight hours for a month to celebrate the revelation of the Koran to Mohammed.

Spotting the moon is a bit more challenging in places like central England than in the Arabian desert, however.

"Here, you don't see the moon for years and years," says Mohammed Khalid on a recent dark afternoon, as a persistent drizzle falls outside his ground-floor office at the Islamic Resource Center here. In fact, "The last time we've seen the sun was a couple weeks ago."

Even in good weather, a new crescent moon can be hard to spot, since it may set before the sky is sufficiently dark. With no central authority to guide them, Muslims outside the Middle East often begin and end Ramadan on different days than their neighbors down the block.

But a recent push to take the guesswork out of moon-spotting is further dividing the Islamic world.

In a hospital laboratory, Birmingham gastroenterologist Monzur Ahmed demonstrates his Moon Calculator Version 0.3 software, released in December and available free via the Internet. Brushing the dust from his computer screen, he selects "London" and "January 8" and gets a full-screen simulation of the night sky, with a thin moon in the lower left-hand corner. MoonCalc also produces a full-color map with a parabola-shaped zone of moon visibility.

Muslims from Malaysia to California are developing similar moon-visibility calculators, and a slew of computer-generated Islamic calendars are slated for publication this year. In recent years, an Ithaca, N.Y., Muslim group called the Committee for Crescent Observation has persuaded most mosques in the U.S. to use such tools to decide weeks in advance when Ramadan will begin.

Saudi Arabian and Egyptian religious authorities, however, have rejected overtures from the observation committee. In the U.K., Islamic scholars met last month and gave MoonCalc the thumbs-down. Traditionalists accuse the moon-calculator advocates of violating the prophet's teachings, sowing discord among Muslims, and harming the simplicity of the religion.

"In Islam, there's no need to use a computer," says Mufti Mohammad Aslam of Dewsbury, England, who serves as secretary general of Jamiat-Ulma Britain, a confederation of conservative mosques. Instead, he says, Muslims facing cloudy skies should rely upon sightings from the Middle East; he plans to spend tomorrow evening calling Saudi Arabia every 30 minutes to see if the moon has been seen there. "If it is an Islamic country, we have to believe it," he says.

The trouble is, Islamic countries differ over moon sightings as much as over politics. In 1995, the newly independent Palestinian Authority snubbed Jordan by starting Ramadan one day earlier than Jordan did. Iran rarely starts and ends Ramadan the same day as archrival Saudi Arabia; Libya's sightings have been as much as two days off; Algeria once suffered a false sighting and had to resume fasting after declaring Ramadan over.

According to Islamic tradition, the moon has appeared if two reliable witnesses testify they saw it. But jet trails and the planet Venus can be confused with a young crescent. Also, there is often prize money for the first person who sees the moon, and "it only takes two people out of one billion to create confusion," Malaysian astronomer Mohammad Ilyas wrote in a 1993 paper calling for scientific verification. He found that 14 out of 36 times Saudis reported sighting a new moon when it would have been physically impossible to see. The Saudis "don't want to be behind anyone," says Omar Afzal, a Cornell University linguistics professor who launched the Committee for Crescent Observation's campaign after falling victim to a premature sighting in 1979.

Mohammed Jibaly, head of a Saudi-oriented religious group in Cincinnati, acknowledges the false sightings but calls them "not very relevant" as long as the witnesses tried to be accurate. Last year, he made a flurry of calls to Nigeria trying to find somebody to vouch for witnesses who spotted the moon there. Mr. Jibaly, who as a physics student used to argue the issue with Prof. Afzal in the Cornell library, says it is "overkill" to use computers to calculate the new moon's appearance.

It is also painfully difficult. Astronomers have no trouble pinpointing the moment when the earth moves between the moon and sun and a new moon is born. But it takes time for the moon to catch enough sunlight to be visible (the current, disputed, binocular-assisted record for spotting the youngest moon is 13 hours, 27 minutes after the alignment occurs).

The precise time of a new moon's visibility depends, among other things, on how high the moon is, how far east of the sun it is, how close the observer is to the equator, and whether lunar mountains are casting shadows that hide the end of the crescent. The computations involve thousands of mathematical operations, and some Muslim scholars are skeptical they really work. "How can you say six months before that it will happen on that day? You're not the one that controls this universe," says Noureddine Hussein Marwan, a London-based member of the Saudi-backed World Muslim League. Besides, some Muslims enjoy not knowing the date of Ramadan until the last minute. "It's very nice: People come to the mosque to find out if it's tomorrow," says Dilwar Khan, leaving the East London Mosque after Friday prayers with a calendar marked "subject to sighting of the moon."

But the uncertainty can be inconvenient, too. School boards in heavily Muslim neighborhoods have demanded a fixed date when students will need vacation for the fast-breaking Eid al-Fitr festival at the end of Ramadan. When Muslim groups in the U.K. sought legislation to compel one day's vacation for Eid, they were told to agree on a single date.

At the Brighton Mosque, Dr. Abduljalil Sajid has already determined Ramadan will start Saturday, and plans to use his laptop computer for verification. He has been able to set prayer schedules in advance and organize a cooking crew to help break the first fast Saturday night. "It will ease life a lot," he says.

Knowing the date in advance also gives advocates of the scientific approach a publicity advantage. Two years ago, the Confederation of Sunni Mosques Midlands in Birmingham got the local television station to broadcast the confederation's predetermined starting date for Ramadan. That raised the hackles of traditional mosques.

This year, though, even the astronomy buffs are divided. The Confederation, using data from the Royal Greenwich Observatory, projects the moon will appear Thursday. MoonCalc's verdict: The moon will show up Thursday in America, but won't be seen before Friday in the rest of the world.

# TEHRAN WANDERLUST: HOT ITEM IN IRAN NOW IS VISA TO VISIT U.S., ONCE THE 'GREAT SATAN'

## Young Population Embraces Coke and Janet Jackson; Islam Leaders Fight Back

### To Study, Perchance to Stay

*October 11, 1996*

TEHRAN, Iran—This country's Islamic government is fond of bashing America for economic sanctions, blaming the U.S. for Persian Gulf instability, even warning of an imminent military attack by the nation once known as the "Great Satan."

But young Iranians have a different reason for resenting America: They can't get in.

"Can you help me get a visa?" a government worker asks. "Why does your government not allow us to visit?" a student wants to know. "Is it possible to get political asylum in the U.S.?" whispers a hotel employee, who says he was denied a visa even though a friend in Hawaii wrote a letter inviting him to visit a factory as a fashion consultant.

Increasing numbers of Iranians are saving, scheming and begging to visit the U.S. Never mind that they are strapped for cash, that there is a deep chill between the two governments, and that the only place an Iranian can get a U.S. visa is outside Iran.

In Istanbul, Turkey, visa applications by Iranians seeking to visit the U.S. are up 30% from last year. In Nicosia, Cyprus, the surge is 50%. In Dubai, the U.S. consulate has begun requiring appointments for visa requests in the summer months, because of the long line of Iranians. Most Iranians say they plan only a brief visit to the U.S., to study or to see relatives. Some privately concede that they might not return.

Many middle-class Iranians have to work three jobs to keep up with prices that double every two years. Half of Iran is under the age of 25, and the young adults are getting rebellious, just as American baby boomers did in the 1960s. They are reading avant-garde novels, dating, dancing—and having run-ins with police.

Iran's "new youth," as some people in Tehran call them, can't remember the 1979 revolution that overthrew the shah and made Iran an Islamic state.

"I love my religion. I love my country," insists 18-year-old Hamed, sitting alone in a Tehran park at night. But he also dreams of becoming a merchant-ship captain and sailing to the U.S. And he loves American movies, which circulate among his friends in video form.

Hamed's strongest impression from the movie "Back to the Future" was seeing the U.S. actor Michael J. Fox in a car with a girlfriend—with no policeman knocking on the window demanding to see a marriage certificate. Hamed talks to his girlfriend only on the phone; for the couple to be seen in public would raise eyebrows.

Yearning for America is common in the developing world, of course. But it is striking in Iran, which takes pains to shield itself from the West. Iran recently banned satellite dishes, forcing Tehran residents to get smaller ones and hide them. President Clinton's 1995 economic boycott of Iran was recently expanded by Congress, and most American products can't be imported directly.

The mood among young people here provides some hope for those seeking a reconciliation between the U.S. and Iran. The political gap is wide, with Washington accusing Iran of sponsoring terrorism and Tehran accusing the U.S. of trying to dominate the Persian Gulf militarily. Still, the two have certain common interests, such as keeping Iraq in check. Some see an opportunity for dialogue after the U.S. presidential elections next month and Iran's in July. "I don't think it would be difficult to sell it to the majority in Iran," says Hooshang Amirahmadi, director of Middle East studies at Rutgers University in New Jersey. But he says perceptions are shallow among Iranian youth: "They know more about Michael Jackson than Jesse Jackson." The government here officially doesn't mind if its citizens travel to the U.S. "We have no problem with the American people—only with the government's policies," an Iranian government spokesman says. But Iran is fighting to avoid losing its intellectuals, and its Islamic ideals, to the West. The country has been offering to return confiscated property and factories to many who fled the country after the shah was deposed. The Iranian media has been playing up tales of disappointed emigrants, such as an Iranian who went to the U.S., wound up working in a gas station, and returned.

The Islamic regime is "getting worried," says a Western diplomat, adding that several religious scholars have proposed suspending all scholarships for overseas study and importing professors to teach.

But religious conservatives are still firmly in power in Iran. Thousands of people still show up for Friday speeches and prayers at Tehran University, where echoes of the 1980s "Great Satan" rhetoric can still be heard in today's chants: "God is great! Down with the U.S.A.! Down with Britain! Down with the hypocrites! Down with Saddam Hussein!"

Young worshipers leaving the grounds offer a list of reasons to hate the U.S.: Its interference with Iranian oil deals, its "horrible" films, its reliance on "Jewish money," its gold-medal victory in Atlanta when the Iranians believe their wrestler deserved it. "America is an aggressive country. They want more than they have," 13-year-old Muhammad Emadi says.

Still, even in working-class South Tehran, links to the U.S. belie the slogans. Asked about America, a hardware salesman in an alley exclaims, "If their foot reaches our country, we'll smash their faces with our fists!" Yet a moment later he pulls a wad of contraband $20 bills from his pocket and says, "Business is great. If people bring me dollars, I'll fix anything." Meanwhile his son is studying in America.

All told, about 300,000 Iranians live permanently in the U.S., more than a third of them in Los Angeles, which some Iranians call "Tehrangeles." Studies show that these Iranians generally do well financially.

Times are tougher in Iran. Grappling with a severe shortage of hard currency, Iran last year banned importation of Western stereo components, cigarettes and candy. "We don't have that much free cash to give to anybody to bring Marlboros into Iran," says Dori Najaf Abadi, a member of the Iranian Parliament.

Yet Marlboros and Coca-Colas can be found all over Tehran, imported from Turkey and Dubai and sold for 10 times the price of local cigarettes and soft drinks. An appliance store downtown displays Black & Decker irons and can openers. "When people hear it's an American company, their eyes go really round and they say, 'Okay, we'll take it,' " a salesman says. Want Western music? Walk into a stereo shop and say a code phrase such as: "I'm a friend of Tapesh." One store salesman named Behrooz pulls a few Janet Jackson compact disks from a drawer and spends an hour talking about his desire to go to the U.S. "I'm a young person. I would love to drive the latest model of car," he says. Instead, he lives with his parents and has no car. His friend Omid doesn't see why the U.S. would be much better. People who spend time in America "only talk about how you wear clothes and where you go and how free you live," he says. But that's enough for a third salesman, Reza, who shows off a photo book from his trip to westernized Dubai: Reza in front of a Pepsi display, Reza with his hand on the bare shoulder of a Filipina girl, Reza at a store filled with American CDs. In Iran, he says, "The government doesn't let you live. You can't even wear a shirt with a brand name on it."

According to Tehran travel agent Abbas Joulaie, "The people less than 30, if the visa will be granted, most of them will not come back." Some tour operators now require cash deposits ranging from $3,000 (for travel to Western Europe) to $13,000 (for Canada).

With a catch in her voice, Nikki, a 24-year-old travel agent, describes walking to Window 2 at the American consulate in Dubai and getting a rejection stamp on her passport even before she could present an invitation letter from her uncle in California. "I just thought, 'These people hate Iranians,' " she says.

"Undoubtedly there is heightened scrutiny for Iranians," says Arthur Helton, who teaches immigration law at New York University School of Law. Consular officials, he says, are well aware that Sheik Omar Abdel Rahman, the blind Egyptian cleric recently convicted of plotting terrorist acts in America, had slipped into the U.S. from Sudan on a tourist visa.

About 500 Iranians a week actually get American visas—10% of the level of, say, the Taiwanese—and only about 500 Iranians a year get political asylum. The State Department doesn't release figures on how often Iranians applying for visas are turned down.

Iranians who have $15,000 or so can try to buy their way into the U.S. Istanbul is a notorious market for false papers. Diplomats say some Iranians have also flown to Latin America, then hooked up with smugglers to get in. Others use Europe, which grants Iranians 120,000 visas a year, as a stepping stone.

Iran is trying to keep its youth diverted. The government recently stopped allowing Danielle Steele novels to be translated into Farsi. But government-run cultural centers have opened throughout Tehran, serving up sports, history films and lectures. A German-Iranian businessman recently got permission to build a Disneyland-style theme park outside Tehran, with Persian characters substituting for Mickey Mouse.

Last month, Iran even hosted an international tennis tournament. "I am not a sportsman, but I like sportsmen," proclaimed a banner-sized quotation from Supreme Leader Ayatollah Khamenei. Male spectators with blue jeans and slicked hair threw occasional quick glances at the stadium's women's section—separated from the men by a 20-foot-wide stairway. But bearded surveillance officers prowled the grounds, driving off any women lingering to talk with foreign players. Italian player Igor Gaudi said three girls had phoned his hotel room in recent days— only to have the line suddenly go dead each time.

In the streets of Tehran, American-style grafitti competes with fading "Down with the USA" murals. There are peace signs, the word "Rap," the word "Love." In a class of 25 English students in fashionable North Tehran, men and women readily reel off the names of favorite actors, all American. The teacher speaks with a perfect American accent. But only one student has actually traveled in the U.S., and the teacher hasn't been there either; American officials in Turkey wouldn't give him a visa. In a discussion about the U.S. minimum wage, he tells students that blacks in America are legally entitled to only half the salary of whites.

"I just want to see what it's like, see how people cross their legs," the teacher says later. "I've spent 25 years saying America's this, America's that, but I don't have the foggiest idea what America looks like."

# 28

# CERTAIN WORK IS FOREIGN TO SAUDIS, BUT THAT'S CHANGING

## Young People Are Paid Now to Learn the Service Jobs Guest Workers Have Done

*September 12, 1996*

JEDDAH, Saudi Arabia—Khalid Al Sharif has just been fired for repeatedly arriving late at the office. Colleagues gather around him to sympathize. 'If I'm supposed to be here at 8 and I come in at 9, why can't I stay until 3:30 instead of 2:30?" the easygoing 27-year-old wonders, before cleaning out his desk.

Tough break, especially coming 11 days before Mr. Sharif was to start his job as a salesman. He was booted from a one-year course, called Passport to Work, offered by CareerCraft, a British outfit that has tapped into a growing business in Saudi Arabia: teaching Saudis a Western work ethic so they can take and hold jobs as restaurant workers, package deliverers, travel agents, salesmen and security guards. Companies trying to fill the jobs pay for the training. A few years ago, most Saudis wouldn't even consider such jobs, leaving them to low-paid Pakistani, Egyptian and Filipino guest workers. But now, as a huge baby boom of Saudis reaches employment age and with government office jobs in decline, Saudi Arabia is trying to break up the ethnic division of labor and send foreign workers packing when their visas expire.

The country is using a combination of stick and sledgehammer. A new edict bars companies from importing secretaries. Another bans foreign laborers from buying cars. In Medina, stores get closed if they don't have a Saudi behind the counter. Saudi Arabia has ordered all companies to increase their native work force 5% each year, and labor inspectors visit work sites to make sure companies aren't just paying dummy Saudi workers token sums just for the use of their names.

"Every job filled by a foreigner is considered a temporary job to be filled by a Saudi whenever it is possible," Deputy Labor Minister Yousef Yacoub Kentab says through his Sudanese translator.

Saudization isn't an easy transition. Foreigners currently hold six out of every seven jobs in Saudi Arabia's service sector, which is blooming with Western franchises like Mail Boxes Etc. and Fuddruckers, as well as with homegrown chains such as Herfy Burgers and Pizza Sheikh. Now, a few companies have begun paying Saudis to consider taking service-sector jobs.

At the year-old Kanoo Training Center in Dhahran—above a Kanoo Globe travel office staffed mostly by Indians—young Saudis get up to $190 a week to take a one-year course in English, computers and placating customers. Teacher Stephen Byrd, who is British, sometimes hurls epithets at students as he pretends to be a traveler with a canceled flight. "You try to make him relax, always smile," says student Muhammad Al Ayash. "You say, 'Yes sir, I'm here to help,' " adds fellow student Abdullah Misfer Al Ghamdi.

"Saudis have great respect for teachers," Mr. Byrd says, but he worries how they will do with real customers. Also, there is no guarantee that they will take the jobs. In Saudi society, a job's security and prestige help determine what kind of wife a man's relatives can find for him and thus can affect the family's social standing. Abdulaziz Al Ogaily, 22, says his parents asked him why he would work for Kanoo, a private company that could fire him at any time. "I told them this was good for the country—it's Saudization—and they were happy with that." The prospect of airline-ticket discounts helped, too.

The list of socially unacceptable jobs is shrinking, slowly. Saudi men (but no Saudi women) now work as flight attendants. Ahmed Bahlaiwa, 38, has held several receptionist jobs but turned down a chance to be assistant manager at a McDonald's. "I won't work in a restaurant," he says, sitting with his Passport to Work classmates. "Why? A job is a job," says 24-year-old Saleh Fallatah.

Mr. Fallatah tried out for the McDonald's job. But when a McDonald's customer spilled a cup of soda, Mr. Fallatah says he asked a Filipino worker to clean up; the worker told him to do it himself, and Mr. Fallatah refused. He didn't get the job.

Headdress-wearing pioneers in service businesses sometimes feel like token Saudis. One young Saudi accountant in Dhahran says his boss wouldn't give him any auditing work for his first three months, until he insisted on a chance to prove himself. Some managers are leery of Saudi employees because they tend to command twice the pay of foreigners—expecting at least $1,000 a month—and they can't be threatened with deportation.

Still, "if they all had an American work ethnic, they would get hired in a heartbeat," says Charles R. Grimm, the American who is running ITT Industries Inc.'s new Jeddah Training Center. In class, teacher John G. Donovan fills his English and computer lessons with homilies like "All work is honorable" and "An honest day's labor for an honest day's pay." When it comes time for role-playing exercises about unsatisfied cable-TV customers or car salesmen late for appointments, the Minnesota native makes sure he and his students move the desks into a circle themselves instead of calling a Pakistani custodian to do it.

CareerCraft takes a similar, if slightly more British, approach. "Always be overpolite in English. That is what is expected of you," says teacher John Culhane, an Irishman, in a lesson on phone manners. But, he warns, don't spend too long asking about the customer's health or family. Saudis typically trade as many as a dozen such pleasantries before getting down to business. They also show unfailing hospitality to visitors, even if that means walking off the job at a busy airline counter to have tea with a friend. CareerCraft director Alan Dolan, an Englishman, says he is constantly blocking visitors at the door, saying, "You can't visit. He's at work."

A bigger challenge is bringing Saudis out of their shells. CareerCraft sends them out to shopping centers to survey customers, which is the kind of thing they never did in secondary school. Mr. Dolan tells students filling out job applications to list something other than "television" as their main interest. When offers come in for lowly courier jobs, he tells students about a graduate who started delivering DHL packages and worked his way up to supervisor.

In Saudia Arabia, though, a note from a well-placed relative or friend is often what it takes to get a job, a promotion, even a telephone line. Saudis call this system wasta (influence) or "Vitamin W." "I hate wasta," says 24-year-old Hisham Ali Alaki, adding that his parents want him to seek a cousin's help in his so-far fruitless job search. "I want a company to take me for me," he says, filling out a CareerCraft application on which he says he is willing to work all hours.

Wasta has kept training courses from expelling some students who have a powerful relative or friend at the sponsoring company. Instead of taking that approach, Mr. Sharif, fired for tardiness, asked Mr. Dolan for one last chance. Mr. Dolan agreed. The following Saturday morning, Mr. Sharif showed up for "work" at 8 sharp.

# 29

# BELIEVE IT OR NOT, TABLOIDS WERE RIGHT ABOUT CHARLES AND DI

## Spending Lavishly Fleshed Out the Sordid Royal Details Early On, It So Happens

*January 29, 1996*

LONDON—Here's an EXCLUSIVE SHOCKER: The rags were RIGHT about the royals ALL ALONG!

Prince Charles and Princess Diana are "drifting apart," declared the *Sun* in 1986. Diana is a "compulsive food binger!" proclaimed the *News of the World* in 1987. The Prince of Wales was caught "canoodling" with an old flame, the Princess had won an army officer's heart, and the dream marriage was over, British tabloids blared in ensuing years.

"Ridiculous," sneered the royals and their defenders. It was all "tittle-tattle" and idle speculation by the "gutter press."

The final score: snooty royalists zero, sleazy tabloids five. Make that six, if Buckingham Palace makes the Waleses' divorce plans official, as the British press recently predicted. The announcement would be a final vindication for the so-called Royal Rat Pack—tabloid reporters who spent years exposing royal troubles, only to be snubbed in British media awards, lampooned as fiction writers in London's broadsheet papers (called the "qualities"), and lambasted by government officials calling for a crackdown on tabloid excesses.

Now, Britain is taking its tabloids more seriously. "By God, didn't the Royal Rat Pack do us proud in telling us what was going on?" wrote former political reporter Alan Cochrane in a mea culpa magazine essay in the *Spectator.* Caroline Miller, a London tea-shop manager, says she, too, used to assume that stories like the one about Diana talking to a suitor who called her "Squidgy" weren't true. Now, perusing the *Daily Mail's* latest Di story, she says, "I think there's lots of things they don't tell you that are even juicier."

Some rat packers have become downright self-righteous. "The difference between tabloids in London and America is that tabloids in America make it up," says Robert Jobson, royal correspondent for the *Daily Express,* who points out he called the Duchess of York, Sarah Ferguson, at home to get one recent scoop. "We're not just plucking stories out of thin air about Michael Jackson eating lions," he says.

Indeed, tabloids spend a royal fortune keeping their reporters close to the royal couple. Flying first class or chartering planes, they have tracked Charles and Diana across Alpine ski slopes and Caribbean beaches, sometimes posing as tourists to observe for hours the couple's body language. The rat pack once spent a week on a yacht and a helicopter, searching the Mediterranean for the royal couple, only to discover the pair had been at sea somewhere else. Sometimes tabloids have simply paid palace employees or others to talk, but they insist that is becoming rare. "I didn't make a single call to anyone this evening to whom I'll pay money," boasts veteran royal reporter James Whitaker of the *Daily Mirror,* relaxing in his study after quizzing three palace insiders about why Diana's personal secretary had just resigned. "Oh, I'll buy them a decent bottle of champagne for Christmas—magnum, say—or claret."

Gutter press, huh? Hanging in Mr. Whitaker's bathroom, near a drawing of him peering through a peephole, is a framed letter asking him to speak at the venerable Oxford Union debating society. Andrew Morton, a former *Daily Star* reporter who wrote a bestselling biography of Diana, has been known to charge other journalists for interviews.

Vindication of the tabloids is all too much for some royalists. "Rubbish," insists Michael Shea, a former Buckingham Palace spokesman. Playing off the tabloids' penchant for circulation-boosting contests, he suggests this one: "Find a fact inside and win a million!" Mr. Shea says that if some Charles-and-Di stories proved later to be accurate, it's only because "circumstances have changed."

*Majesty* magazine's editor, Nigel Evans, has another theory: "There were so many stories around, it was almost inevitable some of them would turn out to be true."

Still, the royal family has been doing more confirming than denying since the Waleses acknowledged their separation three years ago.

Charles admitted to his affair with his then-married friend, Camilla Parker Bowles. Princess Diana, in a November television interview, was asked whether she really suffered from bulimia, had an affair with her riding teacher, and slashed her wrists; "Yes, I did," the once-future queen replied each time.

Buckingham Palace didn't dispute a tabloid scoop that the queen had asked Diana to divorce Charles. But some Fleet Street scoops have indeed fizzled. The *Daily Express* once reported Charles was about to marry Princess Marie-Astrid of Luxembourg. And before settling on bulimia, the tabloids floated pills, pregnancy and anorexia to explain Diana's fluctuations in weight.

Usually, they err on the side of hype. A casual meeting between friends is a "tryst," and every story is an "exclusive," even if every other paper has it. Recently, the Duchess of York somehow spoke "exclusively to the *Daily Express*" on the same flight on which she "opened her heart" to the *Daily Mirror.*

Tacky private-eye methods occasionally get the tabs in trouble with the industry's Press Complaints Commission. Last year, Rupert Murdoch conceded the *News of the World* went "over the top" when it ran a photograph of Princess Diana's sister-in-law entering a "booze and bulimia clinic." The monarchy has won court battles against papers for running a photo of Diana in her gym, publishing a former footman's secrets, and appropriating the royal Christmas-card photo.

But the palace hasn't gone to court in eons to dispute published facts. And in recent years, much of the skinny has come straight from the royals or their cronies, rather than from "downstairs" staff spilling the beans over pints at the Bag O'Nails pub. Richard Kay of the *Daily Mail* recalls that paparazzi once caught him in a car with Diana after an intermediary said the princess wanted to meet with him. Mr. Whitaker of the *Daily Mirror* says he has quoted Prince Charles anonymously as "a friend of the Prince." Says Peter Bond of the *Daily Star:* "This is a bloody joke in many ways. These people use the press."

The tabloids' 10-million-plus readers do get a slightly skewed view of British issues. On January 14, while other papers were writing about education reform, the *People* led with "Topless Diana in TV Shocker!" The following Sunday, the *News of the World* bypassed highway reform and splashed "Di's Midnight Trysts With a Hunk in Black" on its front page.

Clive Goodman, royal editor of the *News of the World,* makes no apologies, saying, "This is a big crisis time" for the Palace. Besides, he boasts, when it comes to accuracy, "Royal reporters have a greater success rate than political reporters."

# 30

# GOOD CONNECTIONS: DESPITE DEREGULATION, RURAL PHONE SUBSIDIES ARE LIKELY TO SURVIVE

## Congress Protects the System Even Though It Distorts Market in Curious Ways

### Tiny Firms With Big Ideas

*November 30, 1995*

PARTOUN, Utah—Here in Utah's western desert, the mail comes twice a week, it's a dusty two-hour drive to the nearest store, and a 100-yard stretch beside the Mormon church is the only paved road. Except on clear nights, even radio reception is scant.

But with telephones, "we've got everything they've got everything they've got in town," says Duane Hicks, standing beside his Hatchet Ranch with its two phone lines.

That's because Beehive Telephone Co. Serves this lightly populated area with high-capacity underground lines and modern digital switching. This enables 40-student West Desert High School to install a two-way educational-TV system. It lets accountant Dean Hayward hook up his computer to Salt Lake City. And rancher Linda Bronson pays only $15.85 a month for basic phone service that includes automatic redialing of a busy number.

Providing all that service costs five times what Beehive's customers pay. But the tiny company, based in nearby Wendover, still makes ample profits—thanks to an elaborate array of subsidies that inflate rates for long-distance and urban users.

It's a system that seems increasingly out-of-date as the industry pushes toward greater competition. But Congress is intent on preserving the "universal service" subsidies despite Republican pledges to cut subsidies and government regulations. As Congress completes a sweeping bill promising to open up competition in communications, it is adopting language limiting competition to protect rural service.

The current system's defenders include state legislatures worried that universal service will erode if phone companies lose revenue. So, despite talk of encouraging competition, many states make it hard to choose a different carrier for local toll calls. Texas gave rural phone companies three years of added protection against competition; Wyoming gave 10 years.

Critics say the system encourages small phone companies to spend money recklessly while discouraging more sensible wireless solutions. It spurs big carriers such as US West Inc. to sell rural exchanges to small companies at a premium because the buyers can collect bigger subsidies. And it keeps rural rates low, however wealthy the customers may be.

Big phone companies generally balance costs internally, charging similar rates in high-cost and low-cost areas. Thus Pacific Telesis Group charges central Los Angeles users more than their true cost to avoid charging higher rates in remote areas, whether farms or ritzy beach communities. US West charges the same in Denver as in ski resorts where wiring homes is costly. Business rates are also inflated to keep residential rates down. In all, the "hidden" subsidies run billions of dollars.

Subsidies for small phone companies such as Beehive are more explicit. They get direct payments from a $1 billion federal fund collected annually from long-distance carriers. Among other things, Beehive wants to tap this fund to bring telephones to a few dozen summer homes at a mountain-lake resort near Zion National Park. The projected cost: $430,000. Though some Utah officials doubt the part-time residents would order phones even at subsidized rates, Beehive's founder, Arthur W. Brothers, insists they would—if only for security systems to protect their expensive homes from snowmobile-riding thieves.

"This is a highly inefficient, unfair subsidy, and any serious student of the issue concluded that a long time ago," says Peter Pitsch, a communications lawyer affiliated with the Hudson Institute in Washington. Many policy makers privately agree. But "it's like fighting apple pie," says Scott Cleland, a telecommunications analyst at the Washington Research Group unit of Lynch, Jones & Ryan, a Baltimore securities firm. "Nobody wants to do anything that will increase rural phone rates."

When Sen. John McCain, an Arizona Republican, tried to replace subsidies with vouchers that poor people could use to get service from any carrier, he could line up only 18 votes. Instead, the Senate bill would probably spread the subsidies to new technologies such as data transmission. Rural considerations are shaping other parts of the telecommunications bills. For example, both the House and Senate versions would increase long-distance competition by letting regional Bell companies enter the market, but both would forbid them to charge lower rates for calls to or from big cities. Universal-service concerns are also making it harder for long-distance companies to win the right to buy local phone service at low rates and resell it.

Both bills require phone companies to let new competitors, such as cable-TV operators, connect with their networks—but a House provision excludes most companies in small towns. Without such interconnections, Robert M. Rogers, chief executive of TCA Cable TV Inc., says it can't offer phone service in Texas towns such as Paris and Tyler "unless they want to make it a long-distance call across the street to your neighbor."

Under the Senate bill, a challenger such as Tyler-based TCA could tap rural phone subsidies—but only after proving to Texas authorities that such payments are in the public interest and would speed deployment of new technology. "Multiple carriers unlikely in rural areas because of entry burdens," concluded a U.S. Telephone Association analysis of the Senate bill. Without subsidies, Mr. Rogers says, companies such as TCA could offer service only to a small town's big customers.

Rural operators say that's exactly why they need protection. David Kneece, whose family runs Pond Branch Telephone Co. in Gilber, S.C., says competitors would ignore his elderly customers, who typically have poor credit and are scattered across 600 square miles of farmland. "They'd come in and cream-skim," picking off lucrative customers such as a truck stop and a factory and thus making it hard for Pond Branch to keep basic rates down to the current $12 a month.

The Organization for the Protection and Advancement of Small Telephone Companies, one of several groups that lobby in Washington for such companies, contends that, without the "support mechanisms," the average rural phone bill would increase by $31.27 a month, or 72%. Rural areas consider good, affordable phone service essential to economic development. The companies say deregulation has made rural bus and plane travel difficult, and a loss of subsidies would inflate phone bills that are already high because many rural calls are toll calls. The companies resist the notion of limiting subsidies to poor people, who already can get other aid. They tried in vain to quash a Federal Communications Commission request for zip-code data to show who benefits from the subsidies. What if wealthy ranchers or movie stars get help? "That's not the point. The point is, it's a high-cost area," says Lisa Zaina, Opastco's general counsel.

Rural companies seem about to get their favorite terms in both bills. The powerful regional Bells back the rural companies, and long-distance carriers have kept quiet on the issue—partly because their two main Senate allies, Democrat Daniel Inouye of Hawaii and Republican Ted Stevens of Alaska, also strongly support rural subsidies. Indeed, most lawmakers now writing a compromise bill are from largely rural areas, and Senate Majority Leader Bob Dole of Kansas backs the rural companies.

Even skeptics seem resigned. "Universal service is a political necessity, and we're going to have to work around it," says Rep. Michael Oxley, an Ohio Republican.

Rutgers University Prof. Milton Mueller says the subsidies emerged in the 1960s for political reasons, after competition—and rural-electrification loans—had already brought phone service to most Americans. Using complex formulas, regulators shifted more and more of the cost of local phone service to long-distance customers. They assumed that customers cared most about basic local rates and that the poor didn't make many toll calls.

However, studies now show people often lose phone service because they can't pay long-distance bills. Meanwhile, affluent people are moving into rural areas; Pond Branch's customers include professionals with lakeside homes who commute 25 miles to Columbia, S.C.

The funding system has grown more complex. Following the 1984 breakup of AT&T, the industry and the FCC set up the National Exchange Carriers Association. NECA collects fees from long-distance carriers and sends monthly checks to local ones. To get payments, a local company usually files studies showing that its spending per line runs at least 15% above the national average. Moreover, those with fewer than 50,000 customers get extra money, regardless of operating costs. And some states have their own funds.

Not surprisingly, small operators spend aggressively. They have installed digital switches and fiber-optic lines faster than the Bell companies have. With extra cash, some rural companies have become wireless wireless pioneers or bought cable-TV systems. And with extra capacity, some offer commercial services. Beehive Telephone uses its computerized switching center to run chat-line services connecting groups of eight people who want to talk dirty.

NECA, the industry group, says it reviews small telephone companies to make sure they follow FCC rules. But the FCC was sufficiently concerned recently about allegedly lax supervision to demand that NECA put more outsiders on its board.

A few big companies with rural customers also pocket subsidies. GTE Corp. says it got $191 million last year. But lately GTE and US West have found it more profitable to sell rural exchanges to operators that can draw full subsidies. US West has sold or plans to sell $1.1 billion of such exchanges. Both companies say the subsidies are just one factor behind the sales. Yet Idaho's regulators blocked 10 US West transactions in October, calling the prices "excessive and unreasonable" and too reliant on federal subsidies.

Such sales also concern the FCC. In 1993, it capped the rapidly growing subsidy fund, and now it seeks to reform the system. One solution would make payouts depend on fixed formulas rather than a carrier's size or cost estimates. Some phone companies have proposed a complicated formula that computes the probable costs of serving an area, by considering such factors as the terrain and rainfall.

In Utah, Mr. Brothers of Beehive Telephone would like to bill the long-distance companies directly. Last year, he quit some subsidy programs and instead charged long-distance carriers 47 cents a minute for each of their calls his system completed. That was 10 times more than normal, but he says his high costs justified it, and the FCC let the rates stand. Thanks to Beehive's chat lines, traffic into its system rose 25-fold, and the company billed AT&T and MCI Communications Corp. over $1 million apiece.

They refuse to pay, and AT&T challenged his rates even though he recently reduced them to a still-high 14 cents a minute. AT&T officials say Mr. Brothers is exploiting the system. He says he is just doing what the universal system intended: bringing quality service to places that otherwise wouldn't have it. "I didn't write the rules," he says with a grin, "but I read the book."

# 31

# CELL PHONES:
# PERFECT IN EMERGENCIES? TRY AGAIN

*April 18, 1995*

For those who sell cellular telephones, 911 has become a magic number.

A brochure for Nokia phones states "Emergency help is one touch away" and shows a worried pregnant mother on a dark street. In television advertisements, Airtouch Communications describes a cellular phone as "your own guardian angel." An industry group gives out "lifesaver" awards to customers who dial 911 to summon help for others. And in surveys, most new cellular customers cite safety as their main reason for signing up.

But for those on the receiving end of 911 calls, cellular phones have been a mixed blessing. In a 911 trade journal article last year, a paramedic described three recent attempts to report different emergencies by cellular phone; he had trouble getting through each time. Dispatchers complain that cellular calls that get cut off can't be dialed back automatically. And unlike calls from wire-based phones, cellular calls don't transmit the location of the caller.

"With cellular phones, people have the capability to report emergencies like they never have before," says S. Robert Miller, 911 director for New Jersey. "But if we don't know where they are, it may do little good."

Now the Federal Communications Commission is considering requiring cellular providers to improve their 911 service. The industry is resisting, saying the costs of what the FCC is proposing are too high and the technology is unproven.

In the 30 years since AT&T Corp. announced it would make 911 the national number for police, fire and medical emergencies, some 90% of telephone lines have gained access to 911. Typically, the call goes to a dispatch center set up by several local governments. And most centers have now added "enhanced 911" technology that puts a caller's location and telephone number on the dispatcher's computer screen.

For reasons of technology and convenience, cellular companies and local officials often route cellular 911 calls to other places, such as a state-police barracks. And the database of numbers and addresses that supplies the location of a fixed telephone is of little use in tracking a phone that constantly moves.

When Amtrak's Sunset Limited train derailed into a swamp outside Mobile, Ala., in 1993, one cellular call put the phrase "Downtown Mobile" on a dispatcher's screen, while another showed "mobile phone." Earlier this year, a landscaper in an unfamiliar part of Ocean County, N.J., dialed 911 from his truck's cellular phone to report that a stranger had collapsed; it took several minutes for emergency crews to figure out the location of the heart-attack victim, who died. Cellular executives say they're trying on their own to find a way to deduce the location of cellular 911 callers. They add that they're working on a "comprehensive solution" that would transmit callers' blood types and other useful information as well.

Under the FCC's proposal, wireless phone providers—including new personal communications services—would have to give 911 calls priority over other calls and have technology in place within five years to pinpoint the location of 911 callers within 125 meters (about 400 feet). Wireless representatives say it could take five years just to develop technical standards for locating callers. And some doubt the technology is even necessary. In comments filed with the FCC, the Rural Cellular Association says most 911 callers are uninjured passersby who know where they are, and claims it's "a matter of conjecture" to say cellular customers want enhanced 911 services.

Joseph Blaschka, a Seattle-area emergency-communications consultant, disagrees. After spotting a car fire near a supermarket recently, he spent several minutes trying to explain to a 911 dispatcher where he was. After hanging up, he spotted a pay phone and called again. His location popped up on a computer screen, and the dispatcher realized the fire truck was heading for the wrong Safeway, Mr. Blaschka says.

Making matters worse, cellular 911 calls sometimes get bounced across county or even state lines. In February, Alaska authorities say, it took several hours for an Army helicopter to find a severely injured snowmobiler whose cellular 911 call had been handled by a faraway center where dispatchers didn't know the terrain.

Of course, such callers are better off than they would be without a cellular phone. In most markets, cellular 911 calls are free, and in some cases, they get through even if the phone isn't signed up for any service.

But Laverne Hogan, director of 911 service for the Houston area, worries that service for everyone will suffer as dispatchers spend more and more time with cellular calls, which she says take two to three times longer to process. The lack of automatic location detection also makes it harder for dispatchers to weed out redundant or fictitious calls. New Jersey officials say one stolen cellular phone produced 92 prank emergency calls, one of which led to a traffic accident that killed a police officer in Paramus.

Since more than 25 million cellular phones are in use already, the industry is unlikely to embrace any technology requiring changes to the instruments—such as location devices that bounce signals off satellites. Other solutions would require big changes in existing cell sites or the signals phones send to the sites.

"We sat on our fat fannies 11 years ago when cellular first came out," concedes William Stanton, who heads a national group of emergency-number administrators. In later years, cellular companies were too distracted by their rapid expansion to pay much heed to 911 officials. Zach D. Taylor, who oversees 911 service in central Oklahoma, says "there was no response" when the local officials who established 911 service in 1989 tried to get the two area cellular companies involved. More recently, he says, the carriers have worked to get cellular calls routed to the closest dispatch station rather than to Oklahoma City. But he says modernization has been "tedious" because he has to deal with corporate lawyers in Seattle, where AT&T Corp.'s McCaw cellular unit is based.

One big question is who will pay for upgrading so that 911 centers can handle cellular calls better. Most telephone bills include surcharges that help phone companies and local governments pay for 911 improvements; a few states have slapped similar surcharges on cellular customers, and others, including Texas and Florida, are considering doing so.

John Cusack, who runs a cellular-funded program in Chicago to teach teenagers how to report emergencies from local phones, notes that disputes over funding have kept Chicago from getting full 911 service for years. "Sometimes you feel a sense that you know public safety is the underlying issue, but money underlies the conversation," he says.

# 32

# PARIAH IN THE SOUTH, WILLIAM T. SHERMAN IS GETTING A MAKEOVER

## The Man Who Burned Atlanta Had Many Fine Qualities

## Civil War History, Revised

*June 9, 1993*

ATLANTA—"War is hell," William Tecumseh Sherman said. But what's really hell is trying to convince Southerners that Gen. Sherman wasn't such a bad guy after all.

In these parts, Gen. Sherman is about as popular as Lucifer. His soldiers, on their march to the sea, were known for murdering livestock and letting women and children starve. They shelled the state capitol building in Columbia, S.C., even after the town surrendered, local historians say. They stole heirlooms and reversed family fortunes. And Gen. Sherman burned Atlanta. In some circles, he is still "Attila the Yankee," or "That Redheaded Demon."

Yet, Gen. Sherman is getting an image makeover these days. Historians are telling Civil War clubs the Union general wasn't just a cold-hearted pyromaniac, and Sherman sympathizers are preparing a humanizing novel and a screenplay.

Ohio troupes recently performed a choral work—"Sherman: Forced to War"—and a ballet that has him grieving over his son's death, helping to find homes for orphans, expressing affection for his troops. "I get the impression those 60,000 guys really did love him," says the ballet's creator, Liz Lerman.

And a new book, "Sherman: A Soldier's Passion for Order," says the general "hated bloodshed" and punished Southern civilians only because he thought it would end the war faster. The book says that Gen. Sherman got blamed for a lot of burning that was actually done by retreating Confederates and that he was polite about his plundering:

When he coveted some Sir Walter Scott novels he had found in a Charleston, S.C., home, he took them—but only after promising to replace them with other books.

"I am not the heartless boar I am often represented," Gen. Sherman, himself, protested in a letter to a critic before marching to Savannah, a city he ended up sparing. John F. Marszalek, author of the Sherman book, agrees, saying the general deserved "respect, admiration and allegiance." But unreconstructed Southerners couldn't agree less. "Sherman is the greatest argument for hell, because if there is no hell, where is William T. Sherman?" says Gordon Cotton, director of the Old Court House Museum in Vicksburg, Miss. James W. Thompson, a Civil War buff in Jackson, Miss., calls Gen. Sherman an "absolute barbarian" and says it's a "disgrace" that Dr. Marszalek teaches history at Mississippi State University. Tom Watson Brown, an Atlanta attorney, says that Gen. Sherman was a war criminal and that his defenders probably "have a streak of hooliganism in them, too—brigandage, vandalism."

Ironically, Gen. Sherman actually loved the South, even though he was a native of Lancaster, Ohio. He had rubbed shoulders with many future Confederates at West Point. Before the war, he had sipped tea with Southerners while stationed at forts in Florida and South Carolina. After unsuccessful stints as a banker and a lawyer, he helped start the military school that later became Louisiana State University, and he hoped ultimately to settle in the state with his family. When South Carolina seceded, Gen. Sherman burst into tears, according to one witness.

The South itself wasn't always so hostile to Gen. Sherman, either. After all, he had sought easy surrender terms. He saw nothing wrong with slavery and thought the South should return to business as usual. After the war, large crowds welcomed the general in Tennessee, Georgia and Louisiana, where he was toasted with champagne during Mardi Gras. And Confederate Gen. Joseph E. Johnston liked his wartime nemesis enough to march in his funeral. It was there that Gen. Johnston contracted pneumonia; he died soon thereafter.

But as Southerners felt the increasing sting of Reconstruction, they found Gen. Sherman a perfect scapegoat. "People knew Sherman, they knew what he looked like," says Charles Edmund Vetter, a sociologist at

Centenary College in Shreveport, La., who wrote a sympathetic book about the general last year. With his scowl, disheveled hair, open coat and the scar on his cheek from a childhood fall off a horse, the general looked "a little bit wacko," Dr. Vetter says, and in fact, Northern newspapers had at one point labeled Gen. Sherman insane.

Sherman-bashing gained strength over the years. In 1908, the governor of South Carolina refused to approve a new U.S. history textbook, until the author squarely blamed Gen. Sherman's troops for burning Columbia. (Some historians believe wind, whiskey and Confederate cotton-burning deserve at least equal blame.)

More recently, Atlantans have been blaming Gen. Sherman for the city's shortage of historical sites—even though real-estate developers have torn down and rebuilt most of the city many times since the war. And Dr. Marszalek, a native of Buffalo, N.Y., says he often is accosted by Southerners who claim Gen. Sherman burned their great-grandfather's barn, thought the maligned general's army didn't get within 100 miles of the place.

On the other hand, Gen. Sherman has groupies, too. Sharon Moody, a native of upstate New York who is now a market researcher in Matthews, N.C., recently had a Sherman figurine made for her five-foot-high version of the New York town house where Gen. Sherman spent his final years. The display includes small replicas of the general's favorite food (spongecake) and drink (bourbon and water). Ms. Moody, whose license plate ("CUMP") honors William Tecumseh, has an old photo of Gen. Sherman in which, she observes, "he's just on the verge of smiling." Red-bearded John Goode likes to portray Gen. Sherman at annual Confederate-surrender reenactments in North Carolina, even though elderly Southern ladies "cuss me like a sailor wouldn't dare to." And Stan Schirmacher, a retired schoolteacher in Arizona, started Sons of Sherman's March to the Sea because his grandfather Gen. Sherman's drummer boy. After getting a few angry letters, Mr. Schirmacher gave his club an alias, Civil War Shack, for use below the Mason-Dixon line.

The South may ultimately surrender to the kinder view of Gen. Sherman. Mississippi State—which was founded by a Confederate general—has distributed copies of Dr. Marszalek's book as thank-you presents to Mississippi politicians. True, the Yellow River Game Ranch, a petting zoo of sorts outside Atlanta, still has a skunk residing in a two-foot mansion labeled "Gen. Sherman's Headquarters." But manager Arthur Rilling, a Texan, could tell that times are changing when he recently heard a schoolteacher explain to her class that the skunk's namesake was a Confederate general.

# PART FIVE

# Finding the Potholes Along the Information Superhighway

Fresh from Atlanta, Danny arrived in the *Journal*'s Washington bureau in the summer of 1993 to take on what were arguably its most boring beats: transportation and telecommunications. Forget the marquee assignments like the White House, foreign policy or Congress, especially in the neophyte Clinton administration; those beats were reserved for more experienced reporters. Danny got acronyms: the ICC, FCC, DOT, etc.

The self-important hot air of Washington always blew cold on Danny's ear. "That's why he grew so disturbed over the excessive use of the term 'information superhighway,' " notes Alan Murray, Danny's bureau chief. Danny wasn't covering Al Gore, but he figured that if the vice president was going to call the Internet a "superhighway," then he was free, as the transportation reporter, to write about it.

The result appeared on February 1, 1994, under the headline "Colliding Clichés and Other Mishaps on the Term Pike."

> The metaphors are piling up on the electronic interstate like jackknifed tractor-trailers, and there isn't an off-ramp in sight.

Danny was quick to give Gore credit for spawning the term.

> As a child, young Al sat in on congressional hearings that decided the color of signs and the size of lanes on the interstates. He says he coined the phrase "information highway" in 1978 during a meeting with computer-industry officials. Most people, interestingly, are willing to give full credit to Mr. Gore for

coming up with the phrase, which he made the center strip of his vice presidential campaign in 1992.

"He had a jaundiced view of Washington's schmoozing," says Jill Abramson, then deputy bureau chief. "Once I persuaded him to go with me to a swank cocktail party crowded with members of the Clinton administration. He only agreed to come because I promised that afterward we would go to a dive in suburban Virginia for duckpin bowling, greasy burgers and lots of beer."

In Washington, Danny hung out at Vegas Lounge, a divey blues bar on P Street, or Planet Fred, a divey bar on Connecticut Avenue that offered salsa lessons, or the Big Hunt, a, well, divey bar off Dupont Circle where the waitresses have tattoos and the chandeliers have hair. ("Better than vice versa," he told colleague John Wilke.) Then sporting a ponytail, he tooled around town in a beat-up yellow pickup, spending weekends playing volleyball on the Mall or driving to the beaches of Maryland's Eastern Shore.

The transportation reporter gloried in finding stories others considered pedestrian—even if that meant writing about "car-killer potholes."

Unlike crews who patch holes only in "reasonably humane conditions" (as the government's classic "Pothole Primer" puts it), Northwestern's Roboplop can run at night, in rain, sleet, snow and freezing cold. And the scientists who built it say it will plug holes faster, better, cheaper and more consistently than humans.

That is, if it ever works.

The best example of Danny's Washington regulatory coverage was his skewering of the Interstate Commerce Commission, which had long outlived its railroad-era mandate to regulate shipping rates This was not the kind of agency any reporter in his right mind would want to write about. That made it fair game.

At a row of desks near gray-draped windows, ICC examiners armed with pencils, yellow highlighting pens and 47-page rule manuals inspect every line of each new filing as though the nation's transportation system rides on it. If a filing, or "tariff," passes muster, it remains in the Tariff Examination Room. Then some year, it is hauled by shopping cart to the Cancelled Tariff Library.

His editor on that story was Ron Shafer, a mild-mannered *Journal* stalwart. While Danny was reporting the piece, Ron told him about a similar *Journal* story he'd written 30 years before, to which Danny responded: "You know, I wasn't even born then." After Danny turned in his first draft, Ron got even. Danny's first line noted that paper at the ICC's was "piling up to the ceiling."

Ron suggested Danny change his lede to read, "paper is climbing right up to the sky" or "as high as an elephant's eye." Danny, of course, didn't have a clue what Ron was talking about.

"Haven't you ever heard the song from 'Oklahoma'?" Ron asked.

No, Danny said, that was before his time.

So Ron called over fellow geezer, news editor Henry Oden, and the two belted out a chorus of "Oh! What a Beautiful Mornin' " in the middle of the newsroom: "The corn is as high as an elephant's eye, an' it looks like it's climbin' clear up to the sky."

After some consideration, Danny delivered his verdict. "I like it."

Not long after Danny's ICC story ran, Congress, which had long discussed abolishing the agency, finally did so.

Here's Danny cutting through the Beltway bog.

*—H.C.*

# 33

# FUTURIST SCHLOCK: TODAY'S CYBERHYPE HAS A FAMILIAR RING

## Glowing Views of the Internet Ignore a Very Old Lesson

### End of Southern Accents

*September 7, 1995*

A new century is at hand, and a fast-spreading technology promises to change society forever. It will let people live and work wherever they please, create dynamic new communities linked by electronics, improve the lot of the poor and reinvent government—unless its use for illicit purposes sparks a crackdown.

It is the dawn of the Internet. Or—rolling back the clock 100 years—the telephone.

Claims about the wonders of "cyberspace" sound all too familiar to those who know the history of the plain old telephone. "Every period has its set of people who are saying, 'There's never been any change like this before,'" says Carolyn Marvin, a communications professor at the University of Pennsylvania in Philadelphia and author of "When Old Technologies Were New." She adds: "People forget all the predictions that didn't come true."

To wit: The telephone would bring peace on Earth, eliminate Southern accents, revolutionize surgery, stamp out "heathenism" abroad, and save the farm by making farmers less lonely. The picture-phone was just around the corner, and in 1912, technology watcher S. C. Gilfillan predicted that a "home theater" would, within two decades, let people dial up symphonies, presidential speeches and three-dimensional Shakespeare plays. The cost would be low and the "moral tone" would be excellent, since only the best material would survive. Novels, orchestras and movie theaters would vanish, and government as we know it might not survive either, he wrote.

Echoes of Mr. Gilfillan filled a conference room at an Aspen, Colo., hotel recently as the well-wired—both politically and technologically—Progress and Freedom Foundation convened a summit on "Cyberspace and the American Dream." By allowing anybody to share information with anyone else, the Internet has made anachronisms of both television and an "irretrievably clueless" government, opined Grateful Dead lyricist turned cyberspace guru John Perry Barlow. Because marketing and distributing products on the Internet costs almost nothing, "only the good stuff will survive," added technology commentator Esther Dyson.

Also stopping by was Alvin Toffler, whose 1970s book "Future Shock" said the world needed more futurists like him because technology was changing society so fast. House Speaker Newt Gingrich is among those convinced, and the Toffler theory of a revolutionary " 'Third Wave' information economy" is part of the new Washington gospel.

In Aspen, Mr. Toffler and others spoke of the Third Wave "demassifying" information companies—even as two TV networks were being acquired by corporations determined to grow bigger. They talked for three hours about the shrinking role of government, while barely noting that Congress is rewriting communications law in sweeping fashion.

Such government and corporate muscle-flexing helps keep futurists afloat. In 1909, as the American Telephone & Telegraph Co. was buying up rivals, social critic Herbert N. Casson wrote that phones were poised to "ring in the efficiency and the friendliness of a truly united people" provided competition and government ownership were quashed so a single provider could do the job. The following year, the company helped fund Mr. Casson's 1910 book on telephone history. (A relentless optimist, he told Americans that the Depression would end if they would just snap out of it.)

As regional Bell companies now try to wrest free of government regulation, modern-day Cassons abound. Writer George Gilder predicts we will soon be able to send limitless amounts of data through the "telecosm" for practically no cost—especially if phone companies are allowed to buy local cable companies. Phone-company executives scoff at the first idea, but they like the second part, and help finance his work. Washington lawyer Peter Huber, another Bell ally, recently wrote a new version of George Orwell's "1984" in which the telescreen is hero, not villain.

To such Pollyannas, the real enemies are the media's Cassandras—who also tend to exaggerate the impact of new technologies. A *Time* magazine cover story in July about Internet porn turned out to be based on dubious research. Likewise, back in 1907 *Cosmopolitan* magazine called telephone companies "Allies of the Criminal Pool-Rooms." Telephones were also blamed for insanity and a total loss of privacy. They would make people "nothing but transparent heaps of jelly to each other," one critic predicted.

Boosters brushed off such talk, and traded jokes about Luddites who stuck paper messages into telephones or asked, "What greases the derned thing?" These days Internet nerds laugh at those who don't know how to turn off their modern speakers. Inspired partly by science fiction, the Internet elite, or "digerati," see themselves as living in the community of "cyberspace" and in scores of "virtual communities" within it—though they must reluctantly return to "terra" for lunch. Of course, any congenial locale can serve as terra. Places with laws restricting Internet use will suffer rapid population loss, warns Michael Vlahos of the Progress and Freedom Foundation.

In similar dramatic tones, telephone enthusiasts spoke about the world of the "ether." H. G. Wells predicted that the telephone would help eliminate traffic congestion by pulling people out of cities. And sociologist Charles Horton Cooley said "an intricate mesh of wider contacts" would turn people's geographical neighbors into strangers.

It didn't happen. Claude Fischer, a University of California professor who pored through marriage records and public announcements for three California towns from 1900 through 1940, found that local attachments remained strong. Even now, some 90% of telephone calls nationwide are local. Predictions about revolutionary social change from technology have a shelf life "roughly equivalent to that of a Big Mac," Prof. Fischer says.

One reason is that forecasters assume technical faults will be solved quickly. But it took decades for the Bell system to eliminate delays and garbled transmissions; until then, cursing at telephone operators was common. At the Aspen summit, Howard Greenspan sat in the audience cursing his laptop computer as it took five minutes to download a summary of what the panelists had just said. "If this is the future, we've got a big problem," he said.

Forecasters also forget that technology can cancel its own effects. For example, the telephone was supposed to break down class barriers decades ago. The average man would have "the power of ancient emperors" to summon anybody, one advertisement claimed. In Britain, the well-heeled feared "triflers and intruders" would use the telephone to bother them needlessly. But unlisted phone numbers, office switchboards and answering machines helped people keep their distance.

Of course, for those who earn their living from the idea of cataclysm, the idea of constancy can be unsettling. Ask Mark Stahlman, an interactive-media consultant who tried to play gadfly at Aspen. The Internet hadn't altered the laws of physics or psychology, he reminded fellow panelists: "There is no revolution."

The foundation's Mr. Vlahos cut him short: "People here accept there's a revolution. If you're saying there's not a revolution, it gets us into an old debate we're not going to have." Mr. Stahlman didn't raise the issue again.

# 34

# COSTLY TALK: WHY PAY-PHONE CALLS CAN GET SO EXPENSIVE AND SPARK COMPLAINTS

## Some Long-Distance Carriers Reward Shops to Sign Up and Then Soak Callers

### Has Competition Gone Awry?

*May 30, 1995*

DALLAS—When you are selling some of the country's most expensive telephone service, it helps if customers don't care what you charge.

Cynthia Whiting, a marketer for Oncor Communications Inc., is pursuing a Cleveland laundromat owner named Nick. If he will choose Oncor as the long-distance carrier for the laundromat's pay phone, she promises him $50 up front plus monthly commission checks. Oncor also will pay the local phone company's switching charge and give him 20 minutes of free long-distance calls.

In the strange world of pay phones, Nick is the customer, and the person doing the dialing is merely an "end user." Like most of Ms. Whiting's customers, Nick says yes without asking how much the end user will pay.

The answer: a surcharge of up to $10, plus an operator charge of about $3, plus per-minute charges typically three times higher than those of AT&T Corp. Those rates, which enable Oncor to pay Nick so much, have helped the company become AT&T's largest competitor in the $7 billion-a-year pay-phone industry.

Not surprisingly, Oncor also is the industry's biggest source of complaints. In its Dallas offices, where Ms. Whiting and 100 other telemarketers sign up new customers, nearly as many sit in an adjacent room taking calls from angry end users.

"It's just so expensive," a shocked caller tells Dwight Harris, who gazes at a computer-screen summary of his $27 bill. Mr. Harris, in a weary monotone, offers each disgruntled caller some free long-distance minutes as calculated by his computer. If the caller persists, Mr. Harris offers to reduce the bill.

Despite such appeasement, 1,024 people last year wrote complaint letters about Oncor to the Federal Communications Commission. One was Norman Shear, a New Jersey contractor who was billed $19.10 for a 10-minute collect call from New York's Queens to his office and $8.47 for a two-minute calling-card call from his office to Queens. "How can the government allow this to happen when deregulation of the phone company was to help everybody, not rape them?" he asked.

Congress wants to deregulate the industry even further on the assumption that more competition will lower prices. But competition over pay phones has made prices soar. Even AT&T charges 65% more than in 1984 for a 10-minute call from a Los Angeles pay phone to New York. Its operator-assistance charges have risen, too.

Government efforts to hold down rates have achieved little. In 1991, FCC staffers pressured some carriers to reduce rates, but Oncor—then called International Telecharge Inc.—slipped through the cracks. A year later, the FCC told Congress that "market forces are securing just and reasonable rates" because callers were dialing special codes to choose cheaper carriers. But market forces also were leading Oncor and similar companies to raise rates and sign up pay phones in poor neighborhoods, where callers often don't use the codes.

Now, the FCC is cracking down on Oncor directly. In March, it fined Oncor $1.4 million for switching 94 phones in the New York subways from AT&T without permission from the Metropolitan Transit Authority. In April, the FCC ordered Oncor to lower its rates or justify them. The company is trying to negotiate a settlement of both matters. FCC officials say they soon will pursue other companies.

"This stuff makes me furious," says Kathleen Wallman, the FCC's top telephone regulator. "There are companies operating out there as traps for the unwary. People deal with them by mistake, not by choice."

The pay-phone industry, too, is furious with Oncor. Its high rates give pay phones a bad name, says Vincent Sandusky, president of the

American Public Communications Council, which refuses to cash Oncor's membership check. The trade group is pushing the FCC to formally cap rates.

However, Republican opposition to new regulations could keep the FCC from doing so. And Oncor—whose 48-year-old founder and sole shareholder, Ronald Haan, has given $31,000 to the Republican National Committee since 1991—still has influence. Last week, Oncor helped spark opposition to a provision in a telecommunications bill that would make it harder for companies such as Oncor to go after Bell pay phones. That language was weakened by the time the bill passed the House Commerce Committee last Thursday.

Oncor is fighting rate caps, too, with leaflets, petitions and personal lobbying. Its officials say they are victims of high costs, counterattacks by AT&T and vicious competition for customers. They say AT&T would have little pay-phone competition if it weren't for companies such as Oncor, which charge more for the same reasons that mom-and-pop stores charge more for bread. "We didn't set out to be the highest-priced carrier," Gregory Casey, vice president for regulatory affairs for the Bethesda, Md., company, told FCC officials recently.

The soft-spoken Mr. Haan did set out to be a major carrier, though. The former telephone-software salesman entered the public-phone business in 1986, and, to bet on it, later sold his software company for $60 million.

Now, he pockets Oncor's annual after-tax profits of about $11 million plus a "modest" salary, the company says. Though Oncor says it will take Mr. Haan another two years to recoup his investment, he lives in high style. He bought a Washington society magazine for his second wife. He married his third wife last year in a lavish ceremony on the French Riviera. The Haans regularly fly by private jet to homes in Boca Raton, Fla., Aspen, Colo., and San Francisco. At first, his customers were hotel chains. His first public-phone company, National Telephone Services Inc., processed long-distance calls for hotel guests and gave hotels a percentage of each bill. But AT&T won back the big ones.

So, Mr. Haan began pursuing small businesses—restaurants, gasoline stations, hospitals and laundromats—that had on their premises pay phones owned by local phone companies. Under a 1988 federal-court ruling, the site owner, not the phone company, picks the long-distance carrier for a pay phone, just as people choose one for their home phones.

As an operator-service provider (OSP), Mr. Haan wanted to become the "zero-plus" carrier for as many phones as possible. That meant receiving any long-distance call that started with a zero rather than an access code; it included collect calls and those using another carrier's calling card. An OSP generally used its own operators and bought long-distance access wholesale. Size was an advantage, Mr. Haan decided. With cash infusions and complicated financial maneuvers, he took over two larger, struggling OSPs in 1991 and created Oncor. The deals gave him a $20 million operator center able to handle a million calls a day in 10 languages.

Mr. Haan was known as a brutal competitor. In its early months, Oncor seemed near failure, but Mr. Haan quickly turned a profit by squeezing creditors, shedding unprofitable accounts, and increasing yields, his managers say. Oncor depicted itself in ads as an astronaut among cavemen and a lion among kittens.

As many as 300 rival OSPs competed against Oncor. Many offered record payoffs to businesses with pay phones. For example, airports that once received 20% of each call's price soon were getting 28%. AT&T started paying commissions, too. Before long, airports could insist on being paid by the number of passengers they handled rather than by the call.

To sign up phones, an OSP sales agent merely sent a form to the local phone company, saying a restaurant or gasoline station wanted to switch carriers. If the owner wasn't available to sign, some agents settled for a waitress or cashier. At times, they sent unauthorized orders by wire, a tactic called "slamming." Oncor concedes some of its agents engaged in such "electronic warfare," but Mr. Haan, in a written response to questions, said, "We got slammed more than anybody."

Nynex Corp. says its pay phones were being switched at least once a month before it took steps to curb slamming last year. Now, Nynex advertisements urge New Yorkers to "look for" its pay phones and "look out" for independents. Yet nearly 40% of Nynex pay phones are linked to obscure OSPs, with Oncor having the biggest share after AT&T.

To stay ahead, Oncor uses a platoon of distributors, outside sales companies. Its favorite is Western Group Communications Inc., of Dallas, whose star salesman is Marvin Brock, an energetic 35-year-old minister with two Bibles in the trunk of his car. He insists on saying "upgrade" instead of "switch" when he strides into bodegas or nightclubs to urge owners to sign up with Oncor. If they do, Mr. Brock collects a fee as long as the phone stays with Oncor. A good phone can bring him more than $20 a month; he especially likes those used by Mexican immigrants to call their relatives collect.

Long-distance salesmen swarm into Dallas's poor neighborhoods. Mr. Brock says one besieged convenience-store owner used an Uzi to show him the door; Mr. Brock says he returned several times and is still after the business.

"They won't take no for an answer," complains Jackie Lay, owner of a new Dallas laundromat. Three OSPs already have sought her single Southwestern Bell pay phone by the time Mr. Brock arrives. "You're not receiving the dollar you're entitled to receive every time someone picks up the phone and dials zero," he tells her. Leaning on her mop, Ms. Lay says the phone is "the least of my worries right now." But Mr. Brock persists, giving her a card for free long-distance calls; it will be renewed if she switches to Oncor. Some weeks later, he signs her up.

Mr. Brock says he tries not to know Oncor's phone rates so that on the rare occasions he is asked he can say "I don't know" and move on. "You've got to spend your time wisely," he says. All that hustling is one reason Oncor's rates are so high. The company says it paid $55 million in commissions last year, or 29 cents of the end user's dollar. Distributors are getting more money, too. Oncor once paid them $15 for every phone they signed up. But distributors would switch phones to Oncor one week and to a rival the next. Keeping them loyal required higher payments—and higher phone bills.

In 1993, for example, Oncor agreed to pay a distributor, Access America Digital Communications Inc., $75 for each new pay phone, and it charged callers an extra 25 cents per minute to recoup the fee. The contract also allowed Oncor to increase the 25-cent surcharge if its profit margin fell below 15%. "Haan doesn't care how many hands are in the pie, as long as the pie is big enough that he gets a big slice of it," says Jack Lake, a former distributor. Oncor disputes that, saying it has tried to limit surcharges.

The high rates of some OSPs became a marketing tool for AT&T. In 1991, television ads urged pay-phone users to hang up and dial AT&T's five-digit access code if they didn't hear AT&T's familiar "bong." The company also introduced "proprietary" cards that don't work on phones wired to other carriers unless the caller dials an access code or 800 number first. AT&T even told people to destroy their old cards. And commercials urge people to dial AT&T's or MCI Communications Corp.'s special 800 numbers for collect calls.

Every time an end user "dials around" Oncor to save money, an Oncor customer misses a commission. To keep customers' checks from shrinking, Oncor raises commission rates. To keep its own revenue constant amid dwindling volume, Oncor acknowledges that it has increased its caller charges—giving people even more reason to avoid the company.

So Oncor cuts costs. It fired 10% of its employees in January. At the Dallas center, it checks phone traffic every 15 minutes and gives operators time off without pay if volume drops even 1%.

Oncor also is chasing independent pay-phone providers as customers. IPPs don't own nearly as many phones as do local phone companies. But they do choose their own long-distance carriers, and a typical IPP controls hundreds of phones. Oncor's trade advertisements promise them "the highest zero-plus commissions you can find anywhere."

Often, that isn't enough. J. Patrick Matthews, vice president of Publicom Inc., a Granger, Ind., IPP, is considering switching 150 phones to AT&T from Oncor. Payments to Publicom for each call would be lower, but most dialers now use access codes to avoid Oncor anyhow, he says. To combat access codes, many IPPs encourage callers to use coins instead. "Call anywhere in the USA for 25 cents a minute," their phones say. Some do more; a California survey found that one in five pay phones there was illegally programmed so that callers couldn't use access codes or 800 numbers. And many pay-phone owners don't post required labels identifying a phone's OSP. At a Texaco station in Dallas, two adjacent phones are labeled "AT&T," but dialing "00" reveals that one is wired to Oncor.

Citing consumer confusion, the FCC in 1992 proposed a plan that would route every pay-phone call to a dialer's regular long-distance carrier—a change that would clobber OSPs such as Oncor. Some OSPs, fearing the end was near, raised their rates even higher.

Oncor and the rest of the pay-phone industry fought the plan, and it hasn't advanced. Now, Oncor and the American Public Communications Council are at odds. The trade group wouldn't let Oncor have a booth at its Las Vegas convention last month, but Mr. Haan set up an unofficial hospitality suite anyway. Oncor executives distributed "No Rate Caps" buttons, plus data showing that some rivals charge just as much.

On the convention floor, Garry McHenry, sales manager for a rival OSP, was rooting for Oncor. Some pay-phone companies may think they are Ma Bell, he said, beer bottle in hand, but "Oncor recognizes the industry for what it is."

Oncor Communications says its average call lasts six minutes. A recent six-minute call to Sparrows Point, Md., from a Daytona, Fla., pay phone, using a Bell Atlantic calling card, generated an Oncor bill of $13.93. A comparable call through AT&T would cost $2.23. Here's how Oncor says it arrived at its bill:

$4.03: Commissions to customers and distributors

$2.57: Cost of sales, including operator center

$2.34: Wages and administrative expenses

$1.61: Payments to long-distance carriers

$1.25: Uncollected or reduced bills

$0.81: Oncor's net income

$0.66: Oncor's corporate taxes

$0.44: Bill collection by local phone company

$0.22: Interest on Oncor's debt

# 35

# THE CASE OF THE ACE ON ICE: FLIERS PROTEST VETERAN'S GROUNDING

## Air-Show Star Bob Hoover, 72, Is Unfit to Fly, FAA Says; Fans Say He Was Framed

*August 17, 1994*

OSHKOSH, Wis.—Fifty years ago, a German pilot shot down Bob Hoover's fighter plane from a seemingly impossible angle. The lanky Tennessean parachuted into the Mediterranean, escaped from a prison camp, won a Purple Heart, and went on to become America's best-known stunt pilot.

"Hoov" flew the same routine for decades: shutting off both engines at 3,500 feet, gliding into a loop, a roll and a full turn, landing on one wheel, and doffing his straw hat to salute the crowd. Occasionally, while rolling his plane over with his left hand, he has poured a glass of iced tea with his right—backhanded.

Mr. Hoover, now 72 years old, was aching to perform here last month at the Experimental Aircraft Association's convention, which attracts 800,000 spectators and is the nation's biggest air show. But instead he was grounded; this time, his own government had shot him down.

Every pilot needs a medical certificate to fly solo, and the Federal Aviation Administration revoked Mr. Hoover's last year after ordering a battery of neurological tests on him. The National Transportation Safety Board upheld the action, saying the aging airman has a "cognitive deficit" and shouldn't be performing edge-of-the-envelope stunts near thousands of fans on the ground.

The reaction from Bob Hoover's fans: Phooey.

"He can outfly every inspector the FAA has," says Rick Grissom, an air-show promoter from Kissimmee, Fla., who says he wouldn't hesitate to let his wife and children fly with Mr. Hoover. Pilots have peppered government officials with protest letters and telephone calls. At Oshkosh, many fans wore buttons reading "Of Course I Support Bob Hoover, Don't You?" and some charged, red-faced, into the safety board's tent to say, "You ought to be ashamed of yourselves." Attorney F. Lee Bailey, who owns six airplanes, defended Mr. Hoover before a safety-board judge in January, and has yet to send him a bill. He says he will even leave O. J. Simpson, a paying client, for a day to take Mr. Hoover's case to the U.S. Court of Appeals in Washington this fall. "One of the finest contributors to American aviation was the victim of a series of moral and ethical pygmies," Mr. Bailey told a hearing officer.

Chuck Yeager, who chased Mr. Hoover around the sky when they were both test pilots (and who says "everything he does is perfect"), helped form a legal-defense fund. Barron Hilton, the Hilton Hotels Corp. chief executive, gave Mr. Hoover a ride on his jet to Oshkosh.

Here, Mr. Hoover, wearing hearing aids and pants that rose up above his navel, was treated like an immortal. During a special tribute, he told 1,000 pilots he was fighting the grounding "for all of you," and he got three standing ovations. Air Force Chief of Staff Merrill McPeak bumped into Mr. Hoover behind the amphitheater and, in a gesture of support, offered to give him the Air Force's fitness test. During a news conference the next day, aviation reporters applauded Mr. Hoover and got him to sign their T-shirts and programs. (He says he has never refused an autograph-seeker, except for an FAA lawyer who had just finished cross-examining him.)

Still, the soft-spoken Mr. Hoover, who says he has earned $500,000 a year as a stunt pilot, was miffed to be earthbound at an air show, with 8,000 planes parked around him. Standing near a runway where a young stunt pilot was flying upside down at an altitude of 10 feet, Mr. Hoover declared that he had been done in by a few bad men at the FAA. "It's a conspiracy," he said.

Mr. Hoover's troubles began at an Oklahoma City air show two years ago. Two FAA inspectors watched him fly, and two months later filed separate reports rapping Mr. Hoover's performance: His flying was "tentative and imprecise," his maneuvers were "not crisp," his announcer lost track of him in the air, and on the ground he needed his staff to "keep track of things." Other performers say Mr. Hoover flew flawlessly, and Mr. Hoover, who scores himself after every performance, gave himself an 8 out of 10. Mr. Bailey subpoenaed a third FAA inspector, Norbitt G. Nester, who told the safety-board judge that his two colleagues had written their negative reports in concert. Mr. Nester testified that one of them was overweight, hated thin pilots and vowed to go after Mr. Hoover because "the old bastard has been around a long time and he is not what he once was."

The inspectors' reports pointed out that Mr. Hoover had been written up for five "incidents" in the past decade, such as improperly flying over the terminal at Oshkosh. Mr. Hoover says most of the citations were trumped up by low-level FAA officials trying to build their reputations by busting a celebrity.

The FAA grounded Mr. Hoover for his performance on the ground, not in the air, though. In day long sessions at two neuropsychologists' offices near his Palos Verdes, Calif., home, Mr. Hoover took tests like connecting numbered and lettered dots and making up stories based on drawings. He got "impaired" scores on several tests, such as repeating a list of 15 words ("drills," "plum," "vest," "parsley") and reciting seven-digit numbers backward. It was "nutty stuff" that had little to do with flying a plane, Mr. Hoover says; the FAA says the tests show how well a pilot adjusts to emergencies.

What's more, a neurologist told the safety-board judge, Richard R. Mullins, that Mr. Hoover's brain scan showed irregularities, possibly from years of drinking, which, he said, also explained Mr. Hoover's bulbous red nose. Mr. Hoover said any brain damage came early in his career; at various times, he was kicked by German captors, struck by an F-84 jet's tail while ejecting, and knocked unconscious while landing a crippled F-100 jet. Mr. Hoover acknowledged having two drinks a day, but said he got his proboscis from his father, who was a teetotaler.

Mr. Hoover decided that the way to convince the government he could still fly was by flying. In the midst of the four-day hearing in Oklahoma City, Mr. Hoover performed his routine for Judge Mullins—with another stunt pilot, Leo Loudenslager, aboard.

Mr. Bailey also showed the judge a videotape from Mr. Hoover's warm-up flight the week before, during which the plane's engine began to sputter over the Pacific. Mr. Hoover nursed the ailing plane back to Torrance, Calif.

And Mr. Bailey pointed out that his client had been hired, as usual, to fly his yellow P-51 Mustang above competitors in air races in Reno, Nev., and Phoenix, guiding the racers to safety (or telling them to bail out) when their engines blew up. (Mr. Hoover was allowed to fly as long as another pilot was with him.)

Judge Mullins, a small-plane pilot himself, ruled that Mr. Hoover should get his medical certificate back. But the NTSB itself overruled him, saying, "We question the relevance of respondent's actual performance skills."

Mr. Loudenslager protests: "They're saying the proof's not in the pudding."

The government has defenders, including James L. Harris, who runs an association of flight surgeons and saw Mr. Hoover's Oklahoma City show. He says a pilot with Mr. Hoover's experience can fly "by rote," until something goes wrong. "If he crashes into a crowd, killing a lot of people, you know who's going to get the blame," Mr. Harris says.

Still, some pilots are convinced Mr. Hoover is really the victim of a larger FAA crackdown on older pilots.

"If they catch the biggest fish in the pond, the little fishies will be really impressed," says Charles Webber, 66, who has been trying for 12 years to prove it is unconstitutional for the FAA to require him to have a medical certificate. Now, in between publishing issues of a newsletter devoted to blasting the agency, Mr. Webber flies a motor glider, for which he needs no medical certificate.

Duane Cole, an 80-year-old former stunt pilot who lost his certificate after an angioplasty, is now giving aerobatic lessons and producing aviation videos and books, which he signs "Happy Flying" in a shaky hand. "Pilots don't have the same rights as criminals," he says. "If you can drive a car, why do you need a medical to fly a little airplane from town to town?"

The FAA won't comment on the Hoover decision because it is being appealed. But it says that more than 99% of recreational pilots get their medical certificates renewed and that several active pilots are approaching the age of 100.

Even Mr. Hoover isn't sure he would want to keep looping and rolling that long. He said he had planned to retire if he ever had a string of poor shows and couldn't regain his form. To make sure he still has the right stuff, Mr. Hoover got an Australian pilot's certificate and started performing in air shows there and in Mexico.

Still, it rankles Mr. Hoover that he can't perform in front of American fans. "They have seen me fly all these years," he says. "I don't like to disappoint them."

# 36

# ROLLING ALONG: ICC KEEPS TRUCKIN' THOUGH IT HAS LOST MUCH OF ITS AUTHORITY

## Rate Regulator, No Longer Able to Regulate Rates, Is Busy With Paperwork

### Sour Spat Over Candy Canes

*April 27, 1994*

WASHINGTON—In a large, dusty room on the fourth floor of the Interstate Commerce Commission building, paper is piling up all over the place. Faded blue and green binders are stacked from floor to ceiling in 14 corridors, as well as on desks and chairs. And every day, five days a week, clerks in T-shirts haul in an estimated 16,000 more pages from the nation's trucking companies.

The papers detail how much truckers intend to charge to ship everything from alpaca wool to zirconium. At a row of desks near gray-draped windows, ICC examiners armed with pencils, yellow highlighting pens and 47-page rule manuals inspect every line of each new filing as though the nation's transportation system rides on it. If a filing, or "tariff," passes muster, it remains in the Tariff Examination Room. Then some year, it is hauled by shopping cart to the Cancelled Tariff Library.

It is a place Franz Kafka would have loved. The tariffs have little meaning. The ICC no longer has the power to regulate the shipping rates listed in the filings. So companies that have products trucked don't protest the rates. In fact, few people can decipher them. And most freight now moves in ways that don't require them.

But this paperwork is the fuel that helps keep Washington's oldest regulatory agency going. Critics say the ICC, created in 1887 to ride herd on emerging railroad monopolies, has had no important function since Congress deregulated the trucking and rail industries in 1980. But the agency has withstood attacks by everyone from Ralph Nader to Ronald Reagan. Over the past several months, attempts to cut its $45 million annual funding have failed on Capitol Hill.

It is, in short, the agency that won't die. "If we can't get rid of the ICC, I don't think we can get rid of anything," says Republican Sen. John Danforth of Missouri.

In Washington, even programs that attract widespread ridicule develop a protective shell. Lawmakers like keeping jurisdiction over independent agencies such as the ICC. Regulated companies don't want to incur a regulator's wrath, and some even feel more secure with the ICC around. New officials at the agency become its champions. Says Gail C. McDonald, the ICC's recently appointed chairwoman: "In being here, I have found we have an important jurisdiction, and I feel the protections we provide the public are important ones."

Others have their doubts. "A lot of what we do is just foolish," one longtime ICC bureaucrat says.

In late 1991, for instance, the agency took up this sticky question: Should candy canes have a classification separate from candy, in a rate table that some truckers use? "A candy cane could be considered a stick of candy which has a crook in the end," argued Bob's Candies, a confectioner in Albany, Ga. But a truckers' group said candy canes take up more space than other sweets. The ICC sifted through briefs, depositions and density tables. It still hasn't ruled. In the interim, Bob's says it has persuaded truckers to carry its candy canes at the candy rate.

Meantime, the ICC also is still working on a 14-year-old dispute over whether railroads were charging too much to ship corn syrup to California from Texas, even though such rates are now determined by the free market.

The agency's 630 employees (down from 2,000 in 1980) try to make their jobs relevant. They write guidebooks, such as 1992's "So You Want to Start a Small Railroad." Fran Grimmett, who has been with the ICC for more than two decades, spends three months a year compiling a list of minority- and women-owned trucking companies. She developed a computer database for the task and now surveys the businesses every year. "I think this is in response to a demand," she says, although "perhaps it didn't start out that way."

All of this activity is overseen by five ICC commissioners (at least two must be Democrats, two Republicans). With less to regulate, the job of ICC commissioner, which pays $115,000 a year, has become a leisurely one. The commission met 11 times last year, but as many sessions were canceled for lack of an agenda.

ICC commissioners can hire five staff members each, but Gregory Walden, a Republican who served as a commissioner most of last year, says he had trouble finding enough work for two. Mr. Walden had a reputation among the ICC staff as hard-working, but says that even after researching each vote thoroughly and proofreading opinions, he had plenty of time to linger over the morning paper.

Commission staffers "are probably among the most frustrated in government service," says Frank Wilner, author of "Comes Now the Interstate Commerce Practitioner," a book about the agency.

At one time, though, the ICC had real power. It set time zones, decreed that trains could be racially segregated and blocked truckers from going into business if they couldn't prove a need for their services. Being an ICC commissioner was second in prestige only to a Supreme Court justice. In 1944, Commissioner Joseph B. Eastman talked about "sitting in dignity and looking down on the supplicants from the elevation of a judicial bench."

The pomp remains evident as one walks under the gargoyles and columns of the ICC building's facade, past busts of four former commissioners. Before ICC meetings, a clerk still intones, "All rise," as the commissioners walk single file to their places behind a long desk, with a mural of the U.S. behind them.

Most of the ICC's clout has evaporated. In the wake of the deregulation of the 1980s, the ICC now can set trucking and rail prices only in situations where competition doesn't exist, something that has become rare. The agency still reviews railroad mergers. And it still processes applications for new trucking or rail service, though it has virtually no power to turn them down. A typical ICC announcement is like the recent one about a $2,500 fine against an Allston, Mass., auto-delivery company for operating without insurance.

Most of the ICC's legal work still emerges from the tariff filing room. The tariffs are complicated because shipping rates change. While some truckers refer to mileage charts or tables, many actually spell out rates for carrying each product to each destination city from each origin city, as well as specifying the discount for each customer. Tariffs alone for Yellow Corp., a motor-carrier holding company, fill 200 binders. And the number of trucking concerns has doubled since deregulation.

Why do all those tariffs still have to be filed, when the ICC no longer regulates trucking rates? "The Interstate Commerce Act hasn't been repealed," declares Charles E. Langyher, chief of the Section of Tariffs. Tariff filings were aimed at preventing truckers from discriminating against certain customers. But now, shippers just call a rival if they don't like a trucker's prices. Mr. Langyher says nobody has made a rate-discrimination complaint in more than a decade. ICC officials say a manufacturer considering locating a factory somewhere could use tariffs to check the local trucking rates. But the manufacturer would face a daunting array of tables, cross references and revisions, as Cathy Stamback demonstrates by thumbing through Schneider National Inc.'s blue binders. Ms. Stamback, who works for one of six tariff-watching firms that rent space at the ICC, says that in 2½ hours she could find what the Wisconsin trucking company charges to ship printed matter to, say, Miami from Oshkosh, Wis. "Some of this belongs across the street," she says, nodding toward the Smithsonian Institution.

The folks at Schneider, like many trucking companies, would be happy if tariffs were, indeed, consigned to history. The company says it will assign four employees and pay $20,000 in filing fees this year to record its rates. To raise prices, truckers must wait at least a week after filing a tariff, a delay that could cost a bundle if fuel prices rose suddenly. But other truckers say they like the tariff-filing requirement because it keeps prices more predictable. Labor groups also support it.

Customers of those trucking companies rely on the ICC for another reason. In the past few years, many have been sued by the bankruptcy trustees of defunct trucking companies for getting lower rates than the tariffs spelled out. Tariff rates were routinely ignored in the 1980s. Richard Johnson, co-owner of a carpet wholesaler in Tampa, Fla., says he didn't even know tariffs still existed until he got two boxes full of bills last year from the trustee of BGR Transportation Co. of Calhoun, Ga.

The ICC has helped him and hundreds like him defeat the trustees' claims. Mr. Johnson says the agency decreed that the tariff that came back to haunt him was invalid in the first place because the now-defunct trucking company never filed the proper paperwork when it changed its name. While Mr. Johnson calls the ICC "filing clerks," he also hopes the agency sticks around.

Under Ms. McDonald, a Democrat, the ICC is trying to make tariffs more relevant. The agency has hired nine new inspectors to read filings. It installed three facsimile machines last month to receive copies of contracts, and it plans to start making tariffs available electronically. The agency has also halved its management ranks, cut paperwork and set up a toll-free telephone number for complaints from citizens ("We call them customers," the agency says). Last week, the commission said it would hold 36 training seminars in 29 states on a tariff law passed by Congress last year. It recently held brown-bag lunches for employees to learn what other employees do.

Congress has an interest in keeping the ICC alive. Despite the agency's lack of real power, the ICC can help lawmakers look important to the folks back home. Members of Congress sometimes pass on complaints to the ICC about moving companies that won't pay after breaking constituents' belongings. And they demand that the ICC hold public hearings when a railroad asks for permission to abandon money-losing stretches of track.

Congressional intervention is largely for show, though. In the past four fiscal years, railroads abandoned enough track to reach Miami from Seattle and back; the track the ICC stopped railroads from giving up would barely make the round trip from Seattle to Tacoma. And the ICC imposed just one fine against an errant mover in that time. (ICC officials say that a phone call is usually enough to get a moving company to shape up, and that the agency puts conditions on many of the rail abandonments it approves.)

Lawmakers' stature depends partly on how many agencies their committees oversee. Proposals to eliminate the ICC have gone nowhere within the Senate and House committees with jurisdiction over the ICC. And when House members outside two such panels offered an amendment last fall to kill the agency's funding, 42 of the 58 committee members voted against it. Rep. John Kasich of Ohio, who cosponsored the amendment, says a fellow Republican "told me he voted against it because I was messing with his jurisdiction."

That support also was evident at a celebration last month to mark the ICC's 107th birthday. The agency formally unveiled a bronze bust of

Clyde Bruce Aitchison, a commissioner from 1917 to 1952, as an eight-man military guard presented the colors and a 20-member chorus sang "God Bless America." House Public Works and Transportation Committee Chairman Norman Mineta displayed an alarm clock that plays "I've Been Working on the Railroad." And the California Democrat told the agency he would defend it against those wanting to cut off "the funding it needs so all of you can do your very, very important jobs."

# 37

# CAR-KILLER POTHOLES HAVE A NEW ENEMY THIS YEAR: ROBOPLOP

## The Vehicle Scans and Fills the Most Pesky Craters

### When It Actually Works

*April 15, 1994*

This country has something like 50 million potholes, and, as Chicago taxi driver Charlie Matthews knows, it takes just one to ruin your day—or your car. Like the one that ate the front end of his Chevrolet Caprice a few years back. Or the one he swears has reappeared at the same spot on Lakeshore Drive ever since he started driving a cab 34 years ago.

"It's like driving an obstacle course," he says. "They need to do something, because what they're doing right now ain't good enough."

What Chicago does right now to attack potholes is what most other cities do: A seven-man crew walks behind a dump truck, scooping grimy patching material into craters and stomping it with their boots. Within an hour, a crew can patch 100 holes. Within months, the patches will be holes again.

But in a basement laboratory at nearby Northwestern University, there sits a machine that would replace the workers: the 20-ton Automated Pavement Repair Vehicle. It carries just two people, but sports $400,000 of high-technology gear, including a 3-D infrared-laser-vision system to scan potholes, two computers to generate a "filling algorithm," a hose to scoop out debris, a hot-air lance to heat the hole and a robotic arm that plops precisely mixed rock and goo— "aggregate" and "emulsion" to those in the trade—into the hole at a force of 60 mph.

Unlike crews who patch holes only in "reasonably humane conditions" (as the government's classic "Pothole Primer" puts it), Northwestern's Roboplop can run at night, in rain, sleet, snow and freezing cold. And the scientists who built it say it will plug holes faster, better, cheaper and more consistently than humans.

That is, if it ever works.

The pothole plugger—actually a converted garbage truck—has had its share of "teething problems," as Richard Johnson, leader of the Northwestern team, puts it. During a recent demonstration for a potential manufacturer, it gurgled to a stop midway through the first hole. Last month, the team fought to prepare the pothole filler for another important showing, but it sat inert for two weeks, four tons of rock stuck in its craw. This week, an exhibition went off smoothly, Mr. Johnson says, though the vehicle's computer-guidance system isn't road-ready yet. The machine's human competitors, shown a drawing while they patch Chicago's narrow North Delphia Street one recent morning, are less than impressed. Can a machine work around manholes, they asked? Can it report a crumbling storm drain or plug a pothole between two parked cars? Can it stop to talk to a homeowner, as supervisor Richard Noreen does? Walking behind his $19-an-hour repair workers, Mr. Noreen says: "Potholes are not easy."

That's certainly true this year, as drivers and their chiropractors already know. Fickle weather has made this spring a particularly prolific pothole period. Water that seeped through cracks in asphalt has frozen and thawed repeatedly, forcing the road above to buckle. Even in a normal year, potholes pose public-policy problems: Scores of highway workers are killed each year while trying to patch the holes, and experts say the holes force the average driver to shake loose $101.12 a year for extra fuel, tire wear and repairs.

In 1989, the federal government offered $1.2 million to anyone who could find a better way to patch roads, and Northwestern's industrial research lab, called BIRL, won the bid. "We knew nothing about repairing holes," says Herbert Underwood, an engineer whose experience was designing transmissions.

They learned. One problem they encountered is that potholes come in all shapes and sizes. A human can tell a manhole from a pothole and can make adjustments while filling the latter. But the machine would get only one look at the depression and patch it out of view of the machine's operator.

Patching materials are unpredictable, too. The pothole plugger apparently choked on an oversized stone during one test run. Rock stopped coming out, but black emulsion fluid kept flowing, turning a pothole into a soup bowl.

Even finding holes for tests has been a challenge. "Our building engineer didn't want us to gouge out the floor," says BIRL scientist John Fildes. At first, they tested the machine's rock-spraying gizmo in an alley behind the lab. The patches seem to have held up, but it is hard to figure out which patches are BIRL's and which are the city's. Now, computer specialist Scott Choi carves test holes out of polystyrene foam (including a heart-shaped pothole for Valentine's Day) and places them under the robot arm at the back of the truck.

In the real world, though, potholes can crop up in less convenient places for the eight-foot-wide truck—near curbs, for instance. The BIRL team considered installing a "side door" to let the robot arm snake out toward tough-to-reach potholes, but dropped the idea because the driver "wouldn't be able to see whether the patching material was striking a pedestrian or hitting a car," says James Blaha, who left the project last fall.

Mr. Blaha says he was discouraged by the expense of automating pothole plugging. He now sells $20,000 human-operated patching kits that fit in a pickup truck. The remaining BIRL researchers insist they can keep their machine's price under $250,000 and say they have had interest from as far away as Japan, Argentina and Poland. But they say they need more money to work out the remaining kinks.

More federal funding is uncertain. On one hand, Transportation Secretary Federico Peña took an interest in the machine after a pothole jolted his car on a road that runs under the 14th Street bridge in Washington. But others worry that the project could be a bottomless pit. James Sorenson, a Federal Highway Administration pavement-repair specialist, recalls the inventor who spent more than $30 million in vain on a machine that would map out asphalt cracks while driving at highway speed.

Some asphalt contractors, such as H. G. "Duke" McCracken of Bernalillo, N.M., say Northwestern shouldn't have sent computers into the battle against potholes in the first place. Mr. McCracken's lower-tech solution is a green truck called "Puff," with a dragon painted on the side. Its snout, controlled with a joystick, can vacuum, torch and "scarify" a pothole before pouring asphalt into it, he says.

Mr. McCracken says the 500-odd potholes he plugged for the city of Albuquerque three years ago are still filled. What's more, Puff won second prize in a local parade. But it is still just a prototype. The pothole business is tough to revolutionize, Mr. McCracken says, because people have been doing it the same way "for years and years and years."

Thirty-one years, in the case of Russell Saletta, Chicago's pavement supervisor. He says his city—which receives 100 pothole complaints each day—has looked at semiautomatic devices, such as Puff, but they all cost two or three times more than the old-fashioned method, commonly known as "throw and go." And some of these "magic wand" patching machines that are supposed to replace human crews have broken down right in front of their demonstrators, he says. "I felt sorry for some of the people."

# 38

# COLLIDING CLICHÉS AND OTHER MISHAPS ON THE TERM PIKE

## The Big Phrase of the Day Is Information Superhighway, and the Traffic Is Terrible

*February 1, 1994*

It's enough to make you beg for a rest stop.

"With bumper-to-bumper traffic expected on the vaunted information superhighway, consumers are apt to be blinded by the glare of oncoming technologies," says *Fortune* magazine. "Remember, some customers will want to be chauffeured, others will want the wheel themselves." But "one way or another, all will be in the driver's seat."

The city of Plano, Texas, should have an "on-ramp" to the information superhighway, a local school official tells a reporter. "We don't want to be too far on the median and too far on the curb."

"The networks," says comedian Sinbad, hosting cable-TV's Ace awards, "are no longer the big HoJo on the information superhighway."

The metaphors are piling up on the electronic interstate like jackknifed tractor-trailers, and there isn't an off-ramp in sight. "I thought we could keep torturing the analogy until people stopped using it," says Allen Rucker, the Los Angeles comedy writer responsible for the Sinbad joke. "We probably failed."

Indeed, the "information superhighway" seems to have unlimited mileage and no brakes. The phrase merged into the fast lane as politicians touted "road maps" for handling rapid changes in telecommunications. Now it's veering out of control.

The media are the biggest road hogs. Consider the accounts of a Los Angeles speech last month by Vice President Al Gore, who claims to have fathered the term "information superhighway." Depending on the story that you read, Mr. Gore was steering down the information superhighway, raising speed limits, installing checkpoints, offering an easier ride, earning his learner's permit or putting the "pedal to the metal." Mr. Gore was seen alternatively as handing industry the keys to the tollbooth or trying to keep disadvantaged people from being "stranded on the shoulder."

Promoters are hitching rides on the "info pike," too. TV ads for MCI Communications Corp. touting the new road have child actress Anna Paquin saying, with an 11-year-old's enthusiasm: "Its speed limit will be the speed of light." David Letterman, in a promo, says his "Late Show" on CBS is "like an information superhighway, without the information."

New twists in the road keep turning up. A telephone trade group talks of wanting to save an "emergency lane" on the superhighway. An NBC official warns of "drive-by shootings on the information superhighway." There are even sharp turns into mixed metaphors—one of them a reference to riverboat gamblers on the mighty thoroughfare.

All of which raises the question: Just what is the information superhighway anyway? The answer is as elusive as the Kansas horizon on I-70.

Some say it's a future network of fiber-optic lines that will stretch across the country, giving everybody hitherto unimagined services through their TV sets. Others say it's the Internet, an existing network that allows people to converse by typing on home computers. Actually, the information superhighway is wide enough to include a slew of activities ranging from off-track betting to videos-on-demand, home shopping and the long-heralded picture phone. Nobody knows whether all that many people will actually want to go with the flow of traffic.

"So far, it's just a lot of puff," says Dennis Baron, a University of Illinois English professor who has been tracking the phrase "information superhighway." Still, he says those who complain about the phrase are merely enshrining it. "If you listen long enough, you'll find them using it, too."

"It's a moronic term," complains Paul Saffo of the Institute for the Future, a Menlo Park, Calif., consulting firm. "Nobody would dare use it on the Internet," he says. Other users would consider them dweebs. But a few minutes later, he is calling Next Inc. workstation computers "the De Lorean of the information highway."

Seagate Technology Inc. chief executive, Alan Shugart, makes fun of the term, too. But aides say that while riding on the New Jersey Turnpike recently, he succumbed to the lure of the road, boasting his diskdrive company was out to put up the signs, sell the maps and own the restaurants on the self-same information superhighway.

Such analogies are causing gridlock in corporate press releases. Thomas Brooksher, a Denver trade-journal publisher, complains that he has to wade through a page of highway expressions before he can figure out just what it is a company is hyping. "If they say 'information highway,' they figure people will read it," he says. "It's like saying 'free sex.'"

The industry has flirted with road imagery since as far back as 1910, when American Telephone & Telegraph Co., in its annual report, promised a telephone system "as universal and as extensive as the highway system." Vice President Gore's father, Sen. Albert Gore of Tennessee, was a big wheel in establishing the Interstate Highway System.

As a child, young Al sat in on congressional hearings that decided the color of signs and the size of lanes on the interstates. He says he coined the phrase "information highway" in 1978 during a meeting with computer-industry officials. Most people, interestingly, are willing to give full credit to Mr. Gore for coming up with the phrase, which he made the center-strip of his vice presidential campaign in 1992.

Now, some folks seem actually to confuse Al Jr.'s highways with Al Sr.'s. Federal Highway Administration officials say they have been asked if they work on the "information superhighway." Talk show host Dick Cavett, kicking off a recent (Information) Superhighway Summit in Los Angeles, said, "When I think of highways, I think of something long and boring that 50,000 people are killed on every year."

And, as was bound to happen, some communications-industry leaders think the metaphor has run out of gas.

But alternatives such as "information canals" and "information skyways" don't have wheels. Technology consultant Charles Morris is promoting "information ocean" (data float around until needed). But even that isn't vast enough for one White House aide, who uses "ideaspace"—discreetly, he says, to avoid offending Mr. Gore.

The vice president isn't yet ready to yield on the "information superhighway." "He still thinks it's an appropriate metaphor," a spokeswoman says. But lately even Mr. Gore has rolled his eyes at what he has wrought: for example, a business worried about becoming "roadkill." Mr. Gore, himself, now sometimes speaks of the metaphor-proof "National Information Infrastructure." Still, the "information superhighway" rolls on. The American Dialect Society voted the phrase Word of the Year for 1993.

# 39

# ROMANCE IN THE AGE OF COMPUTERS: LOTS OF TALK AND NOT MUCH ACTION

*February 13, 1995*

Searching for love on the Internet? There may be plenty of romance in cyberspace, but it isn't always easy to find, as we discovered in a recent dialogue with America Online. By entering a key word, we found news groups that use our search phrase in their name—even if it's only part of another word:

Search phrase: Love.

Results of search for love: Four matching items—alt.pub.cloven-shield (a bulletin board filled with rambling stories set in the Middle Ages), aol.neighborhood.nation.slovenia.soc.culture.slovenia (sample posting: what are your favorite Slovenian albums?) and ont.sflovers. (Ont.sflovers turned out to be a bulletin board for Ontario science fiction lovers, not single female lovers.)

Search phrase: Valentine.

Computer response: No matches were found for this search. Please try a less restrictive search phrase.

Search phrase: Relationship.

Computer response: No matches were found for this search. Please try a less restrictive search phrase.

Search phrase: Friend.

Results of search for friend: Two matching items—alt.tv.friends (fans of the NBC television show "Friends") and comp.unix.user-friendly (fans of the notoriously complex computer-operating system. Sample topic: "Flex++/gflex++ documentation?").

Search phrase: Companion

Computer response: No matches were found for this search. Please try a less restrictive search phrase.

Search phrase: Intelligence.

Computer response: No matches were found for this search. Please try a less restrictive search phrase.

Search phrase: Respect.

Computer response: No matches were found for this search. Please try a less restrictive search phrase.

Search phrase: Talk.

Results of search for talk: 94 matching items. alt.comp.acad-freedom.talk, alt-efftalk, alt-internet.talk-radio, alt-internet.talk.biz arre, alt.internet.talk.haven, alt.internet.talk.of.the.town, alt.internet. talk.shows, alt.kids-talk, alt.radio.talk, alt.soft-sys.tooltalk, alt.tv.talk-shows.daytime, alt.tv.talkshows.late, etc.

# 40

# THERE'S AN EASY SOLUTION TO THIS: LET SANTA DELIVER ALL CANDY CANES

*September 19, 1994*

Who says Washington can't make tough decisions in an election year?

Among other things, the government has recently ruled that Jain art has cultural significance, Nissan Pathfinders are passenger vehicles and candy canes are different from candy.

The candy-cane decision came from the Interstate Commerce Commission after a three-year review. It has Larry Graham, president of the National Confectioners Association, seeing red because it allows trucking companies—in theory, at least—to charge more to ship candy canes. The National Motor Freight Traffic Association, which publishes rate tables that some truckers use to set their rates, has been trying for decades to prove that candy canes are costlier to ship than other candy. It didn't have enough hard evidence until Jane McIntyre, an association official, weighed and measured 417 different candy-cane shipments at loading docks and proved that they take up more space per pound than other candies do. "It's like grading lumber," Ms. McIntyre maintains.

But candy canes are a "real American product," Mr. Graham counters. The Confectioners Association, which had already lost hollow-mold chocolates and marshmallows from the "candy" category, decided to fight to keep candy canes.

The ICC carefully weighed the evidence, including piles of density reports. The candy-cane makers finally lost, but the twist is that they probably have the truckers licked anyhow. Truckers are so eager for business that they are voluntarily shipping candy canes at the lower rate.

Indeed, Ed Emmett, a former ICC commissioner, thinks the candy-cane decision shows the agency's true stripes. "How much money was spent on lawyers and consultants and government employees in this case to set a rate which is virtually meaningless in the real world anyway?" asks Mr. Emmett, who now heads a group of trucking customers.

"If we're not careful, the NMFTA will drag Santa Claus before the ICC for transporting candy canes at the wrong rating."

Actually, the ICC's power to review trucking rates is melting away. Congress passed a law last month saying trucking companies no longer have to file rate documents with the ICC if they don't follow rate tables like the NMFTA's.

# PART SIX

# *Nice Lede!*

In the summer of 1997, Danny returned to the London bureau from a monthlong reporting trip to Iran. Back at the *Journal's* Fleet Street office that Monday morning, he was acting particularly shifty.

"Do you think it's weird that Larry [Ingrassia, London bureau chief and his boss at the time] sent me to do a story on the Iranian election and I'm instead coming back with an Ahed about the world's biggest carpet?" he asked a colleague. (An Ahed is the often-quirky article that runs on page one in the *Journal's* middle column.)

For some reporters, writing about a carpet when you're supposed to be writing about political turmoil could be grounds for dismissal. But this was Danny, who was a master at "ledes"—that first, all-important line of a newspaper story. Like all good opening lines, his lede on the carpet story sucked you in:

> BEN, Iran—This is a small town in search of a really big floor.

Reporter Laurie McGinley sat next to Danny in Washington while he was covering transportation. "One day, he decided to write an Ahed on demolition derbies," Laurie says. "He didn't know what the story was; he just knew there had to be one."

Laurie watched Danny rummage through the wreckage for weeks. Finally, he came out with this:

> TOWER HILL, Ill.—Leonard Pease probably should have chosen an easier sport to reform—like maybe baseball.

Then there was Danny's fighter-pilot story—a rare page-one first-person account about ace-pilot-wannabes.

At the time, Danny was a neophyte in the Atlanta bureau. Somebody told deputy bureau chief Glenn Ruffenach that anyone willing to write a check could go up in vintage fighter planes and participate in mock dogfights. "I knew the story would require actually going up in one of these planes and—frankly—I chickened out," Glenn says. Danny "thought the whole thing would be a kick."

> ATLANTA—Dennis Bachorik enjoys Monet, foreign films and pretending he is a World War II fighter pilot.

The story includes a description of Danny as he reported for flight school.

> Your reporter arrived for duty armed with combat sneakers, a lucky Hawaiian shirt and a double dose of Dramamine. My pilot, Mr. Arrowood, showed me the airsickness bags—"You won't need them," he added—but forgot to explain how the parachute works, which I didn't realize until after takeoff.

Larry Ingrassia recalls his story about Russian fish surgeons who cut open sturgeons to harvest the caviar and then sew the fish back up. "Look!" Danny exclaimed, displaying photographs of the icky procedure to colleagues. "The fish lives!"

Danny filed the story to the unsuspecting Larry, written entirely in verse, playing on the surgeon-sturgeon rhyme. "I thought it was hilarious," Larry recalls. "I sent it to New York with a note saying that I thought they really ought to run the story as filed even though it was way out of the ordinary."

The New York editors were amused but unwilling to break the *Journal* tradition of keeping poetry off the front page. They made Danny rewrite it in prose:

> ASTRAKHAN, Russia—Be aware that patient comfort isn't necessarily a big part of sturgeon surgery. Be warned that knowledge of ichthyological gynecology doesn't necessarily enhance the pleasure of eating caviar.
>
> Now, behold the caviar of the future.

One of Danny's last stories ran on November 14, 2001, the result of the twists and turns that often mark the process of getting a story into the *Journal*.

The story examined the unusual trading of the afghani, the national currency of Afghanistan, and was firmly in the financial-markets territory that Danny rarely covered. But with his eye for the interesting and the absurd, Danny brought the story to life by painting a portrait of the bazaar and the traders in it.

PESHAWAR, Pakistan—As a Muslim, and an ethnic Pashtun, Fazal-e-Maula has some sympathy for the ruling Taliban in Afghanistan. But on September 11, as he watched television replays of airplanes crashing into the World Trade Center in New York, he knew what to do: Buy afghanis.

The afghani, Afghanistan's long-suffering currency, has the perverse tendency to go up whenever sitting governments fall.

The story drew raves. "Your November 14 article on trading in the afghani, Afghanistan's currency, is an example of why I treasure the *Journal*," wrote reader Ryan Baum of Davis, Calif.

Danny wanted the story to run on page one, but Mike Miller, the page-one editor, responded to his proposal with a "classically gentle rejection note," says Amy Stevens, Mike's deputy and a friend of Danny's.

Danny's boss, foreign editor John Bussey, hadn't immediately passed along Mike's rejection note. An hour after sending the proposal, Danny sent Amy an email.

Check one, please:

- Proposal sucked, story sucked.

- Proposal never arrived, story sucked.

- Proposal was okay, story was great, but everyone's freaked out about plane landing in Queens.

- Editors no longer open email because of anthrax fears.

- No point reading foreign stories when Bussey's out of town.

- It's YOU, Danny, YOU, we hate YOU. Now GO AWAY!

Thanks, Danny

Here are some of Danny's ledes and the stories that went under them.

—*H.C.*

# 41

# AMID GLOBAL TURMOIL, WILD TIMES IN TRADING AFGHANIS

*November 14, 2001*

PESHAWAR, Pakistan—As a Muslim, and an ethnic Pashtun, Fazal-e-Maula has some sympathy for the ruling Taliban in Afghanistan. But on September 11, as he watched television replays of airplanes crashing into the World Trade Center in New York, he knew what to do: Buy afghanis.

The afghani, Afghanistan's long-suffering currency, has the perverse tendency to go up whenever sitting governments fall. Mr. Maula, 32 years old, knew that from his 10 years of experience as a currency trader in Peshawar, one of the only places in the world with active trading of afghanis. So as soon as commentators labeled Osama bin Laden the prime suspect in the attack, Mr. Maula says, he figured the Taliban would become a target of the U.S. and "with attacks on the Taliban, the currency would go up."

So it has—94% against the Pakistani rupee, the other currency traded in the Faiz Market here. A small courtyard that functions as an informal afghani currency trading pit here, the market has become hyperactive in recent weeks as the Taliban have taken a pounding. Professional traders such as Mr. Maula, as well as amateurs with time on their hands, have turned neat profits. As Northern Alliance opposition troops approached Kabul, hundreds of dealers, many of them Afghans who fled U.S. bombing, have elbowed and jostled each other, slapping hands to make and accept bids, and cheering when the rate notched up on rumor of Taliban battlefield defeats. "I have taken four aspirins, these people make so much noise," complained Mohammed Ilyas, who sells scarves from a courtyard shop. "I pray to Allah that the Afghanistan issue gets resolved, and these people go back to Afghanistan so I can have a normal business." One day recently, trading continued even as tear-gas fumes wafted over from a nearby demonstration.

"They were crying, but they didn't stop trading."

Even more than currencies in other developing countries, the market in afghanis is unusual. For one thing, the currency hasn't been printed by the Taliban government since it came to power in 1996. Instead, the afghani actually comes from printing presses run by the opposition Northern Alliance, and there are two varieties. Afghanis printed under the auspices of the alliance's late Tajik commander, Ahmed Shaw Masood, are more widely accepted in Taliban areas than those printed by the alliance's Uzbek commander, Abdul Rashid Dostum, though only by the last two digits of the serial number can one tell them apart.

The market exchange rate also varies widely from the bank exchange rate. For example, according to the quoted exchange rate, it cost 4,750 afghanis to buy $1. In the bazaars where trading is done, the afghani is worth a lot less—it costs about 34,000 afghanis to buy $1 (albeit that means the afghani has risen 56% against the dollar since the conflict began, because then it cost 78,000 to buy $1 in mid-September). Similarly, after the recent run-up in the value of the afghani, a rupee is worth 606 afghanis, while the quoted bank rate has it worth only 74 afghanis. It's in places like the Faiz Market where the real action is. Nobody runs the market, and there are no written rules. In 1983, Pakistan's central bank declared that afghanis could be traded without a currency dealer's license. Dealers convene a "Loya Jirga," their version of a traditional Afghan tribal council, to resolve disputes. Like official currency exchanges, Faiz Market keeps regular hours, offers futures trading, and favors big dealers: They're the ones who can make occasional telephone contact with Afghanistan, and in case of shortages they order sacks of afghanis sent across the supposedly closed border.

The afghani's value has plummeted so far over the years that the highest note, 10,000 afghanis, has to be carried in thick stacks to be of any value. Traders quote the exchange rate as the number of Pakistan rupees it takes to buy 100,000 afghanis. That rate was 27,000 in the early 1970s, and fell to around 85 rupees under Taliban rule. Trading become so quiet that Mr. Maula and his brothers considered closing down their shop in 1998.

But September 11 galvanized the market, bringing prospects of a new government, and, perhaps, economic development. Last Saturday's trading is typical. By the time the market opened at 8 a.m., the Northern Alliance opposition captured the city of Mazar-e-Sharif, and the afghani started trading at 154 rupees for 100,000 afghanis, up 10 from the previous day. One of Mr. Maula's traders has been in touch with currency dealers in the Afghanistan capital, Kabul. "We have received news that the rate in Kabul is 160," he whispered. Mr. Maula, sitting crosslegged in his tiny shop, remains cool. "Don't panic. Take your time, we'll wait for the right moment." Toward noon, as hawkers pass by with chewing tobacco and roasted corn, the currency crept up to 164 on talk of further Northern Alliance gains. Suddenly, two traders near Mr. Maula's shop exchanged angry words, and fists start flying. "When the price fluctuates we have such problems," said a bystander. (The brawl was actually over a used-car deal.)

By 1 p.m., the afghan settled down to 160, amid market speculation Gen. Dostum had been arrested. By 1:30, it notches up on rumors the Northern Alliance had captured another town. By 2 p.m., settlement time, Mr. Maula had pocketed big profits for the day.

What moves the afghani market isn't always what's newsworthy from Western eyes. A headline quoting Osama bin Laden saying he had nuclear weapons had no effect. But rumors last month that exiled king Zahir Shah was coming to Pakistan to preside over a new Afghan government briefly pushed the currency above 300 rupees.

Yesterday, the afghani traded at 165 rupees for 100,000 afghanis, up from 155 the day before, showing traders like the Taliban's ouster from Kabul but want to see a new government take control.

Some traders acknowledge mixed feelings about profiting from the demise of the Taliban, which had its roots in Peshawar's religious schools. "It's not my regular job," Younus Khan, a 25-year-old cloth trader with a shaggy Taliban-style beard, said by way of apology, after gaining the equivalent of $1,500 in Saturday's trading. Then his face brightens. "I'll give this money as a donation for jihad purposes," he says.

**Yesterday's Market Activity**
The dollar moved higher against all its major counterparts and reached its best level against the euro since early August as traders aggressively bought the U.S. currency in reaction to reports of military successes in Afghanistan.

The dollar also made solid gains against the yen—touching a high at 121.74 yen—underpinned by the market's growing conviction that the Bank of Japan remains ready to act to counter any signs of significant dollar/yen selling.

Further indications that the American Airlines crash in New York was accidental rather than terrorist-related supported the dollar as well.

"The dollar's value is based on the apparent collapse of the Taliban, which has sparked hopes that things could be moving to a conclusion," said Alex Beuzelin, market analyst at Ruesch International in Washington, D.C.

In late New York trading, the euro was at 88.09 cents, lower than 88.60 cents in London and well down from 89.47 cents late Monday in New York. The dollar rose to 121.67 yen, above 121.15 yen in London and up sharply from 120.39 yen late Monday. The dollar was also at 1.6710 Swiss francs, up sharply from 1.6365 francs. The pound, meanwhile, declined to $1.4411 from $1.4543.

A broad-based return of confidence to the dollar was also reflected in strong gains for the U.S. stock market.

With the euro now barely holding above 88 cents, analysts think the dollar will push ahead in coming sessions.

"The economic and geopolitical news suggests the dollar is going to continue its gains," said Mr. Beuzelin.

The euro, meanwhile, isn't helped by a suggestion by German Chancellor Gerhard Schroeder that he will resign if his request for German troops to help allied forces in Afghanistan isn't passed by the German parliament.

The dollar also rose to an intraday high against the Swiss franc around 1.6720 francs—its highest level since September 11—as traders cut back so-called safe-harbor positions that they had flocked to when it was initially feared that the New York crash was terrorism.

"Since we got this apparent good news from Afghanistan and also the good news that [Monday's airplane crash in New York] wasn't terrorist-driven, we're seeing a major unwinding of Swiss franc positions," said Jan Poser, an economist at Bank Saracen in Zurich.

Following the dollar's fall against the yen Monday, Zembei Mizoguchi, international bureau chief at the Japanese Ministry of Finance, said the ministry would take foreign-exchange market action if it were needed to prevent yen from rising, adding that he believes the "dollar should strengthen," as U.S. economic fundamentals are sound.

The pound fell against the dollar as traders expressed disappointment with sterling's inability to keep up with the U.S. unit—despite the strong U.K. economy and the problems afflicting other major currencies.

Elsewhere, in intraday trading the dollar hit another all-time high against the South African rand at 9.7263 rands to the dollar before slipping back in later trading.

*—Saeed Azhar and John Hardy of Dow Jones Newswires contributed to this article.*

# 42

# SEPARATE PEACE: WHY ETHNIC CLEANSING, ONCE UNDER WAY, IS SO DIFFICULT TO REVERSE

## Few Serbs Who Were Chased From Croatia in 1995 Have Made It Back Home

## A 'Normal Thing' in Balkans

*April 22, 1999*

KNIN, Croatia—Dusan Dujic has a seemingly modest ambition: to die in his own house.

Mr. Dujic hasn't set foot in the small two-story home in this railroad town since he and thousands of other ethnic Serbs fled a Croatian army onslaught called "Operation Storm" in 1995. A city document confirms that he owns the building, but the ethnic Croatians occupying it won't budge, and Croatian officials refuse to evict them.

"I have no country except this one, and it doesn't want me," says Mr. Dujic, a 69-year-old former hotel manager, breaking into tears at a side-walk cafe near his house. "I was a manager. I always had some money," he says. "Now I have to crawl around here like a dog."

Former co-worker Tatjana Grgic, an ethnic Croatian who works in the Red Cross office here, says Mr. Dujic was no Serb nationalist. "He was a good man," she says. "But the war has done what it has done. It's a normal thing."

Normal in the Balkans, perhaps. To Western countries, banishing ethnic minorities from a region is officially abhorrent. The North Atlantic Treaty Organization has responded to Serbia's "ethnic cleansing" of Albanian minorities in the Serbian province of Kosovo with a punishing, four-week bombing campaign. The U.S. vows to return an estimated 600,000 Kosovo refugees to their homes.

The experience of Croatia, Serbia's next-door neighbor, suggests that a massive return is a pipe dream. Croatia, which split from the Federal Republic of Yugoslavia in 1991, has welcomed back fewer than 20% of its 350,000 departed Serbs. Almost all the returnees are elderly people wanting to claim pensions or be buried with their parents.

Serbs are "free to come," says Croatia's assistant foreign minister, Josip Paro. But while proclaiming that policy, Croatia encouraged ethnic Croatians to occupy Serb homes and stalled thousands of Serbs trying to get Croatian citizenship or reclaim their property. Now, it is helping Serbs unload their homes at a steep discount, and is building houses for ethnic-Croat refugees in formerly Serb villages. "It's a slow, bureaucratic ethnic cleansing," charges Ivan Zvonimir Cicak, a Croatian opposition figure and human-rights activist.

Ethnic cleansing tends to stick, and not only because of government policy. Younger Serbs have made new lives in Yugoslavia or in the Serbian-run section of Bosnia, another former Yugoslav republic. Others have emigrated to richer Western countries, or hope to keep their chances of emigration alive by preserving their refugee status. By some estimates, half of those who fled Croatia will never try to return.

Many Croatians, convinced that "war criminals" are coming back, predict trouble from returning Serbs. "I think they should be eliminated," says a Croatian soldier and Operation Storm participant who identifies himself only as Ante, drinking a beer during a rock concert in Knin to benefit war widows. Human-rights activists say several returning Serbs in a nearby village have been killed by fresh mines planted in haystacks.

Even some liberals wonder if separation is best. "We tried one way and it didn't work," says Zagreb architect Nikola Oreskovic, in a bus rolling past Croat villages destroyed by Serbs and Serb villages destroyed by Croats. "Maybe we should try another way."

Ethnic cleansing, horrible as it is, can be effective. Republika Srpska, an almost completely Serb ministate within Bosnia, has enjoyed relative tranquility and growing international acceptance, while tensions are rising between Muslims and Croats who live side by side in Bosnia. Croatia is poor but secure, and when it opened its airspace to NATO for the current bombing raids, the U.S. lifted an arms embargo, despite lingering concerns about Operation Storm.

That operation was "the most efficient ethnic cleansing we've seen in the Balkans," says Carl Bildt, former European Community mediator in the Balkans. "There was a blinking yellow light given to it in 1995, and there hasn't really been any sustained international pressure to reverse it." One of the few critics of the operation, he says acquiescing to ethnic separation would be "horrifying" because the Balkans' ethnic patchwork is so complex.

Croatia denies any ethnic cleansing, noting that it urged Serbs to stay put during Operation Storm. But soldiers also shelled residential areas, killed civilians and let Croats burn and plunder Serb homes, according to a United Nations report. Many intact homes in Knin still bear the painted words "Croat—Don't Touch."

Serbs came here to the Krajina region in the 14th century, when the Turks routed them from Kosovo. The Austro-Hungarian empire gave the Serbs of Krajina (the name means "frontier") free land in exchange for defending the empire's eastern border from the Turks. Serbs became the city dwellers, and the majority in their region, despite Croatian fascists' attempts to exterminate Serbs during World War II. Krajina Serbs broke into armed rebellion in 1991 as Yugoslavia collapsed, and Knin, with its ancient hilltop fortress, became the capital of the Republic of Serbian Krajina.

The republic lasted four years and fell in four days. Knin's Serbs had just minutes to pack on August 5, 1995, when their army warned them to leave. Many thought they would be back within a few days. Mr. Dujic says he was at his cousin's house at a nearby village. He had no time to drive back to Knin to grab the family jewelry. Instead, he and his relatives took his son's car, which had the most gas, and drove to Belgrade, capital of Yugoslavia in the Republic of Serbia.

The flight of about 200,000 Krajina Serbs set off an ethnic chain reaction. Many refugees pushed east into Serb-held territory in Bosnia. In the city of Banja Luka, Josipu Guroljevski, an ethnic Croat, says Serbs pounded on his door August 16 and told him to leave the following morning or die. He and his wife, Stazji, spent a month as refugees before hearing of empty houses in Knin. Croatia gave citizenship to any ethnic Croatian, and eventually 6,000 Croatians from Bosnia would settle in and around Knin.

The Guroljevskis say they went to City Hall and got a list of available houses. Mr. Dujic's house was in the best repair, with room for relatives upstairs. The furniture was overturned, the rooms looted and humid; but after painting and repair, the house became the Guroljevski's home, with an official occupancy permit. A Virgin Mary hangs on the wall. Potted plants sit outside the door.

Mr. Dujic says he wrote a letter to Knin in October 1995, saying he wanted to come back. But even when Croatia allowed Serbs to return, it made it difficult for them to get Croatian citizenship: One consulate where refugees went to get Croatian papers wouldn't allow anybody to enter without Croatian papers, Western officials say. By April 1997, Mr. Dujic had his papers and was staying with his wife in a friend's house as he tried to reclaim the home he had built nearly four decades before.

"Let him wait. We're waiting, too," says Stazji Guroljevski, in Mr. Dujic's living room. She says a Serb is occupying her newly built home in Banja Luka, and "for me they're all the same." Even if their home were empty, the Guroljevskis say fears for their safety would keep them away. And they say they can't afford to buy another home in Croatia, because Mr. Guroljevski received just one month's salary last year from his work as a night watchman at a defunct factory. They might consider a free home, but, "we don't want something worse than this," says Mrs. Guroljevski. Many ethnic Serbs, tired of waiting, are selling out their interests to Croatia's new government Agency for Property Negotiation. One private agent, Augustin Blazevic, says Serbs get about half the value of their homes because "nobody wants to buy a house with somebody inside." Mr. Dujic says he won't sell out.

Croatia, under international pressure, set up housing commissions last year to decide who owns a house and tell the temporary occupier to move somewhere else. On January 15, Mr. Dujic won his decision from Knin's Housing Commission. "This is a piece of paper that means nothing," he says.

Indeed, the Knin Housing Commission has received 585 applications and reviewed 80 cases since September, keeping them in thin yellow folders, but it has returned only eight homes to owners. International monitors say none of those homes were occupied. Knin officials say Croatia's plan doesn't require them to evict people if no other homes are ready.

"We have to be patient," says Ivo Jazinovic, a Croat from Bosnia who is chairman of Knin's five-member (three Croats, two Serbs) housing commission. "Every case that the housing commission works on, it's deciding at least three destinies." Mr. Jazinovic, a 35-year-old engineer with a ready grin, himself occupied a vacated Knin apartment under a law that gave Croats tenancy rights if the renter was gone for more than six months. He knows of only one Croat who has gone back to Banja Luka since the war ended, and says, "My personal attitude in life is that man has to go forward, not backward."

To provide new homes, Croatia presented a $2.5 billion housing plan to international donors in December, but collected just $25 million. Donors are hesitant partly because Croatia is doing "ethnic engineering" as it builds, says Branimir Radev, a monitor with the Organization for Security and Cooperation in Europe.

A case in point is Kistanje, a village near Knin, where the Croatian government has helped move ethnic-Croat immigrants from Kosovo into buildings owned by Serbs. The village is a bizarre mix of burned-out, roofless brick hulks (on one wall sarcastic grafiti proclaims: "We Repaired This for the Owner") and well-lighted clothing boutiques. Some businesses carry the name Janjevo, the town in Kosovo from which most of Kistanje hails.

In a pizzeria, owner Vinko Mazarekic turns down his Rod Stewart compact disk and explains how he arrived. Kosovo's gold and silver mines attracted Croatian settlers centuries before, but Croats as well as Albanians suffered recent persecution. Mr. Mazarekic left in 1993, traveled around Croatia, and finally decided to go to Kistanje because of government aid and low taxes. The government repaired the roof and floor of the bar he occupied, he says. Mr. Mazarekic belittles the returning Serbs.

"They want to expel people who have seven or eight children, to leave everything because of one old man," he says, shaking his head. "We just want to do something useful. It's time to leave us alone."

That's pretty much what Croatia is doing. The government recently started building 170 tidy brick homes in Kistanje. The U.S. has promised $200,000 for the infrastructure. Croatia initially said new ethnic-

Croat immigrants from Kosovo would get the homes, but Western officials protested, so Croatia agreed to reserve 20 homes for returning Serbs.

Croatia has deflected most diplomatic pressure. Dusan Karanovic, a Serb who returned to Kistanje in 1996 only to be evicted from his home by ethnic Croats, gained support from two U.S. ambassadors and the Croatian ombudsman. Still, his Zagreb lawyer, Slobodan Budak, says the case has bounced around the bureaucracy so much that he isn't sure where it now stands. "It's complicated, on purpose," he says.

The Krajina region seems in little danger of going Serb. Before the war, 11% of the citizens in the Knin municipality were Croats. Now Knin is half the size, and 71% Croat. Streets have new Croatian names. At the police station, where a dozen elderly Serbs line up each morning to get documents signed, all the officers are Croats. Serbian staff members were cleared from the hospital and schools as well, and replaced with Croats from Bosnia, says Knin economist and activist Nevena Zunjic.

Residents compete for economic crumbs. The region has rocky soil, a moribund railroad and a small factory that makes screws. Most people live from government handouts of about $100 a month, and even that has been drying up. Croatians from Bosnia say they are second-class citizens because they don't qualify for the free heating-wood and fertilizer given to returning Serbs. The few young Serbs trickling in say they are avoiding being drafted or bombed in Serbia. Elsewhere, Krajina Serbs are looking abroad. In Bar, a port town on the coast of the Yugoslavia republic Montenegro, Serbs recently petitioned the U.N. to go to Western Europe, as some Kosovar refugees are doing. Some Serbs came to Bar because it was the last stop on the railroad line when they fled Croatia. They occupied some abandoned wooden shacks called "the barracks," and they survive by selling fish or cigarettes.

Among the barracks residents is Ranka Milosevic, 43, who owned a tavern in the Croatian mountain town of Slunj. She says a lawyer is trying to retrieve her home from the Croatian villager who occupied it. She wants to sell it. When Ms. Milosevic visited Slunj last year, she syas neighbors had her arrested. "I'll never go back," she says, shaking her head. "We all want to go abroad somewhere."

In Slunj, neighbors dispute her account. Across the town square from Ms. Milosevic's house, a Catholic church that was burned during the 1991 Serb uprising is still being repaired. In the rectory, over brandy, Rev. Petar Bogut notes that the law says nobody should lose property, the church says to love your enemy, and no one accuses Ms. Milosevic of atrocities. Still, he says, covering his face with his hands, "maybe it would be best for her" to stay away.

# 43

# NO OPENINGS: EX-BCCI EMPLOYEES SAY BANK'S NOTORIETY LEFT THEM UNHIRABLE

## Their Lawsuit Alleges 'Stigma' of Affiliation; Opponents Lay the Blame on Racism

## Tony Blair's Wife Leads Fight

*March 1, 1999*

LONDON—If you were a banker, would you hire a man whose resume included a long stint at the most infamous rogue bank of the 1980s?

"I wouldn't take him," says banker Mesbah Islam. "Why should I go into an area that's doubtful or questionable?"

Actually, Mr. Islam is speaking about his own resume. He is a 54-year-old former senior manager of Bank of Credit & Commerce International, which collapsed in 1991 in a fraud and money-laundering scandal. He has spent most of the past eight years on welfare, sending out job letters: 540 at his last count. When he lists BCCI as his last place of employment, he says he gets rejected; when he lists "an international Middle East bank," he says he gets an application form—and then gets rejected.

Now, Mr. Islam and 358 other former BCCI workers in England want the bank to pay for what they say is the "stigma" caused to their careers. They have enlisted one of the most powerful labor lawyers in Britain, Cherie Booth, wife of Prime Minister Tony Blair. And they are getting a serious hearing in the Royal Courts of Justice. The case has dragged on for three months, delved into thorny issues of race and competence, and run up legal costs on the order of $3 million. The workers are breaking new ground in employee law in England, and possibly beyond. The House of Lords overturned an 88-year-old legal precedent to allow the case to go to trial, saying a business could be forced to pay damages for breaking its implicit contract with employees to operate honestly. How much in damages, though, nobody knows: Even Ms. Booth has acknowledged that it is "nebulous" to try to tally damages for the lost income of thousands of jobs the workers may or may not have won if they didn't have the BCCI "badge of uncertainty." The case also is an example of why it is taking so much time and money to finally close the books on BCCI. As of early 1998, the English liquidation, led by the accounting firm Deloitte & Touche, had recovered $2.8 billion, mostly through settlements with BCCI's Middle Eastern backers. But the effort has also run up $604.5 million in costs over six years. The sums left to recover are smaller now, but legal costs are rising, as various lingering BCCI disputes go to court.

The stigma case alone has filled the courtroom with more than 300 bound folders of evidence—and that is just to determine how much compensation, if any, five employees in test cases should receive. After that, wrangling can begin over settlements for the other 354 workers. Courts will also hear a separate claim that BCCI misled workers about its financial condition, and an appeal of the December dismissal of 130 additional "stigma" claims from workers who had signed no-sue agreements with BCCI at the time they were laid off.

"This could easily go another eight years," says Mohammed Qayyum, a former BCCI manager who helped launch the employee legal campaign from his paper-strewn apartment in central London. In a way, the apartment itself was responsible for the legal fight. Like many BCCI workers, Mr. Qayyum took advantage of BCCI's low-interest employee loans, borrowing GBP 100,000 (about $160,000 at the current exchange rate) to buy the flat. After they lost their jobs, he and others stopped paying. "If I didn't have that salary, I wouldn't have taken that loan," Mr. Qayyum says.

Six years of negotiations failed to produce a settlement to pay a reduced amount on the $50 million of loans. "I think there are employees who don't want to settle at any cost," says Bernard Clark, an attorney representing creditors, who so far have received 40 cents on the dollar from the world-wide liquidation. The English liquidators took the former BCCI employees to court. The workers fired back with countersuits on issues ranging from stigma to back vacation pay. The employees have been able to keep up the fight because they qualified for free, government-provided legal aid shortly after losing their jobs. Just as the workers were adding Ms. Booth to their legal team last year, her husband's government was enacting reforms to make it harder for lawyers to use legal aid for cases that don't have a strong chance of success. But Mr. Qayyum says the new rules came too late to affect the stigma case, and that he is certain workers will win some damages.

Stigma is a tricky thing to prove, though.

"Am I not stigmatized?" declares former BCCI loan officer Shafquat Aziz, in his modest home in east London. He points to a stack of rejection letters from banks, airlines, a supermarket chain. But all the letters use boilerplate language, and none mentions BCCI. Mr. Aziz says that during interviews, employers have asked him what happened with the bank. Mr. Aziz, normally garrulous, says he changes the subject when BCCI comes up.

Mr. Aziz, 48, was a schoolteacher before he took his job at BCCI in 1981, answering an advertisement in a local newspaper. He says that BCCI trained him in loan-review procedures, but that his superiors often seemed to violate them. In 1986, he moved to the Oxford Street branch in London. He says he was shocked one day when a Spanish-speaking man was ushered in the back door carrying a garbage bag full of greenbacks.

So if he thought BCCI might be laundering money, why didn't he quit? "Good question," he says, driving his 16-year-old Datsun past BCCI's old Leadenhall Street headquarters, temporarily occupied by Lloyd's Registry. "As an Asian, I knew what my chances would be to find work" outside BCCI, he says.

That is precisely the point the other side is making. Though based in London and later Abu Dhabi, BCCI was founded by a Pakistani and employed mostly South Asians. Lawyers for BCCI's liquidators have produced studies trying to show that people of Pakistani origin have a hard time finding jobs in London. The lawyers say that the more that employees are victims of racial discrimination, the less they are victims of stigma, and thus the less compensation they should receive. But BCCI employees say that approach, in itself, is illegal racial discrimination. Some workers still think BCCI was a good bank destroyed because of its efforts to help developing countries. And that raises another sensitive question: How many BCCI employees actually knew the bank was operating criminally? Soon after the bank was shut down, one liquidator drew cries of protests from workers by saying BCCI was rotten from top to bottom. More recently, after two months of negotiations, the two sides agreed to a list of 41 employees responsible for BCCI misdeeds, including misuse of funds and fictitious loan accounts. Many of those workers have been convicted.

The other employees, including the five test cases, were presumed to be in the clear. But on February 17, the hearing ground to a halt for a week as liquidators presented newly unearthed documents from one former executive's personnel file, in hopes that he would step down as a test case. That didn't happen, and the testimony has now resumed.

Liquidators blame employees' age, lack of skills and half-hearted job searches for their inability to find new work, and they also cite the soft job market in 1991 when BCCI shut down. Job counselors say they agree. "Having the BCCI name on the resume in no way prejudices you," says Shaun McCarthy, group managing director of Jonathan Wren recruiters in London. Still, it is "incredible, given the scale of the frauds" at BCCI, to think the employers weren't hesitating to hire from BCCI, Ms. Booth declares in her opening remarks. She notes that many potential employers lost deposit money themselves.

Preparing for the first two test-case employees, Ms. Booth figures they are in for a grilling. "They're going to get slaughtered," she says, scribbling notes in the hall outside the court at the Thomas More Building here.

Former BCCI clerk Ismail Suleiman Mayet takes the witness stand. The solicitor's barrister, Christopher Jeans, starts questioning why Mr. Mayet once called himself Pakistani on one job application but later signed a statement calling himself Indian. Mr. Jeans points to sloppy penmanship and improper subject-verb agreement in one job application, and asks: "Did you seriously expect to get an interview after sending in a form like that?"

Mr. Mayet's strongest evidence is a 1992 letter from a Saudi company saying the Saudis can't hire Mr. Mayet because of "adverse publicity" surrounding his previous employer. Mr. Jeans labels the letter "bogus," noting that an investigation in Saudi Arabia shows the company was incorporated in 1993. Employees hired their own lawyer in Jidda to help prove the company existed before.

The second test case, former payroll officer Syed Badshah Nawab

Husain, gets three days of cross-examination. Wasn't he doing charity work on BCCI time? No, he insists. Why did he return late from several vacations? "It is the Third World," he explains. Why did he make it seem on job applications that he passed chemistry and physics courses in 1965 even though he hadn't? "I was just in a rush," he says. Why didn't he file more job applications before the stigma case started brewing? He says he was suffering from depression, and also was writing a book. Mr. Jeans even reads a letter from Mr. Husain's personnel file warning that his slow payment of a $13,000 home loan, obtained with BCCI's backing, "gives the bank a bad name."

The idea behind using test cases was to come up with some general guidelines for assessing stigma damages. But the testimony descends deeper and deeper into particular stories. Mr. Husain claims that before he was turned down for a post-office franchise, an interviewer asked him "how many bad habits" he learned at BCCI. The liquidators have called upon the interviewers as witnesses to rebut the claim. Meanwhile, questioning that was expected to last three days is entering its third week.

In Charles Dickens' 1853 novel "Bleak House," a civil suit drags on so long that one participant takes up residence above a Chancery Lane junk shop to follow the machinations in the nearby courthouse. As the BCCI case proceeds, Mr. Aziz has finally found a part-time job at a hardware shop, also off Chancery Lane, and breaks away to watch the proceedings from the gallery. Shaking his head, he whispers, "The solicitors, the liquidators, they're all trying to make money off our misery."

# 44

# FORTUNES OF PEACE: ISRAEL'S NETANYAHU, HIS SUPPORT ERODING, CALLS EARLY ELECTIONS

## Premier's Go-Slow Approach on Withdrawal Alienates Right and Left Alike

### The Opposition Hires Carville

*December 22, 1998*

JERUSALEM—Benjamin Netanyahu came to power in 1996 by appealing to Israel's right wing. His government fell yesterday in a frantic search for the country's political center. After a fractious debate, Israel's Knesset voted not to support Mr. Netanyahu's conditions on further Israeli withdrawals from the occupied territories and then decided, 81-30, to disband and call early elections. The fall of the government in America's main Mideast ally is sure to place the landmark peace deal between the Israelis and the Palestinians in suspension and raise regional tensions.

Yet much as Americans seem at odds with the goings-on in their capital of late, Israelis in general appear much less divided over the peace process than their politicians are. As recently as last week, 70% of the population supported the Wye Plantation accord, a deal brokered by President Clinton under which Israel would withdraw troops from Palestinian areas. Many Israelis say they simply want peace talks to go slower than they did before Mr. Netanyahu became prime minister, but faster than they did after Mr. Netanyahu gained power, and to trust the person conducting the talks.

Indeed, the fall of Mr. Netanyahu's right-wing government shows the difficulties of satisfying a society riven by wide divisions: between young secular Jews in the cafes of Tel Aviv and young Orthodox Jews in the Yeshivas of Jerusalem; between new immigrants and established immigrants; between established European immigrants and established Oriental immigrants. With only a one-person majority in the Knesset, Mr. Netanyahu's Likud coalition veered from hard line to soft to maintain its hold, and it stalled economic reform to keep special interests happy. Yesterday, it paid the price.

Now, Mr. Netanyahu, who at 49 years old represents a new generation of Israeli politicians, has become the first Israeli prime minister to see his government dissolved within two years. "It's inevitable," says Natan Sharansky, one of several cabinet members who had unsuccessfully urged Mr. Netanyahu to try to reach out to the opposition Labor Party. "Just when we're going to the most critical decisions in the history of the Jewish people, they should need to look to a much broader consensus."

Whether Mr. Netanyahu or his rivals can forge a consensus in the coming elections could help determine the future of peace in the Middle East. Already, Palestinian leaders, frustrated with the on-again, off-again way Mr. Netanyahu has carried out withdrawals from the West Bank under the 1993 Oslo peace agreement, are threatening to declare an independent Palestinian state in May. And in coming years, Israel will see even-more-contentious negotiations with the Palestinians over the future of Jerusalem and, presumably, with Syria over a broader Middle East peace.

Palestinian officials would rather work with a non-Netanyahu government. So, too, would Clinton administration officials, though they try not to advertise it. A senior U.S. official involved in the peace process recently warned colleagues that any gloating over the fall of Israel's government or anti-Netanyahu remarks would only help re-elect the Likud bloc—an outcome the administration doesn't want. Last week, Mr. Netanyahu complained when U.S. Commerce Secretary William Daley publicly suggested that it might take an election in Israel to achieve progress on implementing the Wye accord, and when Mr. Clinton said, in Gaza, that Palestinians should pursue peace for the people of Israel, not its government.

Mr. Netanyahu's main rival, Israeli Labor Party leader Ehud Barak, 56, is trying to pattern himself on Bill Clinton in 1992. He even has hired several of Mr. Clinton's advisers from that campaign, including James Carville, and traveled to Germany and Britain to see how left-of-center parties in those countries won victory by turning to the right. Mr. Barak is pledging to focus on Israel's weak economy, and though his rhetoric is different, his prescriptions vary little from Mr. Netanyahu's.

"You need a microscope to see the difference between Netanyahu and Ehud-on policy," says Alon Liel, a Barak adviser. "It just goes by personality."

The trouble is, Israel's second generation of leaders has yet to produce a commanding personality to match Yitzhak Rabin, the Labor prime minister assassinated by a right-wing extremist three years ago. Mr. Barak, a former chief of staff of Israel's armed forces, is a drab speaker who has fumbled some of his attempts to appeal to voters.

He raised an outcry when he said he "would have joined a terrorist organization" if he had been born a Palestinian, later saying it was a slip. Some Labor voters call him "Like Bibi," not just because he was in the same army commando unit as Benjamin "Bibi" Netanyahu, but also because of his habit of political swerving.

Then there's Israel's version of Colin Powell: Amnon Lipkin-Shahak, the 54-year-old army chief of staff who is leaving his post and is expected to help form a party called Center. Mr. Shahak, a well-liked man with a self-deprecating sense of humor, has done little to clarify his views, beyond delivering a subtle dig at Mr. Netanyahu during a recent memorial service for Mr. Rabin. Dubbed "The Prince of Silence," he has nonetheless become a darling of the Israeli media. "People talk so much here that when you have someone who keeps his mouth shut, he's an idol," says Daniel Ben Simon, a columnist for the liberal *Haaretz* newspaper.

The other reason Mr. Shahak is getting so much attention here is that Israel's two main parties both show signs of fading, at least for now. In recent municipal elections, parties representing Russian immigrants and Sephardic Orthodox Jews made big gains, while Labor and Likud posted losses. The two big parties are expected to lose more ground in the coming general elections, too. (The bill approved yesterday would disband the government before its term is to expire in 2000, paving the way for elections sometime in 1999. The bill still must pass a second and third round of voting.)

That makes sense, given that Israelis tend to identify themselves as centrists, according to Dafna Goldberg-Anaby of pollster Gallup Israel. A prime minister who seems less extreme than Mr. Netanyahu could "change the whole atmosphere," she says.

Indeed, even though Russian immigrants have turned Israeli society slightly to the right, polls show a rising percentage of right-wing voters support the general idea of making peace with Palestinians. Twenty-year-old paratrooper Dima Feldman, who emigrated from the Ukraine seven years ago, says he voted for Mr. Netanyahu last time, but won't this time. "He hasn't moved forward the process, and the situation is only deteriorating," he says.

Of course, it is hard to predict how this general longing for peace will play out. Suicide bombings and other terrorist acts have a way of making many Israelis change their minds on their votes; a spate of terrorist attacks before the 1996 election was one reason Mr. Netanyahu prevailed—by a razor-thin majority.

And Israelis aren't writing off Mr. Netanyahu's chances to prevail again. Many politicians are still deciding which faction to join. The Labor Party is in debt, while Mr. Netanyahu, who has raised money successfully from wealthy American Jews, has built a war chest for Likud, though some donors could start channeling funds to opponents from the right.

Still, Mr. Netanyahu is "bruised" by his attempts to keep power, policy adviser David Bar-Illan concedes. "He has made some tactical errors, but the nature of the coalition has made it difficult to continue," he says. "The moment of truth everyone expected has come."

Mr. Netanyahu appeared on the scene as the first of a new generation of Israeli politicians. Forceful, telegenic and ideological, he spent a large part of his career in the U.S. as an Israeli diplomat. But critics say he soon showed an arrogant side: After the election, he made little effort to make peace with Labor, instead forming his ruling coalition from religious parties and other conservative factions.

Mr. Netanyahu's election was the first under a quasi-American system whereby the prime minister is elected directly, rather than by the winning party in the Knesset. That electoral reform was supposed to strengthen the prime minister and lessen the power of small parties. In effect, though, the change fragmented the Knesset further by prompting Israelis to start focusing on narrow parochial issues when casting their votes for Knesset members. "We have really no more parties in Israel; what we have is lobbies," Mr. Bar-Illan says.

Mr. Netanyahu got a reputation for going a bit too far as he struggled to hold together the lobbies. Politicians accused him of offering the same job to more than one person. Israeli radio broadcast his telling a Sephardic rabbi that leftists had "forgotten what it is to be Jewish." A gesture to the Palestinians was often followed by a nod to right-wingers.

Things got tougher when Israel's growth began to slow, partly because of the Asian economic crisis and investors reacting to Middle East tensions. Mr. Netanyahu's religious supporters had backed him with the slogan "Bibi is good for the Jews." This year, bumper stickers appeared asking: "So, Jews, is it good for you?"

This fall, Mr. Netanyahu and Palestinian Authority Chairman Yasser Arafat signed a U.S.-brokered agreement for an Israeli troop withdrawal, in stages. Right-wingers were outraged. That, Mr. Netanyahu's critics say, was a golden opportunity to propose a unity government with Labor. Instead, he pointed to violations by the Palestinians and said Israel would delay its pullback.

Still, the right wing snubbed him. Last week, the finance minister, a Netanyahu loyalist, resigned, complaining that next year's budget was being held hostage by coalition members. When Mr. Netanyahu threatened to call early elections, the head counts in the Knesset stacked up against him. A key defection came from a small party called the Third Way, led by Alexander Lubotzky, the 42-year-old son of Lithuanian immigrants.

Mr. Lubotzky, who may join the new Center party, says that even in the West Bank, where he lives, Jewish settlers would ultimately accept a peace plan if it is acceptable to 70% of the overall population. But if the government scuttles the plan, "soldiers will have to go to war, thinking they are going to war because the prime minister wanted to keep together his coalition." Late yesterday, Mr. Netanyahu presented Labor leaders with a proposal to delay the vote and seek a unity government. They saw it as a cynical ploy. Mr. Barak rose to the podium, cited a list of Netanyahu slights, and said: "It is hard to forget."

Mr. Netanyahu, frowning, watched from his seat on the Knesset floor as his government fell. He then added a torn and crumpled slip of paper to the pile on his desk.

*—Tamar Hausman and Robert S. Greenberger*
*contributed to this article.*

# 45

# STURGEON SURGEONS EXTRACT THE CAVIAR AND SPARE THE FISH

## But Is This Possible Good News For an Endangered Species a Boon to Gastronomes?

*June 30, 1998*

ASTRAKHAN, Russia—Be aware that patient comfort isn't necessarily a big part of sturgeon surgery. Be warned that knowledge of ichthyological gynecology doesn't necessarily enhance the pleasure of eating caviar.

Now, behold the caviar of the future.

Two competing Russian groups, called Ecoresoursy and VNIRO, say they have figured out how to make caviar without killing the fish. In both cases, the sturgeon gets a hormone injection to make it ovulate, and a sort of Caesarean section to remove the eggs. Both groups claim to have a secret method to give the eggs the consistency of normal caviar. The fish returns to the water and eventually spawns again.

It's about time Caspian Sea sturgeons got a break. The prehistoric giants—they have been known to live more than 80 years and reach 12 feet in length—have been fished onto endangered-species lists. The old Soviet Union strictly controlled production, but now the sturgeon is at the mercy of cash-hungry new countries and armed gangs.

"Within a few years, we're going to have to leave the old method and use the new one, without killing the fish," says Elena Chertova, director of Ecoresoursy, a firm that has a six-employee experimental caviar operation in Astrakhan, the Russian caviar capital on the Volga River. Mining caviar could be "just the same as milking a cow," she says.

By the conventional method, it's more mauling than milking. Nets haul in sturgeons before ovulation, when the eggs are still attached to ovaries. Workers kill the fish, pull out the insides, rub the eggs over a strainer to remove ovary tissue, and wash and salt the eggs to make caviar. The caviar industry isn't exactly rushing toward slaughterless caviar. Suzanne Taylor, managing director of Hamburg, Germany-based Dieckmann & Hansen Caviar GmbH, says she imported 100 kilograms of Ecoresoursy's "special" caviar but was disappointed. "It just looks good," she says. For some reason, "the skin is so hard that you keep chewing on the skin." She ended up photographing much of it instead of selling it to shops and restaurants.

Russia's official caviar factories aren't gung-ho, either. Why should they spend to send sturgeons back to sea when outlaws are most likely to catch the fish next time around anyhow? At Astrakhan's open-air fish market, a poacher named Samat describes what he does after catching a rare beluga sturgeon on the Volga at night: whack the beluga on the head, slice the still-living fish's belly from head to tail, scoop out about 10 kilograms (22 pounds) of caviar, and sell it locally for $40 a kilo. (In New York, it would cost 18 times that.)

"I'm sorry for the fish," says the laid-off ship mechanic, "but I have three children to feed." A 175-pound beluga, he adds, is worth an additional $250 dead because sturgeon meat is becoming popular.

So for now, the world's new sturgeon farms are the best hope, according to Igor A. Burtsev of the government-run VNIRO, the Russian abbreviation for the Russian Federal Research Institute of Fisheries & Oceanography. In May, Dr. Burtsev flew to Sarasota, Fla., with 100,000 eggs for the Mote Marine Laboratory's sturgeon farm. In about five years, when Mote strips the sturgeons' first spawn, Mr. Burtsev hopes the farm will keep the mothers alive, using VNIRO's method. Maybe, maybe not. "We don't need that technique at all to be highly profitable," says Steven Serfling, director of the Mote laboratory's aquaculture program. True, he could get caviar out of the same fish 10 times over the course of 20 years, but the fish would get bigger and bigger and use up more and more tank space. Growing new fish might be cheaper.

Dr. Burtsev, a north Russia native with spiky hair, is a patient man. He has a black-and-white photograph of himself performing the world's first successful roe-extraction surgery on a sturgeon way back in 1967; in the photo, he sticks his hand through a slit in the belly of the 3-foot-long patient as an assistant suspends it from its tail.

Twenty years later, another ichthyologist, Sergey Podushka of St. Petersburg, wondered why sturgeon eggs couldn't simply be pushed out the fish's genital orifice with head-to-tail massage. The eggs got backed up in the fish equivalent of fallopian tubes. But if a small scalpel could sneak past the orifice and make a self-healing puncture in one of the tubes . . .

Thus was stitch-free sturgeon surgery born. A recent Podushka paper described the three-man job as follows: "The first man wipes the female's belly with a dry towel and holds a cup for the eggs in his hands. The second man holds the fish's tail, makes the oviduct incision and enlarges the genital opening with a small stick if necessary. The third man holds the fish's head and massages its belly." The surgery lasts 10 minutes.

Clumsy scalpel work can remove the fish's kidney. And wild sturgeons tend to swat their tails during surgery. Still, BIOS, a sturgeon hatchery affiliated with Ecoresoursy, says it has lost no sturgeons with the Burtsev method and only "one or two" with the faster Podushka method. The trouble is, the Burtsev and Podushka methods work only with ovulated eggs. Eggs get a soft outer shell when they leave the ovaries, which makes them perfect for fertilizing with sperm and growing new fish. But try washing and salting them the traditional way, and you end up with mushy-sturgeon-roe porridge.

That problem has stymied efforts in Iran, France and the U.S. to develop death-free caviar. Regulatory concerns about hormones also hampered such research in the U.S., says Serge Doroshov of the University of California, Davis, fishery lab. When he operates on sturgeon, to breed them, he has to use anesthesia, stretchers, flowing water, iodine and surgical gloves. Russia has no such restrictions, and its tradition of tinkering with roe includes developing long-lasting caviar for cosmonauts in the 1960s. Ecoresoursy and VNIRO both say they solved the mushy-egg problem, and will happily reveal how-for a price.

Ecoresoursy won't let outsiders into the room where it makes its experimental caviar. Ms. Chertova, the director, shows a copy of the patent for "way of processing eggs of sturgeon," but quickly pulls the patent away. Does the method use chemicals? "No." Special machinery? "No." Unusual temperatures? "No." Nuclear radiation? "That's too high-level for Russia," Ms. Chertova says, chortling. "Everything is very easy."

Well, not everything. Ecoresoursy doesn't yet have its own sturgeons; it uses eggs that the BIOS lab extracts for fishhatching but rejects as unhatchable. And Ecoresoursy would have to surmount tough new international rules limiting exports of caviar: The rules, though designed to save the sturgeons, have no exemption for caviar extracted without killing the fish. Meanwhile, VNIRO is working on taste refinements; ovulated eggs seem to take on the characteristics of the grassy, soily river-bottom where they would end up if nature took its course. Asked to submit its work for taste-testing in Europe, the VNIRO team offers some caviar (a jar of eggs taken from live sevruga caviar) and some caveats ("It's not the best batch," "European experts don't know much about Russian caviar").

In London, John L. Stas, a caviar trader for 10 years, dons a white hat and lab coat and enters a tasting room. His company, W.G. White Ltd., imports 8 tons of caviar a year from Russia and Iran, though he hasn't heard of caviar from live fish. "It's a lovely color," Mr. Stas says, dipping a mother-of-pearl spoon into VNIRO's jar. He puts a blob of light-gray sevruga eggs on his fist, and tastes. "It's very unusual. . . . It's not unpleasant. . . . It's very rubbery." An egg goes down the wrong pipe. The coughing lasts 10 minutes.

# 46

# ROCKY TAKEOFF: LEBANON SCRAMBLES TO REBUILD AN AIRPORT BATTERED BY CIVIL WAR

## A Sunken Ship and Air Raids Set Construction Back, but the Project Rolls On

### Hijackers Could Stand By

*April 6, 1998*

BEIRUT, Lebanon—Mark Conway helped design airports in Denver and Chicago. Those were tough assignments, but at least he got to visit the job sites.

Mr. Conway, a Chicago-based consultant, was hired to help write a master plan for Beirut's airport in 1992, when the U.S. still barred its citizens from entering Lebanon because of terrorism. Mr. Conway had to work in Cairo, Egypt, from photos and Lebanese government records.

Record-keeping wasn't too diligent during Lebanon's civil war, though. After drafting a proposal for two new parallel runways, Mr. Conway learned that a new mosque with a high minaret sat at the end of one runway. "I believe the mosque was built by Hezbollah," he says. Goodbye, parallel runways.

The rebuilding of Beirut's airport ranks among the more challenging recent international construction projects. During 15 years of war, the airport was frequently shelled, shot up and shut down. It was a preferred destination for hijackers, including those of a TWA jet who dumped the body of an American passenger onto the tarmac in 1985. The war also interrupted an expansion project, and when peace broke out in 1990, Lebanon had a half-finished, bullet-ridden terminal, a decimated national airline—and little cash.

Lebanon is still chaotic, but it is making the new Beirut International Airport a reality. On Friday, passengers departed from a new terminal, with escalators, skylights and nine spacious departure lounges, instead of the tattered old terminal, where the cafeteria serves only cheese sandwiches, and posters of Syrian President Hafez al-Assad and his sons are taped onto metal columns. A second nine-gate concourse and two new runways are being built, one of them stretching more than a mile into the Mediterranean Sea. A new highway will whisk passengers past slums, straight to downtown.

Whether the airport will pay off economically is harder to say. The project is already more than a year behind schedule and potentially $100 million over its $460 million budget. Lebanon officials still don't know how much money the airport will spend and raise, or even who will run it.

Lebanon's civil-aviation authority is nominally in charge, but it is so weak that it needed cabinet approval to hire some temporary janitors. The airport's lenders, which include Kuwait and the European Investment Bank, insisted that Lebanon create a strong, independent authority. But a proposal to create a new authority has stalled in Parliament, as factions compete for control. When the airport opened in 1954, Beirut was the financial hub of the Middle East, and carriers used Beirut as an overnight stop between Europe and East Asia. Now, airlines need fewer refueling stops. Dubai's airport, one-fourth as busy as Beirut's before the war, replaced it as a transit hub during the civil war. It's four times busier than Beirut's airport.

Lebanon's prime minister, a construction tycoon named Rafic Hariri, is convinced Beirut can regain its role as a tourist and business center. Even before he became prime minister in 1992, he hired the Cairo-based engineering firm Dar Al Handasah to design a world-class financial center and an airport worthy of it.

"He said, 'My idea is not just an airport, I want a convention center, and a shopping center,' " recalls Nabil Nassar, former senior partner at Dar Al Handasah. "He's the eternal optimist." Mr. Hariri's highflying notions quickly collided with reality. Dar Al Handasah was stuck with a half-built terminal designed 16 years before. It had too little room between its two concourses for many wide-body jets to maneuver between. At a meeting in Damascus, Syria, with Lebanese government officials in 1991, planners suggested starting from scratch.

"For political reasons, they didn't want to do that," says Riad Mneimneh, Dar Al Handasah's director of operations. Officials feared demolishing work done under the past government might raise an outcry.

In 1994, as construction was almost under way, Mr. Hariri forced a major design overhaul by decreeing—after a visit by European consultants—that retail space in the new terminal should be multiplied by 10, planners say. And despite airline objections, he insisted on two new runways. One with a man-made peninsula poking into the sea would reduce downtown noise. The other would allow nonstop flights to Los Angeles and Singapore.

To build it all, the government picked a joint venture of Germany's Hochtief AG and Lebanon's Consolidated Contracting Co., low bidder at $485 million. Rolf Klockow, the Hochtief engineer leading the job, recalls visiting Beirut in 1967, before the war, and seeing clear beaches from the airport all the way downtown.

But the war "created an undisciplined situation," Mr. Klockow says on a recent afternoon, driving past wartime refugees' illegal tenements and an unlicensed garbage dump unearthed during construction. Also, a beach hotel called Costa Brava sat smack at the end of the eastern runway, blocking the planned route of a highway diversion needed to free space for one of the new runways.

Hussein Bdeir, a Lebanese Shiite, says he got permission to build the Costa Brava resort in 1985, by paying "at least $1 million" to the appropriate officials. Mr. Bdeir also helped raise funds in Africa for Nabih Berri's Amal militia during the war, so he appealed to Mr. Berri—now speaker of Lebanon's Parliament—to save Costa Brava from the wrecking ball. The resort went down last August, but only after a $5 million settlement and nearly two years of wrangling.

The project presented other unusual challenges. To lay ground for the marine runway, the project managers needed to strip 13 million cubic feet of rock from a mountain near the sea, and they needed cement. Druze leader and cabinet member Walid Jumblatt offered a package deal: the mountain, which he owned, and cement from a plant he partly owns. A 40-year-old shipwreck in the path of the marine runway couldn't be budged; contractors filled it with sand and built over it. In 1996, Israeli air raids scared off many workers for weeks.

Indeed, Beirut's image as a war zone has haunted the project, especially when the government tried to raise funds by selling off profitable parts of the airport. Getting someone to build and run the parking garage—usually an easy sell at airports because parking garages mint money—took two separate international marketing efforts; finally, a Kuwaiti company agreed. The company is also low bidder—actually, the only bidder—to build and run the airport's luxury hotel, near the site of the U.S. marine barracks bombed in 1983.

Still, Lebanon managed to raise $38 million by awarding a contract to build and manage airport shops to a group including Phoenicia Trading Partners, a Lebanese concern that ran the airport's existing duty-free shop through most of the war. The group has been ready since September, with detailed plans for a cigar-smoking lounge, duty-free shops and private-brand stores that could give the airport another $10 million a year as its cut of sales. Walid A. Saleh, Phoenicia's managing director, says the "big risk" now comes from construction delays, and passenger traffic that's below expectations.

Airlines have been trickling back to Beirut, which now has 31 carriers. Luring more flights will be a challenge because Beirut already has some of the highest ticket taxes and airline-landing fees in the region. Also, the U.S. still hasn't lifted a ban on American airlines flying to Beirut. President Reagan enacted it in 1985, citing security concerns, after the hijacking of TWA flight 847 to Beirut.

At the time of the TWA hijacking, Jalal Haidar was a young security adviser at the airport, and Billie Vincent was in charge of security at the Federal Aviation Administration. In 1993, Mr. Vincent, now retired, persuaded Lebanon to hire his private consulting firm to help beef up Beirut's airport security. He hired Mr. Haidar, who left Lebanon during the war, to return. Touring the new terminal recently, Mr. Haidar showed off the results: state-of-the-art metal detectors and security doors at the gates that require both a key code and the swipe of a photo card to open.

He acknowledged hardware alone won't get the ban lifted, though. American officials worry that Hezbollah sympathizers could penetrate the airport through relatives or through the squatters' tenements overlooking the runways. An urban-renewal project is supposed to relocate some of the airport's neighbors, but funding has been scant.

Syria, with about 40,000 troops in Lebanon, is keeping Hezbollah under control, but the Syrians are part of another problem: The airport hosts a bewildering array of officers, in blue, green, camouflage and plain clothes. One recent afternoon, as Lebanese immigration officials tried to reason with a hysterical arriving passenger, a plain-clothes Syrian struck him in the head and dragged him through the terminal.

Mr. Haidar got security workers to consent to background checks and identity badges. But as late as September, airport officials hadn't met with airlines to discuss space requirements at the new airport. A team from Parsons Brinckerhoff, the U.S. transportation-consulting firm, toured the terminal in November and found an empty shell, with no escalators, no X-ray machines and no new employee manuals.

"We said, 'You want it open when?' " recalls Julia Brickell of Parsons Brinckerhoff. She told Lebanese officials they might have to turn the whole operation over to a professional airport manager.

Prime Minister Hariri had a different plan. Middle East Airlines, the bloated, money-losing state airline, was having trouble cutting its payroll, in part because it had to keep an even balance of Muslims and Christians. The airline, Mr. Hariri said, should shift hundreds of maintenance workers to a new company that would operate telescopic passenger bridges and keep the airport running.

Confusion still reigns. In February, Mr. Haidar was hired to help run the new company. He says it's an independent company, but the airline says it owns it. Half the airline's board had been replaced because of a kickback probe. One recent afternoon, sitting in his still-undecorated Middle East Airlines office, board member Rafic Kazan refused to read meeting minutes until they were reprinted with his name ahead of Mr. Haidar's.

Older airport employees didn't trust Mr. Haidar, either. They were loyal to airport director Chafic Abboushi, a short man with a furrowed brow who has been at the airport since it opened. On a tour of the old terminal's communication center—where one of the doors says "typist"—Mr. Abboushi and other 40-year veterans recall how they used to peer over a fourth-floor window to give planes the all-clear when the control tower was under attack.

The prime minister wanted the long-delayed terminal running by April 3. So Mr. Haidar soothed older workers by saying the best of them would get jobs. The clock was ticking, loudly. A sandstorm stopped work for a day. A rainstorm exposed leaks in the skylights. The cables for the new electronic-ticketing computers still hadn't arrived, eight days before opening. Mr. Abboushi was helping airlines move into their new offices, but couldn't tell them how much they'd be paying.

"I'm starting to rethink it," a bleary-eyed Mr. Haidar said then, stepping into a check-in area strewn with emergency-power systems, still in boxes.

On Friday, though, Mr. Abboushi watched as British Airways checked in passengers for the new terminal's first flight. He followed them through two security checks, and stepped outside to watch a telescopic bridge unfold, letting 160 passengers aboard. Then he watched the Airbus jet take off, 10 minutes late.

"It was perfect," he says. "It was nice and smooth. It was wonderful."

# 47

# LOOMING LARGE: THIS PERSIAN RUG SHOULD SET A RECORD

## Less Certain Is Who Will Buy a Carpet That Is So Big It Needs a Soccer Stadium

*June 30, 1997*

BEN, Iran—This is a small town in search of a really big floor.

It should be a bare floor, big enough to accommodate about 6,000 people, with no columns breaking up the space. And it should be crying out for the subtle decorative touch of the world's largest hand-woven carpet, with a third of an acre of beige, brown and blue swirls and flowers. Working in two shifts in a converted fire station at the top of a hill, 84 women have spent two years on the carpet so far, and it is only half finished. The asking price, yet to be arrived at, could be as high as $1 million. There is nary a buyer in sight.

"I would like to see it in a great exhibition hall—a big room, where anyone who walked in would say, 'Vuy!' ('Wow!')" says 21-year-old Mehrandokht Aghaie, sitting on a 100-foot-long bench at a huge loom, tying knots with woolen yarn around hanging silk threads and then swiping the excess with a razor blade.

Perhaps a European soccer stadium could put it on display when there isn't a game being played, says Farhad Shams, a sponsor of the project.

It's crazy to make such a big carpet on speculation, says Karim Mirzamani, a Tehran exporter. The market is so bad that for six months he hasn't even been able to get foreign orders for carpets of any size. The U.S., once the biggest market for Persian rugs, is off-limits now because of trade sanctions. Iran's taxes and currency regulations—and low-wage competition from India, Pakistan and China—have hurt the rug trade. Persian-carpet exports dropped nearly 35% last year, to $602 million.

Still, Iranians can't stop making carpets. By some estimates, the industry occupies one of every seven Iranians. "People in the villages don't have anything better to do," says Nasrollah Arvarian, 31, a weaver in the village of Sefid-Dasht, down the road from Ben (population 8,000). He has invested his life savings (about $21,000) in two living-room-size rugs that he and his family are weaving at home. His wife, Nargess, who sometimes works through the night, is bug-eyed from staring at tiny knots. "The doctors say I have to stop, but this is my job," she says.

And certain Iranians can't stop making big carpets. That's the weakness of Elyas Abdi, 47, the designer behind Ben's megarug. He was raised in the rug-trading center of Isfahan. He says the 500 people in his family tree all have been in the carpet trade. His business card reads: "producers of the biggest carpets in the world." He says, "Every time I come up with a big carpet, I have to start another one to break the record." Mr. Abdi says he sold a 6,451-square-foot carpet to a buyer in Dubai. But for two decades his dream has been to weave the ultimate carpet: 50 meters long and 30 meters wide. That is an area of more than 16,000 square feet.

Mr. Abdi says he copyrighted the design, which includes a record-breaking six main flowers. But for years, he couldn't find a carpet trader willing to bankroll the project.

Then he found the Behezisti Foundation. Financed by the government and private-donation boxes, the foundation is a sort of workfare project, Iranian style. It helps get jobs for widows, orphans and girls who have "gone astray," to keep them on the moral track, according to Siavosh Ahmadi, Behezisti general manager in the city of Shahrekord in western Iran. Actually, he says, "We do not find jobs for them, we create jobs for them." In his region, which includes Ben, that means supporting about 400 carpet-weaving projects. Most girls, and some boys, in Iranian villages know how to weave carpets by the time they reach their teens.

Mr. Abdi says he was sitting with some foundation people, listening to them complain about how hard it is to come up with new job-creation schemes, when he made his pitch for the megarug. He signed a deal with Behezisti in 1995 to provide about $160,000 in start-up funds. A job announcement about the project in Ben's mosque brought a crowd of 250 women to the site, many of them wondering whether the carpet was a joke.

Big rugs do have a history in Iran. In the 1950s, the shah ordered a series of approximately 1,550-square-foot rugs for his palaces. One of them is still on display, under eight dining-room tables in the north Tehran palace, now a museum. "It's the biggest carpet one could ever make," says one of the security guards, who tended the palace before the revolution, too. "I'd bet my eyes on it."

Bad idea. The Guinness Book of Records lists a 54,000-square-foot carpet made with gold-enriched silk in eighth-century Baghdad as the biggest, though it no longer exists. Oman recently commissioned a very big carpet from Iran for its new Sultan Qaboos Mosque, but it is being woven in four pieces. At the Dubai Shopping Festival, Persian carpet dealer Abdul Rahim Forootan made headlines with his 8,600-square-foot "world's biggest carpet." "It's the biggest on the market," he explains, though the market for megacarpets is so quiet that he never actually had to unfurl the rug.

Handling big carpets takes some muscle. Every six weeks, Mr. Abdi brings in six men from Isfahan to raise the loom so the women, who earn 2½ cents for every 100 knots, or about 50 cents an hour, can keep working at eye level. The yarn and silk threads for the 500-million-knot carpet together weigh seven tons, and the pylons supporting the steel loom are sunk more than three feet into the ground. When the carpet is finished, the team will break down the outer wall of the fire station and, with a crane, load the rug onto an 18-wheeler. If he can muster the manpower to unroll it, Mr. Abdi would like to stop and display the completed rug in Ben.

So far, there hasn't been a flood of interest from buyers, the rug's sponsors concede. They say the Red Crescent, Iran's version of the Red Cross, considered buying the carpet to resell for hard currency with which to buy medicines, but a new director put the kibosh on the plan. The Behezisti Foundation plans to tout the rug at a carpet exhibition in Tehran in September. Its brochure will say the carpet is "the symbol of Iranian people, because of their patience, fine work and humbleness."

Maybe so, but big carpets are more trouble than they are worth, according to Sefatollah Taghi Khani, curator of Tehran's carpet museum. The museum keeps one of the shah's leftovers in the basement, and air-ing it once a year takes 15 people, he says. "It's so damn difficult to move, even though it's one of the thinnest carpets ever made." Besides, Mr. Khani says, the bigger the rug, the more chance it will house insects.

Another problem, says Mohammed Reza Hakami, a Tehran carpet dealer: Carpets become more valuable when people have walked on them. That is one reason rug dealers and some buyers will leave their new rugs on the sidewalk for a few days. But "nobody could over cover such a big carpet."

Besides, "They're cheating when they make the big carpets," says Shoukoufeh Sadeghi, weaving a rug with her three sisters in Sefid-Dasht. She shows how some big-carpet weavers save time by skipping knots, a trick called farsi boff. She says, "It's like machine made. I call it counterfeit." Mr. Abdi says there is no farsi boff in his rug. He doesn't see why anyone would want to walk on a piece of art. And, as for bugs, he is using tobacco and mothballs to keep them away.

# 48

# IF ONLY KING SOLOMON WERE HERE TO SETTLE THIS NASTY DISPUTE

## Both Ethiopia and Yemen Claim Queen of Sheba as Their Native Heroine

*May 2, 1997*

AXUM, Ethiopia—Her name was Makeda, better known as the Queen of Sheba. The Bible records that she ruled a rich kingdom from here, according to locals who tell legends about the wise, beautiful African queen. Soon, Ethiopians hope, her tomb here will be found. . . .

MARIB, Yemen—Her name was Bilqis, better known as the Queen of Sheba. The Koran records that she ruled a rich kingdom from here, according to locals who tell legends about the wise, beautiful Arab queen. Soon, Yemenis hope, her tomb here will be found. . . .

Which version is correct? Maybe neither. Archaeologists have found plenty of inscriptions from the ancient Sabean kingdom on old stones in Ethiopia and Yemen. Strangely, none mention a Makeda or Bilqis. Nor do any mention a female ruler from 950 B.C., when the queen is supposed to have reigned. Indeed, nothing that old has been found among the ruins in Axum or Marib. But that hasn't stopped Ethiopia and Yemen from laying claim to the Queen of Sheba. Both countries are trying to pump up tourism, and Western travelers seem to like nothing more than a familiar name in an unfamiliar setting.

"Land of the Queen of Sheba," proclaim travel posters in Yemen. Tour guides in Marib give her credit for building the ancient Marib dam and praying at two temples that now bear her name. Guests who ask about her at the modern Bilqis Hotel get an elaborate information sheet ("She never made important decisions without consulting her ministers and advisers.") "I guess it's good business," says German tourist Martin Rettenmayr, browsing in the hotel.

About 600 miles west across the Red Sea in Axum, where a new international airport will soon replace the town's gravel runway, tourist shops sell stone carvings of Sheba marrying King Solomon or suckling their child. Tour guides in this dusty mountain town point out the throne room at the reconstructed Queen of Sheba's Palace, and the queen's multihued goblet in the local museum; both palace and goblet are actually from around the sixth century, archaeologists say. "It's all a lot of hot air," says Colombian tourist Camillo Mejia, sipping Ethiopian red wine at the Makeda restaurant after comparing his guide's explanations with his guidebook's.

Yemen and Ethiopia are both encouraging archaeologists to dig deeper for proof of Sheba. "There is no smoke without fire," says Yusuf Abdulla, director of Yemen's General Organization for Antiquities and Museums. In the past, Yemen wasn't exactly a hospitable place to practice archaeology. American explorer Wendell Phillips, who started excavating Marib's Moon Temple of Sheba in 1952, had to run for his life four months after arriving when local tribesmen became convinced his team was actually prospecting for gold. Civil wars later put a crimp on excavations.

Last month, however, Yemen's government reached an agreement with the late Dr. Phillips's American Foundation for the Study of Man to excavate the oval-walled temple with the help of ground-penetrating radar. That kind of spending will require corporate sponsors. "Their eyes light up when you talk about the Queen of Sheba," says archaeologist William Glanzman of the University of British Columbia, who figures if his team finds evidence of the queen, Yemen would have a tourist attraction on par with the pyramids of Egypt.

In Ethiopia, a civil war made ancient sites off-limits to archaeologists for two decades. Now, three foreign teams are digging in and around Axum for a few months each year. Ethiopian officials want the digs to go year-round, and are training home-grown archaeologists to help. More is at stake than tourist dollars. Yemen, which had 75,000 tourists last year, prides itself as being the root of ancient culture and trade, on both sides of the Red Sea. Ethiopia, with 107,000 tourists in 1996, takes pride in its ties to ancient Zion; modern-day Ethiopian emperors such as Menelik II and Haile Selassie took pains to show they were descended from Solomon and Sheba. "From Sudan up to Yemen she was queen," says Aba Walde Amanuel, a robed priest at Menelik II's tomb in Addis Ababa, who believes the queen's remains are in Ethiopia's Lake Tana. "In Somalia, do they say the Queen of Sheba was from Somalia? No, only Yemen people say this." Well, not exactly. Sheba-envy is spreading. An Egyptian magazine earlier this year bragged, "The Queen of Sheba was an Egyptian Queen." Her name has been slapped on ruins in Iran, the United Arab Emirates and elsewhere, according to German archaeologist Burkhard Vogt, who has launched several digs in Marib. He thinks the queen was probably the head of a Sabaen spice-trade colony near the current border of Jordan and Saudi Arabia; one theory holds that she visited Solomon as part of a trade dispute.

The Bible isn't much help. It details all the gold and spice Sheba brought to Solomon, but doesn't say where she came from. It says he answered all her questions, but doesn't say what they were. In the Koran, Solomon sends for Sheba and convinces her to become a Muslim (after examining her legs, apparently to verify she wasn't a genie).

But in the Kebra Negast (a 14th century Ethiopian text), Sheba comes from Ethiopia to see Solomon, and he tricks her into sleeping with him and bearing a son, who brings the ark of the covenant to Axum. (Tourists are allowed to see the church that allegedly contains the ark, but are barred from seeing the ark itself—which, according to other accounts, is also said to be buried in Egypt or Israel).

Axumites have no doubt the Queen of Sheba was real. One local history book even records the name of her trade minister, "Tarmin." Dingil Atesbaha, a local hairstylist, demonstrates on a village girl the queen's braided coiffure, with rows radiating from a tight braid along the hairline. Teferi Tesfay, a tour guide who worked on a dig last summer, says his heart leapt when he uncovered a skull: If it is the queen's, he thought, "I'll be a hero." It was more than a millennium off, though.

Izghinamen Ghebreyesus, who runs the Ancient Handicraft Shop in Axum, insists that Ethiopian villagers have found coins from the Queen of Sheba's reign. In a low voice, Mr. Ghebreyesus confides that he has some to sell, and to prove he is a legitimate dealer he retrieves from a wooden safe a 23-year-old letter from the Carnegie Museum. He keeps the letter folded to hide the text, but the first line is briefly revealed: "We are sorry we cannot use any of the . . ." Yemenis also can cite rich details about the queen. At the Throne of Bilqis in Marib, 14-year-old Mohamad Ahmed Ali sells oranges, guards the fenced-off altar and pillars, and gives the temple's history, complete with enchanted orchards, genies and magic walkways on which the queen traveled.

But where is Sheba now? Ali Saleh al Mahouren, a white-bearded farmer passing by, gives the answer: in a nearby mountain cave filled with treasures. Unfortunately, a strange force, strong enough to bend a Kalashnikov assault rifle, has kept explorers away, he says. "The government wants to enter, but it can't," Mr. Mahouren says, before scurrying off for afternoon prayers. Local officials say they don't know anything about a cave. Antiquities official Sadiq Said Othman acknowledges that none of the bones and coins excavated at the throne date back to the Queen of Sheba. Still, he says, "Too many people think she came from Ethiopia. In Ethiopia, what is there? Nothing. Where is the Palace of Sheba? They haven't anything at all."

# 49

# DEMOLITION DERBY, A LAWLESS SPORT, GETS SOME RULES

## They Are Wildly Unpopular, and Honored in the Breach; Mr. Pease Is the Poorer

*October 4, 1994*

TOWER HILL, Ill.—Leonard Pease probably should have chosen an easier sport to reform—like maybe baseball.

Still, Mr. Pease is a demolition derby man. And after driving on the Midwest car-crash circuit for 16 years (which works out to about 23,000 collisions), Mr. Pease decided derbies needed some discipline.

So last year, he rolled out the National Demolition Derby Association. The NDDA polled drivers and drafted 59 "uniform rules and regulations" for all derbies to use. It trained officials to spot cheaters who weld steel plates into their frames, "sandbaggers" who fail to hit another care hard at least once a minute as is required, and team drivers who improperly gang up on one car. The NDDA also awarded victory points for the top drivers, who, Mr. Pease insists, have as much talent as those who enter the Indianapolis 500. He had visions of fast-food sponsorships and national TV coverage for derbies, which were last featured on ABC's "Wide World of Sports" in 1970.

But Mr. Pease's dream has slammed into some brick walls.

Most derby promoters snubbed him. One promoter told drivers they couldn't paint profanities on their cars unless they wrote "NDDA" after them. Another, George Sims of Auto Race Promotions Inc., in St. Louis, ejected Mr. Pease when he showed up to tally points and sell NDDA T-shirts. Mr. Sims also wrote his own new rule: Any driver belonging to a "national organization" would lose amateur status and be disqualified. "He's trying to professionalize a sport that won't take professionalism," says Mr. Sims, a rotund 47-year-old who runs derbies without budging from his chair.

Indeed, derby drivers aren't easy to corral. Bill and Regina Mc-Dermith, promoters certified by the NDDA, say they left a Carlyle, Ill., Lions Club derby under police guard after enforcing a rule against smashing into a driver-side door. Two drivers were barred for life from the NDDA—one for decking Mrs. McDermith, and another for jumping on a rival driver's hood and trying to kick him. Membership now stands at 120.

Nowhere has recruiting been tougher than in Mr. Pease's central Illinois hometown of Tower Hill, population 700. Here, NDDA opponents wear "Phil's Buddy" shirts, as in Phil Watson, Mr. Pease's former brother-in-law. Mr. Watson, an iron worker, was in his first derby before he was old enough to drive. He and his buddies spend hundreds of hours and dollars readying their Chryslers for battle, and they have protested that the NDDA rules restrict their artistic license. For example, they like to strengthen the seams with hundreds of screws, an NDDA no-no, though Mr. Pease did that sort of thing himself when he was a metal worker.

During the Tower Hill Fall Festival derby, the Chryslers make rock-solid "clang" sounds when hitting nonfriends-of-Phil. "They won't hit each other," driver Bill Morrison says with disdain, as he perches on a garbage can and watches the derby in his "I Ain't Nobody's Buddy" T-shirt. "Big surprise," another onlooker mutters when Mr. Watson wins first place, and $400.

Derbies were a lot simpler when they began in the 1950s. One bit of folklore tracks their birth to pedestrians cheering a fender bender at an Ohio intersection, but historians credit the first derby to Larry Mendelsohn, a stock-car promoter in Islip, N.Y., who realized that people go to car races hoping to see crashes. The formula: Put a hundred cars in a ring, declare the last surviving car the winner and let the junkyard carry off what's left.

Complications soon arose. To keep insurance companies happy, some promoters forbade head-on collisions. Weary firefighters won a two-engine-fires-and-you're-out rule. Hearses, limousines and Chrysler Imperials were banished from most events to keep an even playing field. And environmental regulators started cracking down on antifreeze spills.

But the sport's biggest problem is that it is running out of good cars.

Demo drivers say that 1978 was the last year Detroit built them to last. Some fairs are reduced to staging derbies with compact cars, pickup trucks, school buses, bicycles, lawn mowers or bed frames. Drivers lucky enough to spot an old Chevy Impala might pay $200 just for the shell, so now they try to preserve cars through several derbies.

That requires teamwork, as Terry Hadley explains before a derby of Mr. Sims's in Cape Girardeau, Mo. Calling themselves Tag Team Motor Sports, Mr. Hadley and his friends weld iron beams to one another's doors before derbies, sledgehammer the bodies back into shape after each heat and nudge the old heaps loose if they get stuck in competition. "It's just like if a a neighbor needs help putting his roof up, I help him," Mr. Hadley says, inspecting his 1976 Impala as the words "kiss me like we're lovers" squeal from a country song on the fairground loudspeakers.

Backing up and bashing anything in the way is the main driving technique for the Tag Team and the others in Mr. Sims's derby. The steering wheel of Mike Maglone's Ford Pinto falls off after one collision. First-time driver Mitch Dukes gets his car stuck atop Norman Sadler's. "It's controlled mayhem," says a grinning Mr. Sims.

The NDDA's derby in Du Quoin, Ill., promises a more "professional atmosphere," as driver Keith Tyree puts it during his inspection before the race. Mr. Pease, jumping onto Mr. Tyree's open-bed trailer, checks the 1973 Caprice's tires, bumpers and every inch in between. Soon, there are 11 cars in line for inspection, and as many undergoing last-minute blowtorch surgery to remove illegal welds.

Mr. Tyree says he likes NDDA events because they don't attract big teams of drivers. Still, once he gets to the pits, Mr. Tyree is drawn into ad hoc alliances with two other drivers. "It's all politics," he explains, climbing through his open windshield to begin a six-car heat, the three winners of which will advance to the final round. He and his allies proceed to gang-bash Bart Steines's Pontiac, which has no recognizable front or back end left by the time officials issue a warning about team driving.

Even worse, the drivers prove skilled at evading one another, in order to save their cars for the later rounds in the contest. One driver scoots off the racetrack as the second heat begins. Soon, spectators are slumping in their seats, and Mr. Pease is pacing in the announcer's booth. "Come on, let's see some hitting," he begs drivers over a loud-speaker. The heat finally ends after a car with "Snafu" painted on it gets stuck on the track's log boundary.

To Mr. Sims, scenes like that just prove his point: Team driving is inevitable, and good drivers are boring. It is the difference between a fist-throwing amateur boxer and a professional pugilist who "throws more head bobs than punches," he says.

Mr. Pease says he is starting to feel battered himself. He says he couldn't even get local stations to televise the Du Quoin "Illinois State Championship," and the Hardees restaurant chain sponsored a golf tournament instead. His only promoter, Mr. McDermith, is talking about bolting. And the NDDA took a $2,500 bath in Du Quoin, not counting the hedge it will have to replace near the "Victory Lane" sign.

Mr. Pease says demolition derbies cost him little more than whiplash when he was a young driver. But now that he is a 41-year-old, unpaid demolition-derby traffic cop, the sport has claimed his life savings, some $60,000. "I gave till it hurts," he says.

# 50

# SKY WARRIORS TAKE WOULD-BE FLYBOYS ON FLIGHTS OF FANCY

## Off They Go, Gunning Down Sons, Lovers and Bosses In Mock Aerial-Dogfights

*August 28, 1991*

ATLANTA—Dennis Bachorik enjoys Monet, foreign films and pretending he is a World War II fighter pilot. The computer-systems manager, who idolized the chain-smoking, fast-living flyboys of yesteryear, always felt that he, too, could have been an ace fighter. This summer, he got his chance. With his silk "Army Air Corps" scarf waving in the breeze, he climbed into a fighter plane, ready to engage in battle and rattle off favorite movie lines like: "Bandits at two o'clock."

Apparently, a lot of folks lust for the wild blue yonder. "I didn't think there were this many Walter Mittys out there," says Earl "Stinger" Arrowood, cofounder of Sky Warriors. The Atlanta outfit sets up aerial shootouts by sending people like Mr. Bachorik up in a fighter plane equipped with laser guns and experienced backup pilots who seize control when necessary, rather like driving-school instructors.

Since opening in November, Sky Warriors has taken aloft more than 400 civilians itching to find out whether they have the Right Stuff. Scott Zifferer, who owns a computer software company, is convinced he does. After a Sky Warriors dogfight, he went out and bought a surplus T-34 plane used by Chile's air force and had it painted to look like one from the U.S. Navy.

Around the nation, dogfights have taken off. Adventurers who don't want to leave home can strap themselves into a chair and fight opposing pilots on computer screens, courtesy of GE Information Services. Cost: $10.95 an hour.

Thrill seekers who don't mind going outside but aren't thrilled about heights can spend $35 to sit in the jet-fighter cockpit at the Air Combat

School of Arlington, Texas, and shoot Tomcats on an eight-foot-wide video screen. (Look for franchises soon.) Air Combat USA, in Fullerton, Calif., offers for $300 rides and target practice at mock Scud missile launchers and opposing planes.

And for $490, Sky Warriors stages hour-long simulated dogfights, complete with real laser-shooting guns and smoke. How real is it? "You lose touch of the fact that it's your father or brother—it's much more 'the enemy,'" says Douglas Coles, 19, who says he forgot it was his father, Michael Coles, a New York investment banker, in the other plane.

Even McGee's boyfriend was so engrossed in air battle with her that he growled into his two-way radio, "Die, you dog!"

Many customers have pilot licenses but are bored with simple flying. Frank Rider, tired of strafing railroad yards with imaginary bullets from a small plane, wanted something that could fight back. "Every pilot has that little drop of blood that makes him think or wish he were a World War I fighter," says the soft-spoken blimp builder from Boulder, Colo.

But non-pilots have "Top Gun" fantasies, too. Peter Doyle, who works for a lawn maintenance company in Seymour, Conn., says that since his Sky Warriors encounter, he watches "Top Gun" constantly— fast-forwarding through the boring love-interest stuff to his favorite scene: Tom Cruise on the flight deck, preparing for the climactic air engagement.

To psych the inexperienced for battle, Sky Warrior pilots encourage flyers to remember the enemy's past transgressions. One father, taking aim at his teen-age son's plane, pulled the trigger and shouted through the two-way radio, "Clean your room!"

Dogfights can be therapeutic. Business associates gun down each other, lawyers fight clients, and husbands take on wives.

While her husband, Dennis, was trying to maintain consciousness, Marilynn Bachorik, a mild-mannered special-education teacher, was flying rings around his plane and shouting, "Whee." Mr. Bachorik didn't mind getting beat up by his wife. Now, when he watches air battles in famous movies like "Twelve O'Clock High," starring Gregory Peck as a World War II flight commander, he leans sideways in his chair and starts grunting with the imagined gravitational force against his head. He calls his wife in to watch. "Hey, Marilynn. Dogfight!"

Elgin Wells, an Atlanta jazz musician, says he didn't think he could shoot at his 74-year-old father, a former fighter pilot. But he managed, and they ended up in a draw. The younger Mr. Wells, 41, stepped out of his plane wearing a sweatshirt that read, "He didn't touch me" in the front. "It's a little kid's fantasy," he says. "You get to work out your aggressive side."

It's also a good way to vent workplace aggression. "It was a rare and unique opportunity to shoot at my boss without killing him and therefore rendering myself unemployed," says software executive Mark Theiler, who tried to gun down his boss, Mr. Zifferer.

Some companies are even using the flights of fancy as a military version of Outward Bound. California's chapter of Young Presidents Organization, a collection of chief executives who typically travel to tame resorts to discuss regional economies or geopolitics, will engage in dogfights next year. Gary F. Thompson, an insurance executive organizing the trip, explains: "A bonding takes place that you can't accomplish over a conference table."

Sky Warriors cofounder Michael J. Brady is himself a frustrated fighter pilot. After attending West Point and finding that his eyesight wasn't good enough for the military, he bought a military training plane from Federal Express Corp. founder Frederick W. Smith. He and fellow pilot Mr. Arrowood would chase each other's tails and shout "Rat-a-tat-tat" over their radios.

It was so much fun that they rigged three Beechcraft T-34A planes with laser guns and devices that cause a plane to smoke when hit by a laser. Then they assembled a squadron of former military pilots, and called themselves Sky Warriors.

Sky Warriors clients—er, pilots—put on olive drab jumpsuits over their penny loafers and select a helmet painted like those of "Top Gun" heroes. During a 90-minute briefing they learn what to expect when entering G-LOC, or gravitationally induced loss of consciousness: You lose vision, and then "go to sleep for a few seconds."

Safety pilots get the plane airborne, do some steering—or all of it if the pilot blacks out—and run three video cameras. One trained at the pilot's head, called the hero-cam, catches all the right moves: such as scoring a kill. Wrong moves, such as nearly stalling a plane, can be edited out.

"You think you're on a mission in Iraq, flying F-15s," says Robin

Walker, a British airplane insurance executive. Actually it's not even close to real combat, in which pilots use radar to shoot from miles away, rarely get into dogfights and fly in all weather. Sky Warriors are grounded when it rains to keep the cameras dry.

In real war, too, pilots don't break off the fight to meet deadlines.

Your reporter arrived for duty armed with combat sneakers, a lucky Hawaiian shirt and a double dose of Dramamine. My pilot, Mr. Arrowood, showed me the airsickness bags—"You won't need them," he added—but forgot to explain how the parachute works, which I didn't realize until after takeoff.

We flew some hard turns and some vertical "barrel rolls," at 170 m.p.h., squashing me, a la Gumby and Pokey. After an hour of trying to chase down the enemy—in this case high-school teacher Danny Jones—I was sweating, panting and remembering fondly the ground scenes in "Top Gun."

Thankfully, Mr. Jones's pilot announced he had to return to base for a 4 p.m. appointment, but my pilot mercilessly overshot the runway, and made a hard turn for a second approach. He explained why this was necessary, but the words didn't quite penetrate the air-sickness bag around my face. "It's the heat," Mr. Arrowood said. Another Sky Warriors leader assured me later, "It has nothing to do with testosterone."

# APPENDIX 1

*From the* North Adams Transcript

# GOING TO THE TOP WON'T GET YOU TO BOTTOM OF BUREAUCRACY

*August 28, 1986*

NORTH ADAMS—Imagine, please, being stuck in a huge flaw in the system. I mean a crack 30 feet deep, so narrow that nobody will admit it's there.

Now, imagine being freed from the crack, and by a fluke coming face to face with the man who helped put you there.

This is how I felt on discovering a note Monday on the top file of my desk: "Alan Mackey, Mass. Commissioner of the Registry of Motor Vehicles, will be here Monday August 25. We need a story and photo. Joe." Like Ahab with the white whale, I would face my tormentor at last.

Let me explain.

I bought a car, in June, in California. The next day I drove it to Massachusetts, arriving in seven days.

So far, I believe, I had committed no crime (except, perhaps, on a small stretch of highway in Utah, when my car became officially broken in and I had to see if it could exceed 60 mph without crumbling).

I began work here, eagerly awaiting the arrival of my title and license plates from California, whose motor vehicle department has a backlog so long that there is a waiting list to apply to stand in line to request to register.

And I would have gone on waiting in peace had an accident not popped up on the police scanner one day, or had I not foolishly agreed to cover it. But, then, at the *Transcript* we do not negotiate coverage. The accident was across the street from the police station, and as I turned into the parking lot I was stopped by an officer.

The officer was just doing his job, and doing it quite well, when he told me he had seen me driving in Massachusetts for over 30 days, and I was therefore unregistered and would have to pay a $100 ticket and leave the car where it stood until I could register it here.

The next day, I realized I could not register it here; I had no title. The crack, at this point, was plain to me: California was too slow, Massachusetts was too fast. But I assumed there was some way out of it.

I called the California Department of Motor Vehicles in Sacramento. I called the Massachusetts Registry of Motor Vehicles in Boston. I called the dealer who sold me the car. I called the mayor, my congressman and the state representative who heads the committee that deals with such things. I called my mother.

There way no way out. Massachusetts demanded the title and nothing less. California said that, according to their computer, my title would not be sent for another two weeks. The dealer said he was sorry and he would express mail something-or-other notarized. The state legislator said the number of people who had ever had the same problem as I was probably five, not a significant voting block. My mother said to quit my job and come home.

Two weeks later, the title arrived and I registered my car, but if you have ever been throttled by a faceless bureaucracy, you will understand the relish with which I introduced myself to Mr. Mackey (The Registrar! In the flesh!) Monday morning. I savored my chance to confront him with The Gross Injustice.

I duly took notes, and Mike Finkle took pictures, as Mr. Mackey explained a new computer system the North Adams office would receive in April, the last month of the Registry's six-month phasing in of high technology.

Then I put down my notepad and began my diatribe. I had repeated my tale in 20 conversations with 12 separate authorities in seven different cities, so I had the act down—complete with "as a citizen of the commonwealth" and "denied me the mode of transportation necessary for my livelihood" and ending with "forced upon me the unwanted role of lawbreaker." You get the idea.

Mr. Mackey looked wounded. (He was wounded, I might add, with a foot injury that he said he had received at another registry office—I can only guess how).

"You shouldn't have gone through all that trouble," he said. "You should have called the ombudsman."

The ombudsman? THE OMBUDSMAN!!? I spent five hours running up a phone bill not seen since the *Transcript* called James Michener five times in Alaska. I went 10 days without a car. I could have called the ombudsman?

Mr. Mackey almost had my apologies. I was ready to express gratitude that he had hired a person to make an exception for me and pull me out of the crack.

But Mr. Mackey had commenced a Platonic dialogue on my situation with his assistant, William Hutch.

Mr. Mackey said I should have been able to register without a title, provided I had a bill of sale.

Mr. Hutch responded that this provision only holds for automobiles carrying a bank lien.

Mr. Mackey said a manufacturer's statement of origin, along with California's temporary registration, might have sufficed.

Mr. Hutch said that a California temporary registration does not constitute proof of title for the purpose of the Massachusetts registry.

Ah, the evil Mr. Hutch—there is always an extra legality to keep you from your freedom.

The dialogue was all to familiar, and I was thinking about the four stories I had to write before deadline as the men advanced into more and more intricate details of registration law. Mike and I shook their hands and escaped.

It was not until Tuesday afternoon that I was able to bring myself to call the ombudsman.

By my motor's honor, I swear that the following is an accurate transcription of what happened when I dialed 617-727-3800 as per Mr. Mackey's instructions.

"Hello, Registry."

"Hi, I would like to speak to the ombudsman."

"To whom? I didn't get the name."

"The ombudsman."

"Is that a person's name who works here?"

"No, OMBUDSMAN. It's a title."

"Oh, he works in title!"

"No, no. It's not a name. It's a thing. It's in the dictionary. Ombudsman."

"We're no better off than we were before. Spell it."

"O, M, B, U, D, S, M . . ."

"N?"

"M as in motor, A, N."

"No."

"No?"

"No."

"No what?"

"Is that all one word?"

"Yes. Ombudsman."

I would see I was getting nowhere, so I scrambled through my notes and actually managed to find a name, Jacqueline Dooley, whom Mr. Mackey had described as "both my hands."

"Let me speak to Jacqueline Dooley."

"One minute."

When I reached Ms. Dooley, after being put on hold and trying to explain myself a few more times, I discovered a helpful, pleasant lady. She said the registry could not do a thing for me, but after I whined a bit she said the people in title could probably have worked something out by "flagging" my registration.

Now, that's a new one. "Flagging." I had not heard that in any of my 21 conversations with 13 people in seven cities.

She said she was glad that I had called, and she would be sure to share this "flagging" trick with the subordinates I had spoken with when my car was still unregistered.

I decided not to pursue the matter with the people in titles. The thing was moot, after all.

And my conversation with Ms. Dooley had left me with a good feeling I didn't want to jinx. I still was not sure if the bureaucrats could have helped me escape from the crack they had created.

# REGISTRY SAGA, PART 2: INTREPID
# REPORTER-DRIVER OUTLASTS CHIEF

*April 25, 1987*

I, for one, was a little saddened to see Alan Mackey step down as registrar of the Registry of Vehicles this week. I had almost come to think of him as a friend, after all the trouble we have put each other through in the last year.

Last summer, faithful *Transcript* readers will recall, my car and I became outlaws, briefly, when Mr. Mackey's workers couldn't find a way for me to register it legally.

Last month, because of another Registry quirk, I once again had to violate my friend Mr. Mackey's laws, driving a car without a license for a week or two. I have been meaning to apologize to him, and perhaps this is as good a chance as any.

My troubles with the Registry began when I drove a new car from California to Massachusetts. I was stopped by a North Adams police officer on my 30th day in the Commonwealth and given a $100 ticket for driving an unregistered vehicle.

I soon realized I had no way of registering my vehicle here, due to an utterly bizarre set of circumstances that had to do with Massachusetts stubbornly demanding a document that California lazily refused to send.

After driving illegally for a week, I finally registered my car. A few weeks later, Mr. Mackey visited North Adams, and I was sent to write a story about him.

He told me all about a computer that would be installed in the Registry office to end various glitches caused by paper records.

I told him about my glitch. We argued about it a bit. Then he said, "You should have called the ombudsman."

An ombudsman is defined as a government official who handles complaints and "helps to achieve equitable settlements." True, that is something of a contradiction in terms when it comes to the Registry, but out of curiosity, I telephoned Boston and said I wanted to speak to the ombudsman. The word "ombudsman," readers might remember, threw the receptionist into a hopeless state of confusion. When I finally reached the ombudsman, Jacqueline Dooley, we had an engaging, if useless, conversation about my registration woes, and she even thanked me for calling.

End of story. Or so I thought. Last month, I head from Mr. Mackey again.

This time, he was far less pleasant. In fact, he had a photocopied signature at the bottom of a computerized letter informing me that I would have my license suspended in two weeks because I was in court default.

Not being fond of the word "default," I went to court and asked what this thing was all about. It was the ticket. Remember the ticket? Neither did I. I assumed the charge against me had been dropped when the Registry people realized that it was unwarranted. Nobody had demanded payment, so everything was OK, right?

(Oh, folly that rules our lives, letting us forget The Uncompleted Task until it has grown so foul and formidable that Hercules himself could not slay it!)

Nothing had been dropped. The ticket still stood. The hearing I requested had been held without me . . .

Wait! How could they hold the hearing without telling me?

"We sent you two notices," the clerk said, showing me two envelopes with "return to sender: address unknown" stamps on them. The notices had been sent to my old address, from which I moved a few days after getting the ticket.

"And you also hung up on me when I tried to tell you on the phone," the clerk said with a scrowl.

Now wait. Drive an unregistered vehicle, maybe. Forget to tell people my new address, conceivably. But hang up on an employee of the Trial Court of the Commonwealth of Massachusetts, District Court Department, Northern Berkshire Division? Never.

Then I remembered: The *Transcript* newsroom, 30 minutes after deadline, the busiest time of the morning. Hairs are being pulled, death threats are being screamed across the room, fingers are flying at 120 words per minute.

In this setting, with my right hand still typing my final story, I phoned the District Court to check the court date of an upcoming assault and battery trial.

When I identified myself, the clerk said, "You have a motor vehicle violation." It's those parking tickets, I thought. I told her I would speak with her after deadline; now, could I please have that court date?

That afternoon, I paid the parking tickets and forgot to call her back. Mea culpa.

But why didn't the court people send my notice to the *Transcript*? And why couldn't they get my address from the Registry of Motor Vehicles?

"We're not an investigative agency," said the clerk.

Well, OK, but can't I file some kind of appeal?

"You had your appeal, and you missed it," said the magistrate. "The only thing we can do now is collect your money."

I took the next logical step. I called the Registry. Remember the ombudsman? So did I, so that's who I asked to speak with.

"The who?"

"The Om-buds-man."

"Is that a name?"

"No, it's not a name, it's a title. It means somebody that helps people with problems."

"Oh, it's a title."

"Yes."

"Is it a new title or a duplicate?"

After a few more minutes of this, I was turned over to the new ombudsman (Ms. Dooley had retired, much to my dismay), who passed me on to somebody else, who told me, "There's nothing we can do for you. Your problem is with the court."

I don't give up easily, as you can tell. I telephoned a prominent city attorney. He said he would investigate my options and get back to me.

"Is one of the options jail?" I asked.

"It could very well be," he answered.

Not long ago, a Berkshire County man got a full year in the slammer. A YEAR for driving on a revoked license. Sure, reporters will gladly serve time for protecting a source, or something like that, but for unlicensed driving? Not me, Jack. I paid the fine the day before the Registry was scheduled to suspend my license. I paid cash—they wouldn't take my check.

But my problems were not over. Remember Alan Mackey's computer? Neither did I. It came back to haunt me.

It seems that half of the system had been installed when I presented my court receipt to the local Registry office, the half that tells North Adams that Boston plans to suspend a license. But not the half that tells Boston to lift the suspension.

The director of the Registry office here had to mail that information instead.

"I don't know how long it will take for them to process it," he said. "They have a huge backload in Boston now." I've spent the last two days trying to iron out this guy's problem, he said, showing me some other innocent's wrongly suspended license.

Well, couldn't I get written proof that I came in with the court's receipt, just in case I get pulled over for having mudstains on my truck and the officer finds out I have a suspended license? "We can't do that with the new computer," he apologized.

You see, not only is California unable to communicate with the Massachusetts registry, not only is the court system unable to communicate with the Registry, but the Registry is also unable to communicate with itself.

Mr. Mackey is going to Florida now. He wants to spend more time with his family. Really, I don't blame him. And I wish his successor luck.

# ACKNOWLEDGMENTS

If ever there were people I would want with me in a foxhole, it is the staff of *The Wall Street Journal*. In a year when we lost four of our best journalists—Jeff Cole, Bruce Ingersoll, David Rosenberg and, now, Danny—the reporters and editors here have shown what they are made of.

When so many of us were falling apart, Paul Steiger pulled us back together. Peter Kann, Karen House and Steve Goldstein worked tirelessly to try to secure Danny's release. John Bussey dropped everything and flew to Pakistan, where he stayed for six weeks. Asra Nomani, Steve Levine, Robert Frank, Peter Waldman, Larry Ingrassia and countless other reporters and editors in the *Journal*'s bureaus all over the world scoured old articles and harassed public and private officials in an unwavering effort to help Danny.

In the Washington bureau, where I work, I witnessed this up close. Jerry Seib, calm, steady and dogged, was on the phone day and night. Carla Robbins called every contact she had, and then called them again, and again. David Wessel, David Cloud and John Wilke followed the examples of Carla and Jerry, showing every day that as journalists, we are always human beings first.

The Pearl family had the wrenching task of watching events unfold from afar. The strength of Danny's father, Judea, his mother, Ruth, and his sisters, Tamara and Michelle, was palpable, and the love and laughter that had shaped their incredible son and brother soon became clear.

Mariane Pearl showed us courage.

Barney Calame, Steve Adler and Roe D'Angelo made this book happen.

Danny was my friend for 10 years. I would not have gotten through the past two months without the emotional support of several people. On one of my darkest days, Phil Kuntz drove me across the Chesapeake Bay Bridge, because I wanted to drive fast and listen to Springsteen on the car stereo. Dawn Blalock, Shailagh Murray, John Sellers, Bob

Davis, Dana Milbank, Sara Calian, Michael Phillips, Veda Simpson and Nicholas Kulish propped me up. Tom Jennings yelled at me when I needed it. My sisters—Marlene, Janice and Alyson—let me grieve. My mother, Calista, made me have faith again.

Finally, Alan Murray, for six years my boss at *The Wall Street Journal,* showed me that the most important trait in a journalist is the ability to care.

—Helene Cooper
April 8, 2002

# ABOUT THE AUTHOR AND EDITOR

**Daniel Pearl** was named South Asia bureau chief of *The Wall Street Journal*, based in Bombay, India, in December 2000. He joined the *Journal* as a reporter in Atlanta in November 1990 and moved to Washington, D.C., in 1993 to cover transportation. In January 1996 he moved to London, and in February 1998 he began reporting from the *Journal's* Paris bureau. Mr. Pearl had been a reporter for the *North Adams* (Mass.) *Transcript* in 1986; the Springfield, Mass., *Union News* in 1987 and the *Berkshire Eagle* in Pittsfield, Mass., in 1988, where he won an American Planning Association Award for a five-part series on land use. A Princeton, N.J., native, Mr. Pearl graduated from Stanford University with a bachelor's degree in communications.

**Helene Cooper,** assistant bureau chief in *The Wall Street Journal's* Washington bureau, worked with Daniel Pearl in Atlanta, Washington and London. She now leads a *Journal* team covering international economics and regulatory policy. Prior to joining the *Journal* in 1992, Ms. Cooper was a reporter for the *Providence* (R.I.) *Journal-Bulletin*. In 2000, Ms. Cooper won the Raymond Clapper Award for Washington reporting, and in 2001, the National Press Club's Sandy Hume Award, presented to an outstanding journalist under the age of 35.